THE ROUGH GUIDE

GERMAN

PHRASEBOOK

Compiled by

LEXUS

ROUGH
GUIDES

www.roughguides.com

Credits

Compiled by Lexus with Horst Kopleck
Lexus Series Editor: Sally Davies
Rough Guides Reference Director: Andrew Lockett
Rough Guides Series Editor: Mark Ellingham

First edition published in 1995.
Reprinted in 1996, 1997 and 1998.
Revised in 1999.
This updated edition published in 2006 by
Rough Guides Ltd,
80 Strand, London WC2R 0RL
345 Hudson St, 4th Floor, New York 10014, USA
Email: mail@roughguides.co.uk.

Distributed by the Penguin Group.

Penguin Books Ltd, 80 Strand, London WC2R 0RL
Penguin Putnam, Inc., 375 Hudson Street, NY 10014, USA
Penguin Group (Australia), 250 Camberwell Road, Camberwell,
Victoria 3124, Australia
Penguin Books Canada Ltd, 10 Alcorn Avenue, Toronto,
Ontario, Canada M4V 1E4
Penguin Group (New Zealand), Cnr Rosedale and Airborne Roads,
Albany, Auckland, New Zealand

Typeset in Bembo and Helvetica to an original design by Henry Iles.
Printed in Singapore by Toppan Security Printing Pte. Ltd.

© Lexus Ltd 2006
272pp.

British Library Cataloguing in Publication Data
A catalogue for this book is available from the British Library.

ISBN 13: 978-1-84353-626-0
ISBN 10: 1-84353-626-9

7   9   8   6

The publishers and authors have done their best to ensure the
accuracy and currency of all information in The Rough Guide
German Phrasebook however, they can accept no responsibility for
any loss or inconvenience sustained by any reader using the book.

Online information about Rough Guides can be found at our
website www.roughguides.com

CONTENTS

Introduction

The Rough Guide German phrasebook is a highly practical introduction to the contemporary language. Laid out in clear A-Z style, it uses key-word referencing to lead you straight to the words and phrases you want – so if you need to book a room, just look up 'room'. The Rough Guide gets straight to the point in every situation, in bars and shops, on trains and buses, and in hotels and banks.

The main part of the Rough Guide is a double dictionary: English-German then German-English. Before that, there's a section called **Basic Phrases** and to get you involved in two-way communication, the Rough Guide includes, in this new edition, a set of **Scenario** dialogues illustrating questions and responses in key situations such as renting a car and asking directions. You can hear these and then download them free from **www.roughguides.com/phrasebooks** for use on your computer or MP3 player.

Forming the heart of the guide, the **English-German** section gives easy-to-use transliterations of the German words wherever pronunciation might be a problem. Throughout this section, cross-references enable you to pinpoint key facts and phrases, while asterisked words indicate where further information can be found in a section at the end of the book called **How the Language Works**. This section sets out the fundamental rules of the language, with plenty of practical examples. You'll also find here other essentials like numbers, dates, telling the time and basic phrases. In the **German-English** dictionary, we've given you not just the phrases you'll be likely to hear (starting with a selection of slang and colloquialisms) but also many of the signs, labels, instructions and other basic words you may come across in print or in public places.

Near the back of the book too the Rough Guide offers an extensive **Menu Reader**. Consisting of food and drink sections (each starting with a list of essential terms), it's indispensable whether you're eating out, stopping for a quick drink, or browsing through a local food market.

Gute Reise!
have a good trip!

Basic
Phrases

Basic Phrases

yes
ja
yah

no
nein
nine

OK
okay

hello
hallo

good morning
guten Morgen
g**oo**ten m**o**rgen

good evening
guten Abend
g**oo**ten **ah**bent

good night
gute Nacht
g**oo**t-uh naкнt

goodbye
auf Wiedersehen
owf-v**ee**derzayn

please
bitte
b**i**tt-uh

yes please
ja bitte
yah

thanks, thank you
danke
d**a**nk-uh

no thanks
nein danke
nine

thank you very much
vielen Dank
f**ee**len

don't mention it
bitte
b**i**tt-uh

how do you do?
guten Tag!
g**oo**ten tahk

how are you?
wie geht es dir/Ihnen?
gayt ess deer/**ee**nen

fine, thanks
danke, gut
dank-uh g**oo**t

nice to meet you
freut mich
froyt mish

excuse me
(to get past)
entschuldigen Sie!
ent-sh**oo**ldigen zee
(to get attention) Entschuldigung!
ent-sh**oo**ldigoong
sorry: (I'm) sorry

tut mir leid
toot meer lite

sorry?
(didn't understand) wie bitte?
vee bitt-uh

I see/I understand
ich verstehe
ish fairstay-uh

I don't understand
das verstehe ich nicht
nisht

do you speak English?
sprechen Sie Englisch?
shpreshen zee eng-lish

I don't speak German
ich spreche kein Deutsch
ish shpresh-uh kine doytch

could you say it slowly?
könnten Sie das etwas
langsamer sagen?
kurnten zee dass etvass langzahmer
zahgen

could you repeat that?
können Sie das noch einmal
wiederholen?
kurnen zee dass noKH ine-mahl

could you write it down?
könnten Sie es aufschreiben?
kurnten zee ess owf-shryben

I'd like a ...
ich möchte gern ein ...
mursht-uh gairn

I'd like to ...
ich würde gern ...
voord-uh

can I have a ...?
kann ich ein ... haben?
kan ish

how much is it?
was kostet das?

cheers!
(toast) Prost!
prohst

it is ...
es ist ...

where is it?
wo ist es?
vo

is it far from here?
ist es weit von hier?
fon heer

how long will it/does it take?
wie lange dauert es?
vee lang-uh dowert ess

Scenarios

1. Accommodation

is there an inexpensive hotel you can recommend?
▶ können Sie mir ein günstiges Hotel empfehlen?
[**kur**nen zee meer ine g**oo**nstigess hot**e**l empf**ay**len]

tut mir Leid, aber es scheint alles ausgebucht zu sein ◀
[t**oo**t meer lite **ah**ber ess shynt **al**-ess **ow**ss-geb**oo**кнт ts**oo** zine]
I'm sorry, they all seem to be fully booked

can you give me the name of a good middle-range hotel?
▶ können Sie mir ein gutes Mittelklasse-Hotel nennen?
[**kur**nen zee meer ine g**oo**tess m**i**ttel-klassuh-hotel n**e**nnen]

mal sehen, möchten Sie im Zentrum sein? ◀
[mal z**ay**-en m**ur**shten zee im ts**e**ntroom zine]
let me have a look; do you want to be in the centre?

if possible
▶ wenn möglich
[venn m**ur**glish]

macht es Ihnen etwas aus, etwas außerhalb der Stadt zu sein? ◀
[m**a**кнt ess **ee**nen **e**tvass owss **e**tvass **ow**sserhalp dair shtat ts**oo** zine]
do you mind being a little way out of town?

not too far out
▶ nicht zu weit außerhalb
[nisht ts**oo** vite **ow**sserhalp]

where is it on the map?
▶ wo ist es auf dem Stadtplan?
[vo ist ess owf daym sht**a**tplahn]

can you write the name and address down?
▶ können Sie mir Namen und Adresse aufschreiben?
[**kur**nen zee meer n**ah**men oont adr**e**ss-uh **ow**f-shryben]

I'm looking for a room in a private house
▶ ich suche ein Zimmer in einem Privathaus
[ish z**oo**кн-uh ine ts**i**mmer in **ine**-em priv**ah**t-howss]

2. Banks

bank account	das Bankkonto	[**ba**nk-konto]
to change money	Geld wechseln	[gelt **ve**kseln]
cheque	der Scheck	[shek]
to deposit	einzahlen	[**ine**-tsahlen]
euro	der Euro	[**oy**-ro]
pin number	die PIN-Nummer	[**pin**-noomer]
pound	das Pfund	[pfoont]
to withdraw	abheben	[**ap**-hayben]

can you change this into euros?
▶ würden Sie das bitte in Euro umtauschen?
[v**oo**rden zee dass b**i**ttuh in **oy**-ro **oo**m-towshen]

wie möchten Sie Ihr Geld?
[vee m**ur**shten zee eer gelt]
how would you like the money?

small notes	big notes
▶ kleine Scheine	▶ große Scheine
[kl**ine**-uh sh**ine**-uh]	[gr**oh**ss-uh sh**ine**-uh]

do you have information in English about opening an account?
▶ haben Sie Information auf Englisch, wie man ein Konto eröffnet?
[h**ah**ben zee informats-**yoh**n owf **eng**-lish vee man ine k**o**nto air-**ur**fnet]

ja, was für ein Konto möchten Sie?◀
[ya vass f**oo**r ine k**o**nto m**ur**shten zee]
yes, what sort of account do you want?

I'd like a current account
▶ ich möchte ein Girokonto eröffnen
[ish m**ur**shtuh ine J**ee**ro-konto air-**ur**fnen]

Ihren Pass, bitte ◀
[**ee**ren pas b**i**ttuh]
your passport, please

can I use this card to draw some cash?
▶ kann ich mit dieser Karte Geld abheben?
[kann ish mit d**ee**zer k**a**rt-uh gelt **ap**-hayben]

Sie müssen zum Schalter gehen ◀
[zee m**oo**ssen tsoom sh**a**lter g**ay**-en]
you have to go to the cashier's desk

I want to transfer this to my account at the Dresdner Bank
▶ ich möchte das auf mein Konto bei der Dresdner Bank überweisen
[ish m**ur**sht-uh dass owf mine k**o**nto by dair dr**ay**zdner bank **oo**ber-v**y**-zen]

OK, aber wir müssen Ihnen dieses Gespräch berechnen ◀
[OK **ah**ber veer m**oo**ssen **ee**nen d**ee**zess geshpr**ay**sh ber**e**shnen]
OK, but we'll have to charge you for the phonecall

14

3. Booking a room

shower	die Dusche	[d**oo**sh-uh]
telephone in the room	Zimmertelefon	[ts**i**mmer-telefohn]
payphone in the lobby	Münzfernsprecher in der Eingangshalle	[moonts-fairn-shpresher in dair **ine**-gangs-hal-uh]

do you have any rooms?
▶ haben Sie Zimmer frei?
[h**ah**ben zee ts**i**mmer fry]

für wie viele Personen? ◀
[f**oo**r vee f**ee**l-uh pairz**oh**nen]
for how many people?

for one/for two
▶ für eine Person/für zwei Personen
[f**oo**r **ine**-uh pairz**oh**n/f**oo**r tsvy pairz**oh**nen]

ja, wir haben Zimmer frei ◀
[ja veer h**ah**ben ts**i**mmer fry]
yes, we have rooms free

▶ für wie lange?
[f**oo**r vee l**a**ng-uh]
for how many nights?

just for one night
nur für eine Nacht ◀
[n**oo**r f**oo**r **ine**-uh n**a**кнt]

how much is it?
▶ was kostet es?
[vass k**o**stet ess]

neunzig Euro mit Bad und siebzig Euro ohne Bad ◀
[n**oy**ntsish **oy**-ro mit baht oont z**ee**ptsish **oy**-ro **oh**n-uh baht]
90 euros with bathroom and 70 euros without bathroom

does that include breakfast?
▶ ist das inklusive Frühstück?
[ist dass inkl**oo**z**ee**v-uh fr**oo**sht**oo**ck]

can I see a room with bathroom?
▶ kann ich ein Zimmer mit Bad sehen?
[kann ish ine ts**i**mmer mit baht z**ay**-en]

ok, I'll take it
▶ gut, ich nehme es
[g**oo**t ish n**ay**m-uh ess]

when do I have to check out?
▶ wann muss ich das Zimmer räumen?
[vann mooss ish dass ts**i**mmer r**oy**men]

is there anywhere I can leave luggage?
▶ kann ich irgendwo mein Gepäck unterstellen?
[kann ish **ee**rgentvo mine gep**e**ck **oo**nter-shtellen]

4. Car hire

automatic	der Automatikwagen	[owtom**ah**tik-vahgen]
full tank	ein voller Tank	[f**o**ller tank]
manual	ein Auto mit Gangschaltung	[**ow**to mit gang-shaltoong]
rented car	das Mietauto	[m**ee**t-owto]

I'd like to rent a car
▶ ich möchte ein Auto mieten
[ish m**u**rsht-uh ine **ow**to m**ee**ten]

für wie lange? ◀
[f**oo**r vee lang-uh]
for how long?

two days
▶ zwei Tage
[tsvy **tah**g-uh]

I'll take the ...
▶ ich nehme den ...
[ish n**ay**m-uh dayn]

is that with unlimited mileage?
▶ ist das ohne Kilometerbeschränkung?
[ist dass **oh**n-uh keelo-m**ay**ter-beshrenkoong]

ja ◀
[yah]
it is

kann ich bitte Ihren Führerschein sehen? ◀
[kann ish b**i**ttuh **ee**ren f**oo**rerschine **zay**-en]
can I see your driving licence, please?

und Ihren Pass ◀
[oont **ee**ren pas]
and your passport

is insurance included?
▶ ist Versicherung inbegriffen?
[ist fairz**i**sheroong **i**nbegriffen]

ja, aber die ersten hundert Euro müssen Sie selbst bezahlen ◀
[yah **ah**ber dee **air**sten h**oo**ndert **oy**-ro m**oo**ssen zee zelpst bets**ah**len]
yes, but you have to pay the first 100 euros

könnten Sie eine Anzahlung von hundert Euro leisten? ◀
[k**ur**nten zee **ine**-uh an-tsahloong fon h**oo**ndert **oy**-ro l**y**sten]
can you leave a deposit of 100 euros?

and if this office is closed, where do I leave the keys?
▶ und wo gebe ich die Schlüssel ab, wenn dieses Büro geschlossen hat?
[oont vo g**ay**b-uh ish dee shl**oo**ssel ap venn d**ee**zess b**oo**ro geshl**o**ssen hat]

werfen Sie sie in den Kasten dort ◀
[**vair**fen zee zee in dayn k**a**sten dort]
you drop them in that box

5. Communications

ADSL modem	das ADSL-Modem	[ah-day-ess-**el**-modem]
at	at	
dial-up modem	das DFÜ-Modem	[day-ef-**oo**-modem]
dot	Punkt	[poonkt]
Internet	das Internet	
mobile (phone)	das Handy	[h**e**ndy]
password	das Passwort	[p**a**s-vort]
telephone socket	der Telefonstecker-	[telef**oh**n-shtecker
adaptor	adapter	-adapter]
wireless hotspot	der Hotspot	

is there an Internet café around here?
▶ gibt es hier in der Gegend ein Internetcafé?
[geept ess heer in dair g**ay**gent ine **i**nternetkafay]

can I send email from here?
▶ kann ich von hier Emails schicken?
[kann ish fon heer emails sch**i**cken]

where's the at sign on the keyboard?
▶ wo ist das at-Zeichen auf der Tastatur?
[vo ist dass **at**-tsyshen auf dair tastat**oo**r]

can you help me log on?
▶ können Sie mir helfen einzuloggen?
[k**u**rnen zee meer h**e**lfen **ine**-ts00loggen]

can you put me through to ...?
▶ können Sie mich mit ... verbinden?
[k**u**rnen zee mish mit ... f**air**binden]

can you switch this to a UK keyboard?
▶ können Sie das auf eine britische Tastatur umstellen?
[k**u**rnen zee dass owf **ine**-uh br**i**tish-uh tastat**oo**r **oo**m-shtellen]

I'm not getting a connection, can you help?
▶ ich bekomme keine Verbindung, können Sie mir helfen?
[ish bek**o**mm-uh k**ine**-uh fairb**i**ndoong k**u**rnen zee meer h**e**lfen]

where can I get a top-up card for my mobile?
▶ wo bekomme ich eine Nachladekarte für mein Handy?
[vo bek**o**mm-uh ish **ine**-uh na**кн**-lahduh-kart-uh f**oo**r mine h**e**ndy]

zero	five
null	fünf
[nool]	[f**oo**nf]
one	six
eins	sechs
[**ine**-ss]	[zeks]
two	seven
zwei	sieben
[tsvy]	[z**ee**ben]
three	eight
drei	acht
[dry]	[a**кн**t]
four	nine
vier	neun
[feer]	[noyn]

6. Directions

hi, I'm looking for Ortlerstraße
▶ hallo, ich suche die Ortlerstraße
[hallo ish zOOKH-uh dee ortler-shtrahss-uh]

hi,
Ortlerstraße,
do you know
where it is?
hallo, wo
ist bitte die
Ortlerstraße?
[hallo vo ist
bittuh dee
ortler-shtrahss-
uh]

tut mir Leid, nie gehört ◀
[toot meer lite nee gehurt]
sorry, never heard of it

can you tell me where Ortlerstraße is?
▶ können Sie mir sagen, wo die Ortlerstraße ist?
[kurnen zee meer zahgen wo dee ortler-shtrahss-uh ist]

ich bin auch fremd hier ◀
[ish bin owKH fremt heer]
I'm a stranger here too

where?
wo?
[vo]

which direction?
welche Richtung?
[velshuh rishtoong]

▶ um die Ecke
[oom dee eck-uh]
around the corner

▶ bei der zweiten Ampel links
[by dair tsvyten ampel links]
left at the second traffic lights

▶ es ist dann die erste Straße rechts
[ess ist dann dee airstuh shtrahss-uh reshts]
then it's the first street on the right

abbiegen [ap-beegen] turn off	gegenüber [gaygenOOber] opposite	links on the left	Straße [shtrahss-uh] street
an dem ... vorbei [an daym ... forby] past the ...	geradeaus [gerahduh-owss] straight ahead	nächste [naykst-uh] next	vor [for] in front of
dort drüben [dort drOOben] over there	gleich nach [glysh naKH] just after	neben [nayben] near	weiter [vyter] further
		rechts [reshts] on the right	zurück [tsoorOOck] back

18

download these scenarios as MP3s from:

7. Emergencies

accident	der Unfall	[**oo**nfal]
ambulance	der Krankenwagen	[**kr**anken-vahgen]
consul	der Konsul	[**k**onzool]
embassy	die Botschaft	[**boh**tshaft]
fire brigade	die Feuerwehr	[**foy**-er-vair]
police	die Polizei	[polits**ī**]

help!
▶ Hilfe!
[h**i**lf-uh]

can you help me?
▶ können Sie mir helfen?
[k**ur**nen zee meer h**e**lfen]

please come with me! it's really very urgent
▶ kommen Sie bitte mit mir! es ist wirklich sehr dringend
[**k**ommen zee b**i**ttuh mit meer ess ist **vee**rklish zair dr**i**ngent]

I've lost (my keys)
▶ ich habe (meine Schlüssel) verloren
[ish h**ah**b-uh (m**i**ne-uh shl**oo**ssel) fairl**o**ren]

(my car) is not working
▶ (mein Auto) ist nicht in Ordnung
[(mein **A**uto) ist nisht in **o**rdnoong]

(my purse) has been stolen
▶ (mein Portmonee) ist gestohlen worden
[(mine port-monn**ay**) ist gesht**oh**len v**o**rden]

I've been mugged
▶ ich bin überfallen worden
[ish bin **oo**berfal-en v**o**rden]

wie heißen Sie? ◀
[vee h**ice**-en zee]
what's your name?

können Sie mir bitte Ihren Pass zeigen? ◀
[k**ur**nen zee meer b**i**ttuh **ee**ren pas ts**y**gen]
I need to see your passport

I'm sorry, all my papers have been stolen
▶ tut mir Leid, aber alle meine Ausweispapiere sind gestohlen worden
[t**oo**t meer lite **ah**ber **a**l-uh m**i**ne-uh **ow**ss-vice-pap**ee**r-uh zint gesht**oh**len v**o**rden]

8. Friends

hi, how're you doing?
▶ hallo, wie gehts?
[hallo vee gayts]

OK, und dir? ◀
[OK oont deer]
OK, and you?

yeah, fine
▶ ja, ganz gut
[yah gants goot]

not bad
▶ nicht schlecht
[nisht shlesht]

d'you know Mark?
▶ kennst du Mark?
[kennst doo mark]

and this is Hannah
▶ und das ist Hannah
[oont dass ist hannah]

▶ ja, wir kennen uns
[yah veer kennen oonss]
yeah, we know each other

where do you know each other from?
▶ woher kennt ihr euch?
[vohair kennt eer oysh]

we met at Daniel's place
▶ wir haben uns bei Daniel kennen gelernt
[veer hahben oonss by daniel kennen gelairnt]

that was some party, eh?
▶ das war vielleicht eine Party, oder?
[dass vahr feelysht ine-uh party ohder]

einmalig ◀
[ine-mahlish]
the best

are you guys coming for a beer?
▶ kommt ihr mit auf ein Bier?
[kommt eer mit owf ine beer]

▶ cool, gehen wir
[kool gay-en veer]
cool, let's go

▶ nein, ich treffe Sarah
[nine ish tref-uh sarah]
no, I'm meeting Sarah

see you at Daniel's place tonight
▶ dann bis heute Abend bei Daniel
[dann biss hoyt-uh ahbent by daniel]

bis dann ◀
[biss dann]
see you

download these scenarios as MP3s from:

9. Health

I'm not feeling very well
▶ es geht mir nicht gut
[ess gayt meer nisht goot]

can you get a doctor?
▶ können Sie einen Arzt holen?
[**kur**nen zee **ine**-en artst **ho**hlen]

▶ wo tut es weh?
[vo toot ess vay]
where does it hurt?

it hurts here
▶ es tut hier weh
[ess toot heer vay]

▶ tut es ständig weh?
[toot ess sht**e**ndish vay]
is the pain constant?

it's not a constant pain
▶ es tut nicht ständig weh
[ess toot nisht sht**e**ndish vay]

---

can I make an appointment?
▶ kann ich einen Termin machen?
[kann ish **ine**-en tairm**ee**n mak**H**en]

can you give me something for ...?
▶ können Sie mir etwas für ... geben?
[**kur**nen zee meer **e**tvass f**oo**r ... **gay**ben]

yes, I have insurance
▶ ja, ich bin versichert
[yah ish bin fairz**i**shert]

antibiotics	die Antibiotika	[antibi**o**tika]
antiseptic ointment	eine antiseptische Salbe	[anti**ze**ptish-uh **za**lb-uh]
cystitis	eine Blasenentzündung	[bl**ah**zen-ent-ts**oo**ndoong]
dentist	der Zahnarzt	[ts**ah**nartst]
diarrhoea	der Durchfall	[d**oo**rshfal]
doctor	der Arzt	[artst]
hospital	das Krankenhaus	[kr**a**nken-howss]
ill	krank	
medicine	das Medikament	[medikament]
painkillers	die Schmerztabletten	[shm**ai**rts-tabletten]
pharmacy	die Apotheke	[apot**ay**k-uh]
to prescribe	verschreiben	[fair-shr**y**ben]
thrush	eine Pilzinfektion	[p**i**lts-infeks-yohn]

10. Language difficulties

a few words	ein paar Wörter	[ine pahr **vur**ter]
interpreter	der Dolmetscher	[**do**lmetsher]
to translate	übersetzen	[oober**zet**sen]

Ihre Kreditkarte wurde abgelehnt ◀
[**eer**-uh krayd**eet**-kart-uh **voo**rd-uh ap-gelaynt]
your credit card has been refused

what, I don't understand; do you speak English?
▶ wie bitte, das verstehe ich nicht; sprechen Sie Englisch?
[vee **bi**ttuh dass f**air**shtay-uh ish nisht; shpr**e**shen zee **eng**-lish]

die ist nicht gültig ◀
[dee ist nisht g**oo**ltish]
this isn't valid

could you say that again?　　　　**slowly**
▶ können Sie das wiederholen?　　　▶ langsam
[**kur**nen zee dass veeder-h**oh**len]　[**la**ngzahm]

I understand very little German
▶ ich verstehe nur sehr wenig Deutsch
[ish fairsht**ay**-uh n**oo**r zair **vay**-nish doytsh]

I speak German very badly
▶ ich spreche sehr schlechtes Deutsch
[ish shpr**e**sh-uh zair shl**e**sht-ess doytsh]

Sie können mit dieser Karte nicht bezahlen ◀
[zee **kur**nen mit d**ee**zer kart-uh nisht bets**ah**len]
you can't use this card to pay

▶ verstehen Sie?　　　　**sorry, no**
[fairsht**ay**-en zee]　　　▶ nein, tut mir Leid
do you understand?　　[nine t**oo**t meer lite]

is there someone who speaks English?
▶ spricht hier jemand Englisch?
[shpr**i**sht heer **yay**mant **eng**-lish]

oh, now I understand　　　**is that ok now?**
▶ ach so, jetzt verstehe ich　▶ ist das jetzt in Ordnung?
[ach zo yetst fairsht**ay**-uh ish]　[ist dass yetst in **o**rdnoong]

11. Meeting people

hello
- hallo
[hallo]

hallo, ich heiße Claudia ◄
[hallo ish hice-uh klowd-ya]
hello, my name's Claudia

Graham, from England, Thirsk
- ich bin Graham; ich komme aus Thirsk in England
[ish bin graham ish komm-uh owss thirsk in eng-lant]

kenne ich nicht, wo ist das? ◄
[kenn-uh ish nisht, vo ist dass]
don't know that, where is it?

---

not far from York, in the North; and you?
- nicht weit von York entfernt, im Norden, und Sie?
[nisht vite fon york ent-fairnt im norden oont zee]

ich komme aus Berlin; sind Sie alleine hier? ◄
[ish komm-uh owss bairleen zint zee al-ine-uh heer]
I'm from Berlin; here by yourself?

---

no, I'm with my wife and two kids
- nein, meine Frau und meine zwei Kinder sind dabei
[nine mine-uh frow oont mine-uh tsvy kinder zint da-by]

---

what do you do?   ich arbeite im Computerbereich ◄
- was machen Sie beruflich?   [ish arbyt-uh im computer-berysh]
[vass maкнen zee berooflish]   I'm in computers

me too
- ich auch
[ish owкн]

here's my wife now
- hier kommt meine Frau
[heer kommt mine-uh frow]

freut mich, Sie kennen zu lernen ◄
[froyt mish zee kennen tsoo lairnen]
nice to meet you

---

12. Post offices

airmail	Luftpost	[looft-posst]
post card	die Postkarte	[posst-kart-uh]
post office	die Post	[posst]
stamp	die Briefmarke	[breef-mark-uh]

what time does the post office close?
▶ wann schließt die Post?
[vann shleest dee posst]

um siebzehn Uhr Montag bis Freitag ◀
[oom zeep-tsayn 00r mohntahk biss frytahk]
five o'clock weekdays

is the post office open on Saturdays?
▶ ist die Post samstags geöffnet?
[ist dee posst zamstahks ge-urfnet]

bis Mittag ◀
[biss mittahk]
until midday

I'd like to send this registered to England
▶ ich möchte dies per Einschreiben nach England senden
[ish mursht-uh deess pair ine-shryben naкн eng-lant senden]

gut, das macht zehn Euro ◀
[g00t dass maкнt tsayn oy-ro]
certainly, that will cost 10 euros

and also two stamps for England, please
▶ und auch zwei Briefmarken nach England, bitte
[oont owкн tsvy breef-marken naкн eng-lant bittuh]

do you have some airmail stickers?
▶ hätten Sie ein paar Luftpost-Aufkleber?
[hetten zee ine pahr looft-posst-owf-klayber]

do you have any mail for me?
▶ ist Post für mich gekommen?
[ist posst f00r mish gekommen]

Auslands...	Inlands...	postlagernd
international	domestic	poste restante
Briefe	Pakete	
letters	parcels	

13. Restaurants

bill	menu	table
die Rechnung	die Speisekarte	der Tisch
[**resh**noong]	[sh**py**z-uh **kart**-uh]	[tish]

can we have a non-smoking table?
▶ können wir bitte einen Nichtrauchertisch haben?
[**kur**nen veer **bi**ttuh **ine**-en **ni**sht-rowкHer-tish **ha**hben]

there are two of us
▶ wir sind zu zweit
[veer zint ts00 tsvite]

there are four of us
▶ wir sind zu viert
[veer zint ts00 feert]

what's this?
▶ was ist das?
[vass ist dass]

es ist eine Fischsorte ◀
[ess ist **ine**-uh **fi**sh-sort-uh]
it's a type of fish

es ist eine regionale Spezialität ◀
[ess ist **ine**-uh rayg-yohn**ah**l-uh shpetsi-alit**ayt**]
it's a local speciality

kommen Sie herein, ich zeige es Ihnen ◀
[**ko**mmen zee hair-**ine** ish **tsyg**-uh ess **ee**nen]
come inside and I'll show you

we would like two of these, one of these, and one of those
▶ wir hätten gern zwei von diesen, eins von diesen und eins von denen dort
[veer **he**tten gairn tsvy fon **dee**zen ine-ss fon **dee**zen oont ine-ss fon **day**nen dort]

▶ und zu trinken?
[oont ts00 **tri**nken]
and to drink

red wine
▶ Rotwein
[**roht**-vine]

white wine
▶ Weißwein
[**vice**-vine]

a beer and two orange juices
▶ ein Bier und zwei Orangensaft
[ine beer oont tsvy or**on**jen-zaft]

some more bread please
▶ noch etwas Brot bitte
[noкH **et**vass broht **bi**ttuh]

▶ wie hat es Ihnen geschmeckt?
[vee hat ess **ee**nen geshm**eck**t]
how was your meal?

excellent, very nice!
▶ wunderbar!, sehr schön!
[**voo**nderbar zair shurn]

▶ noch etwas?
[noкH **et**vass]
anything else?

just the bill thanks
▶ nur die Rechnung, danke
[n00r dee **resh**noong **da**nk-uh]

14. Shopping

kann ich Ihnen behilflich sein? ◀
[kann ish **ee**nen beh**i**lflish zine]
can I help you?

can I just have a look around?
▶ kann ich mich kurz umschauen?
[kann ish mish koorts **oo**m-show-en]

yes, I'm looking for ...
▶ ja, ich suche ...
[yah ish z**oo**KH-uh ...]

how much is this?
▶ wie viel kostet dies?
[vee feel k**o**stet deess]

zweiunddreißig Euro ◀
[tsvy-oont-dr**y**ssish **oy**-ro]
thirty-two euros

OK, I think I'll have to leave it; it's a little too expensive for me
▶ ich glaube, ich muss es lassen, es ist mir ein bisschen zu teuer
[ish gl**ow**buh ish mooss ess l**a**ssen ess ist meer ine b**i**ss-shen ts**oo** t**oy**-er]

wie ist es hiermit? ◀
[vee ist h**ee**rmit]
how about this?

can I pay by credit card?
▶ kann ich mit Kreditkarte bezahlen?
[kann ish mit krayd**ee**t-kart-uh bets**a**hlen]

it's too big
▶ es ist zu groß
[ess ist ts**oo** grohss]

it's too small
▶ es ist zu klein
[ess ist ts**oo** kline]

it's for my son – he's about this high
▶ es ist für meinen Sohn – er ist etwa so groß
[ess ist f**oo**r m**ine**-en zohn – air ist **e**tva zo grohss]

▶ darf es sonst noch etwas sein?
[darf ess zonst noKH **e**tvass zine]
will there be anything else?

that's all thanks
▶ nein danke, das ist alles
[nine d**a**nk-uh dass ist **a**l-ess]

make it twenty euros and I'll take it
▶ für zwanzig Euro nehme ich es
[f**oo**r tsv**a**ntsish **oy**-ro n**ay**m-uh ish ess]

fine, I'll take it
▶ gut, ich nehme es
[g**oo**t ish n**ay**m-uh ess]

der Ausverkauf	sale	die Kasse	cash desk
geöffnet	open	umtauschen	to exchange
geschlossen	closed		

download these scenarios as MP3s from:

15. Sightseeing

art gallery	die Kunstgalerie	[koonst-gal-leree]
bus tour	eine Stadtrundfahrt	[shtat-roont-fahrt]
city centre	das Stadtzentrum	[shtat-tsentroom]
closed	geschlossen	[geshlossen]
guide	der Führer	[foorer]
museum	das Museum	[moozay-oom]
open	geöffnet	[ge-urfnet]

I'm interested in seeing the old town
▶ ich würde gerne die Altstadt sehen
[ish voord-uh gairn-uh dee alt-shtat zay-en]

are there guided tours of the town?
▶ gibt es eine Stadtführung?
[geept ess ine-uh shtat-fooroong]

tut mir Leid, es ist voll ausgebucht ◀
[toot meer lite ess ist foll owssgebooKHt]
I'm sorry, it's fully booked

how much would you charge to drive us around for four hours?
▶ wie viel würde es kosten, wenn Sie uns vier Stunden lang herumfahren?
[vee feel voord-uh ess kosten venn zee oonss feer shtoonden lang hairoom-fahren]

can we book tickets for the concert here?
▶ können wir die Konzertkarten hier buchen?
[kurnen veer dee kontsairt-karten heer booKHen]

ja, auf welchen Namen? ▶ was für eine Kreditkarte?
[yah owf velshen nahmen] [vass foor ine-uh kraydeet-kart-uh]
yes, in what name? **which credit card?**

where do we get the tickets?
▶ wo bekommen wir die Karten?
[vo bekommen veer dee karten]

holen Sie sie einfach am Eingang ab ◀
[hohlen zee zee ine-faKH am ine-gang ap]
just pick them up at the entrance

is it open on Sundays? **how much is it to get in?**
▶ ist es sonntags geöffnet? ▶ wie viel kostet der Eintritt?
[ist ess zonntahks ge-urfnet] [vee feel kostet dair ine-tritt]

are there reductions for groups of 6?
▶ gibt es Ermäßigungen für Gruppen von sechs Personen?
[geept ess air-mayssigoongen foor groopen fon seks pairzohnen]

that was really impressive!
▶ das war wirklich beeindruckend!
[dass vahr veerklish be-ine-droockent]

16. Trains

to change trains	umsteigen	[**oo**m-shtygen]
platform	der Bahnsteig	[**bah**nshtike]
return	die Rückfahrkarte	[r**oo**ck-fahrkart-uh]
single	einfach	[**ine**-faKH]
station	der Bahnhof	[**bah**nhohf]
stop	die Haltestelle	[**halt**-uh-shtell-uh]
ticket	die Fahrkarte	[**fahr**kart-uh]

how much is ...?
▶ wie viel kostet ...?
[vee feel **k**ostet ...]

a single, second class to ...
▶ einfach zweiter Klasse nach ...
[**ine**-faKH tsv**y**ter kl**a**ss-uh naKH ...]

two returns, second class to ...
▶ zwei Rückfahrkarten zweiter Klasse nach ...
[tsvy r**oo**ck-fahrkarten tsv**y**ter kl**a**ss-uh naKH ...]

for today	for tomorrow	for next Tuesday
▶ für heute	▶ für morgen	▶ für nächsten Dienstag
[f**oo**r h**oy**t-uh]	[f**oo**r m**o**rgen]	[f**oo**r **n**ayksten **d**eenstahk]

Sie brauchen einen Zuschlag für den Intercity ◀
[zee br**ow**kHen **ine**-en ts**oo**shlahk f**oo**r dayn intercity]
there's a supplement for the Intercity

möchten Sie einen Platz reservieren? ◀
[**m**urshten zee **ine**-en plats rezairv**ee**ren]
do you want to make a seat reservation?

Sie müssen in Frankfurt umsteigen ◀
[zee m**oo**ssen in frankfoort **oo**m-shtygen]
you have to change at Frankfurt

is this seat free?
▶ ist dieser Platz frei?
[ist d**ee**zer plats fry]

excuse me, which station are we at?
▶ Entschuldigung, welcher Bahnhof ist das hier?
[ent-sh**oo**ldigoong v**e**lsher b**ah**nhohf ist dass heer]

is this where I change for Heidelberg?
▶ muss ich hier nach Heidelberg umsteigen?
[mooss ish heer naKH heidelberg **oo**m-shtygen]

English → German

A

a, an* ein(e) [**ine**(-uh)]
10 marks a bottle 10 Mark
pro Flasche
about: about twenty etwa
zwanzig [**etvah**]
at about 5 o'clock gegen fünf
Uhr [**gay**gen]
a film about Germany ein
Film über Deutschland [**oo**ber]
above über [**oo**ber]
abroad im Ausland [**ow**sslant]
to go abroad ins Ausland
gehen
absolutely (I agree) genau
[gen**ow**]
accelerator das Gaspedal
[**gah**ss-pedahl]
accept akzeptieren
[aktsept**ee**ren]
accident der Unfall [**oo**nfal]
there's been an accident es
hat einen Unfall gegeben
[geg**ay**ben]
accommodation die
Unterkunft [**oo**nter-koonft]
accurate genau [gen**ow**]
ache der Schmerz [shmairts]
my back aches mein Rücken
tut weh [toot vay]
across: across the road über
die Straße [**oo**ber]
adapter der Adapter
address die Adresse
[adr**e**ss-uh]
what's your address? was ist
Ihre Adresse? [**eer**-uh]

address book das Adressbuch
[adr**e**ssbooKH]
admission charge der Eintritt
[**ine**-tritt]
adult der Erwachsene
[airvaksen-uh]
advance: in advance im
voraus [**fo**rowss]
aeroplane das Flugzeug
[fl**oo**ktsoyk]
after nach [naKH]
after you nach Ihnen [**ee**nen]
afternoon der Nachmittag
[na**KH**mit-tahk]
in the afternoon am
Nachmittag
this afternoon heute
Nachmittag [**hoy**t-uh]
aftershave das After-shave
aftersun cream die Après-
Lotion
[apr**ay**-lohts-yohn]
afterwards danach [dana**KH**]
again wieder [**vee**der]
against gegen [**gay**gen]
age das Alter [**al**-ter]
ago: a week ago vor einer
Woche [for **ine**-er]
an hour ago vor einer Stunde
agree: I agree ich bin
einverstanden [**ine**-fair-
shtanden]
AIDS Aids
air die Luft [looft]
by air mit dem Flugzeug
[fl**oo**ktsoyk]
air-conditioning die
Klimaanlage [kl**ee**ma-anlahg-
uh]

airmail: by airmail per Luftpost
[pair **loo**ftposst]

airmail envelope der Luftpost-
Briefumschlag [**loo**ftposst breef-
oomshlahk]

airport der Flughafen [fl**oo**k-
hahfen]

to the airport, please zum
Flughafen bitte [tsoom]

airport bus der Flughafenbus
[fl**oo**k-hafenbooss]

aisle seat der Sitz am Gang

alarm clock der Wecker
[**veck**er]

alcohol der Alkohol

alcoholic alkoholisch [alko-
hohlish]

all: all the boys alle Jungen
[**al**-uh]

all the girls alle Mädchen

all of it alles [al-ess]

all of them alle

that's all, thanks das ist alles,
danke

allergic: I'm allergic to ... ich
bin allergisch gegen ... [ish bin
al**lair**gish gay**gen**]

allowed: is it allowed? ist es
erlaubt? [air**lowpt**]

all right okay

I'm all right ich bin okay

are you all right? bist du/sind
Sie okay?

almond die Mandel

almost fast [fasst]

alone allein [al-**ine**]

alphabet das Alphabet [alfa-
bayt]

a	ah	j	yot	s	ess
b	bay	k	kah	t	tay
c	tsay	l	el	u	oo
d	day	m	em	u	oo
e	ay	n	en	v	fow
f	eff	o	oh	w	vay
g	gay	p	pay	x	eeks
h	hah	q	koo	y	**oo**psilon
i	ee	r	air	z	tset
				ß	ess-tset

Alps die Alpen

already schon [shohn]

also auch [owkн]

although obwohl [op**vohl**]

altogether insgesamt

aluminium foil die Alufolie
[**ah**loo-**fohl**-yuh]

always immer

am*: I am ich bin [ish]

a.m.: at seven a.m. um sieben
Uhr morgens [oom – o**or**]

amazing (surprising) erstaunlich
[airsht**own**lish]

(very good) fantastisch

ambulance der Krankenwagen
[**kran**ken-vahgen]

call an ambulance! rufen Sie
einen Krankenwagen [**roo**fen
zee **ine**-en]

America Amerika [am**ai**reeka]

American (adj) amerikanisch
[amairik**ah**nish]

I'm American (man/woman) ich
bin Amerik**a**ner/
Amerik**a**nerin

among unter [**oo**nter]

amount die Menge [**meng**-uh]

(money) der Betrag [bet**rahk**]

amp: a 13 amp fuse eine

dreizehn-Ampere-Sicherung [ampair zisheroong]
and und [oont]
angry wütend [vootent]
animal das Tier [teer]
ankle der Knöchel [knurshel]
anniversary (wedding) der Hochzeitstag [hoKH-tsites-tahk]
annoy: this man's annoying me dieser Mann belästigt mich [belestisht mish]
annoying ärgerlich [airgerlish]
another ein anderer [ine anderer]
can we have another room? können wir ein anderes Zimmer haben?
another beer, please noch ein Bier, bitte [noKH ine]
antibiotics die Antibiotika [anti-bee-ohteeka]
antifreeze das Frostschutzmittel [frost-shoots-mittel]
antihistamine das Antihistamin
antique: is it an antique? ist es antik? [anteek]
antique shop das Antiquitätengeschäft [antikvitayten-gesheft]
antiseptic das Antiseptikum
any: have you got any bread/tomatoes? haben Sie Brot/Tomaten? [hahben zee]
sorry, I don't have any tut mir leid, ich habe keine [toot meer lite, ish hahbuh kine-uh]
anybody jemand [yaymant]
does anybody speak English? spricht jemand Englisch?
there wasn't anybody there es war keiner da [kyner]
anything etwas [etvass]

dialogues

anything else? sonst noch etwas?
nothing else, thanks sonst nichts, danke [nishts, dank-uh]

would you like anything to drink? möchten Sie etwas trinken? [murshten]
I don't want anything, thanks ich möchte nichts, danke [nishts]

apart from abgesehen von [ap-gezay-en fon]
apartment die Wohnung [vohnoong]
apartment block der Wohnblock [vohnblock]
appendicitis die Blinddarmentzündung [blint-darm-ent-tsoondoong]
aperitif der Aperitif [apairee-teef]
apology die Entschuldigung [ent-shooldigoong]
appetizer die Vorspeise [for-shpize-uh]
apple der Apfel
appointment der Termin [tairmeen]

dialogue

good afternoon, how can I help you? guten Tag, kann ich Ihnen behilflich sein? [**goo**ten tahk, kan ish **ee**nen be**hil**flish zine]

I'd like to make an appointment ich möchte einen Termin vereinbaren [fair-**ine**-bahren]

what time would you like? welche Zeit wäre Ihnen recht? [**velsh**-uh tsite **vair**-uh **ee**nen resht]

three o'clock drei Uhr [**oor**]

I'm afraid that's not possible, is four o'clock all right? tut mir leid, das ist nicht möglich, ist vier Uhr in Ordnung? [**mur**glish]

yes, that will be fine ja, das ist mir recht [meer]

the name was ...? Ihr Name war ...? [eer **nahm**-uh vahr]

apricot die Aprikose [apri**kohz**-uh]

April der April [a-**prill**]

are*: we are wir sind [veer zint]

you are du bist/Sie sind [doo .../zee]

they are sie sind [zee]

area die Gegend [**gay**gent]

area code die Vorwahl [**for**vahl]

arm der Arm

arrange: will you arrange it for us? können Sie das für uns regeln? [**ray**geln]

arrival die Ankunft [**an**koonft]

arrive ankommen

when do we arrive? wann kommen wir an? [van **ko**mmen veer an]

has my fax arrived yet? ist mein Fax schon angekommen?

we arrived today wir sind heute angekommen

art die Kunst [koonst]

art gallery die Kunstgalerie [**koo**nstgal-leree]

artist der Künstler [**koo**nstler]

as: as big as so groß wie [zoh grohss vee]

as soon as possible so bald wie möglich [**mur**glish]

ashtray der Aschenbecher [**a**shen-besher]

ask fragen [**frah**gen]

I didn't ask for this das habe ich nicht bestellt [dass **hahb**-uh ish nisht be**stellt**]

could you ask him to ...? könnten Sie ihn bitten ...? [**kur**nten zee een **bitten**]

asleep: she's asleep sie schläft [shlayft]

aspirin das Kopfschmerzmittel [**kopf**-shmairts-mittel]

asthma das Asthma [**ast**-mah]

astonishing erstaunlich [airsht**own**lish]

at: at the hotel im Hotel at the station am Bahnhof

at six o'clock um 6 Uhr [oom]
at Günter's bei Günter [by]
athletics Leichtathletik [**ly**sht-at-laytik]
attractive attraktiv [atrakt**eef**]
aubergine die Aubergine [ohbair**jee**n-uh]
August der August [owg**oo**st]
Australia Australien [owstr**ah**lee-en]
Australian (adj) australisch [owstr**ah**lish]
I'm Australian (man/woman) ich bin Australier [owstr**ah**lee-er]/Australierin
Austria Österreich [**ur**ster-rysh]
Austrian (man/woman) der Österreicher [**ur**ster-rysher]/die Österreicherin
(adj) österreichisch [**ur**ster-rysh-ish]
the Austrians die Österreicher
Austrian Alps die österreichischen Alpen
Austrian Tirol Tirol [tee-**rohl**]
automatic (car) der Automatikwagen [owto-m**ah**tik-vahgen]
automatic teller (US) der Geldautomat [**g**elt-owtomaht]
autumn der Herbst [hairpst]
in the autumn im Herbst
avenue die Allee [all**ay**]
average (not good) mittelmäßig [**m**ittel-maysish]
(ordinary) durchschnittlich [**d**oorsh-shnitt-lish]
on average im Durchschnitt
awake: is he awake? ist er

wach? [va**k**H]
away: go away! gehen Sie weg! [**g**ay-en zee vek]
is it far away? ist es weit? [vite]
awful furchtbar [**f**oorsht-bar]
axle die Achse [**a**x-uh]

B

baby das Baby
baby food die Babynahrung [-nahroong]
baby's bottle das Fläschchen [**f**lesh-shen]
baby-sitter der Babysitter
back (of body) der Rücken [r**oo**cken]
(back part) die Rückseite [r**oo**ck-zite-uh]
at the back hinten
can I have my money back? kann ich mein Geld zurückbekommen? [tsoor**oo**ck-bekommen]
to come back zurückkommen
to go back zurückgehen [**g**ay-en]
backache die Rückenschmerzen [r**oo**cken-shmairtsen]
bacon der Speck [shpeck]
bad schlecht [shlesht]
a bad headache schlimme Kopfschmerzen [shlimm-uh]
badly schlecht [shlesht]
bag die Tasche [**t**ash-uh]
(handbag) die Handtasche [**h**ant-tash-uh]

(plastic) die Tüte [toot-uh]

baggage das Gepäck [gepeck]

baggage check (US) die Gepäckaufbewahrung [gepeck-owfbevahroong]

baggage reclaim die Gepäckrückgabe [gepeck-roock-gahb-uh]

bakery die Bäckerei [becker-ī]

balcony der Balkon [bal-kohn]
  a room with a balcony ein Zimmer mit Balkon [ine tsimmer]

bald kahl

ball (large) der Ball [bal]
  (small) die Kugel [koogel]

ballet das Ballett [bal-ett]

ballpoint pen der Kugelschreiber [koogel-shryber]

Baltic Sea die Ostsee [ost-zay]

banana die Banane [banahn-uh]

band (musical) die Band [bent]

bandage der Verband [fairbant]

bank (money) die Bank

bank account das Bankkonto [bank-konto]

bar die Bar

bar of chocolate die Tafel Schokolade [tahfel shoko-lahd-uh]

barber's der Frisör [frizur]

basket der Korb [korp]
  (in shop) der Einkaufskorb [ine-kowfs-korp]

bath das Bad [baht]
  can I have a bath? kann ich ein Bad nehmen? [naymen]

bathroom das Bad [baht]
  with a private bathroom mit

eigenem Bad [ī-gen-em]

bath towel das Badehandtuch [bahduh-hant-tookH]

battery die Batterie [batteree]

Bavaria Bayern [by-ern]

Bavarian Alps die Bayrischen Alpen [by-rishen]

be* sein [zine]

beach der Strand [shtrant]

beach mat die Strandmatte [shtrant-mat-uh]

beach umbrella der Sonnenschirm [zonnen-sheerm]

beans die Bohnen
  runner beans die Stangen-bohnen [shtangen-]
  broad beans dicke Bohnen [dick-uh]

beard der Bart

beautiful schön [shurn]

because weil [vile]
  because of ... wegen ... [vaygen]

bed das Bett
  I'm going to bed ich gehe zu Bett [ish gay-uh tsoo]

bed and breakfast Übernachtung mit Frühstück [oobernakHtoong mit frooshtook]

bedroom das Schlafzimmer [shlahf-tsimmer]

beef das Rindfleisch [rint-flysh]

beer das Bier [beer]
  two beers, please zwei Bier, bitte [bitt-uh]

beer mug der Bierkrug [beerkrook]

before vorher [forhair]
before that davor [dafor]
before me vor mir
begin: when does it begin?
wann fängt es an? [van fengt
ess an]
beginner (man/woman) der
Anfänger [anfeng-er]/die
Anfängerin
beginning: at the beginning
am Anfang
behind hinten
behind me hinter mir
beige beige [bayJ]
Belgian (adj) belgisch [belgish]
Belgium Belgien [bel-gee-en]
believe glauben [glowben]
below unten [oonten]
below ... unter ... [oonter]
belt der Gürtel [goortel]
bend (in road) die Kurve [koorv-
uh]
Berlin Wall die (Berliner)
Mauer [(bairleener) mow-er]
berth (on ship) die Kabine
[kabeen-uh]
beside: beside the ... neben
dem/der ... [nayben daym/dair]
best beste [best-uh]
better besser
are you feeling better? geht
es dir/Ihnen besser? [gayt ess
deer/eenen]
between zwischen [tsvishen]
beyond jenseits (+gen) [yayn-
zites]
bicycle das Fahrrad [fahr-raht]
big groß [grohss]
too big zu groß [tsoo]

it's not big enough es ist nicht
groß genug [nisht – genook]
bike das Rad [raht]
(motorbike) das Motorrad
[motohr-raht]
bikini der Bikini
bill die Rechnung [reshnoong]
(US: money) der Geldschein
[gelt-shine]
could I have the bill, please?
kann ich bitte bezahlen? [kan
ish bitt-uh betsahlen]
bin der Abfalleimer [apfal-
ime-er]
bin liners die Mülltüten [mooll-
tooten]
binding (ski) die Bindung
[bindoong]
bird der Vogel [fohgel]
biro® der Kugelschreiber
[koogel-shryber]
birthday der Geburtstag
[geboorts-tahk]
happy birthday! herzlichen
Glückwunsch zum
Geburtstag! [hairts-lishen
gloockvoonsh tsoom]
biscuit das Plätzchen [plets-
shen]
bit: a little bit ein bisschen [ine
biss-shen]
a big bit ein großes Stück
[grohssess shtoock]
a bit of ... ein Stück von ...
a bit expensive etwas teuer
bite (by insect) der Stich [shtish]
(by dog) der Biss
bitter (taste etc) bitter
black schwarz [shvarts]

Black Forest der Schwarzwald [shvarts-valt]

blanket die Decke [deck-uh]

bless you! Gesundheit! [gezoont-hite]

blind blind [blint]

blinds die Jalousie [Jalloozee]

blister die Blase [blahz-uh]

blocked (road, sink) verstopft [fairshtopft]

block of flats der Wohnblock [vohnblock]

blond blond [blont]

blood das Blut [bloot]

high blood pressure hoher Blutdruck [bloot-droock]

blouse die Bluse [blooz-uh]

blow-dry (verb) fönen [furnen]

I'd like a cut and blow-dry schneiden und fönen, bitte [shnyden oont]

blue blau [blow]

blusher das Rouge [rooJ]

boarding house die Pension [pangz-yohn]

boarding pass die Bordkarte [bortkart-uh]

boat das Boot [boht]
(for passengers) das Schiff [shiff]

body der Körper [kurper]

boil (water, potatoes) kochen [koKHen]

boiled egg ein gekochtes Ei [gekoKHtess ī]

bone der Knochen [k-noKHen]

bonnet (of car) die Haube [howb-uh]

book das Buch [booKH]
to book buchen [booKHen],

bestellen [beshtellen]

can I book a seat? kann ich einen Platz reservieren lassen? [rezair-veeren]

dialogue

I'd like to book a table for two ich möchte einen Tisch für zwei Personen bestellen [ish mursht-uh ine-en tish foor tsvy pairzohnen]

what time would you like it booked for? für wann ist die Reservierung? [rezair-veeroong]

half past seven halb acht

that's fine das geht in Ordnung [gayt in ortnoong]

and your name? Ihr Name, bitte? [nahm-uh]

bookshop die Buchhandlung [booKH-hantloong]

bookstore (US) die Buchhandlung

boot (footwear) der Stiefel [shteefel]
(of car) der Kofferraum [koffer-rowm]

border (of country) die Grenze [grents-uh]

bored: I'm bored ich habe langeweile [ish hahb-uh lang-uh-vile-uh]

boring langweilig [langvile-ish]

born: I was born in Manchester ich bin in Manchester geboren

[ge**boh**ren]

I was born in 1960 ich bin neunzehnhundertsechzig geboren

borrow leihen [**ly**-en]

may I borrow ...? kann ich ... leihen?

both beide [**by**-duh]

bother: sorry to bother you with this es tut mir leid, Sie damit zu belästigen [ess toot meer lite zee dahmit tsoo be**les**tigen]

bottle die Flasche [**flash**-uh]

a bottle of dry white wine eine Flasche trockenen Weißwein

bottle-opener der Flaschen-öffner [**flash**en-urfner]

bottom (of person) der Hintern

at the bottom of the hill am Fuß des Berges [**fooss**]

box die Schachtel [**shakH**tel] (larger) der Karton

box office die Kasse [**kass**-uh]

boy der Junge [**yoong**-uh]

boyfriend der Freund [**froynt**]

bra der BH [**bay-hah**]

bracelet das Armband [**armbant**]

brake die Bremse [**bremz**-uh]

brandy der Weinbrand [**vine**-brant]

bread das Brot [**broht**]

some more bread, please noch etwas Brot, bitte [**etvass**]

white bread das Weißbrot [**vice**-broht]

brown bread das Graubrot [**grow**-broht]

wholemeal bread das Vollkornbrot [**follkorn**-broht]

break (verb) brechen [**bresh**en]

I've broken ... mir ist ... kaputtgegangen [meer – kap**oot**-gegangen]

I think I've broken my wrist ich glaube, ich habe mir das Handgelenk gebrochen [ge**brokH**en]

breakdown die Panne [**pann**-uh]

breakdown service die Pannenhilfe [**pann**en-hilf-uh]

break down (in car) eine Panne haben [**ine**-uh pann-uh **hah**ben]

I've broken down ich habe eine Panne

breakfast das Frühstück [**frOOsht**OOck]

English/full breakfast ein englisches Frühstück [**eng**-lish-ess]

break-in: I've had a break-in bei mir ist eingebrochen worden [by meer ist **ine**-gebrokHen **vor**den]

breast die Brust [**broost**]

breathe atmen [**aht**men]

breeze die Brise [**breez**-uh]

brewery die Brauerei [**brower**-**ī**]

bridge (over river) die Brücke [**brOOck**-uh]

brief kurz [**koorts**]

briefcase die Aktentasche [**akten**-tash-uh]

bright (light etc) hell

bright red hellrot [hell-**roht**]

brilliant (idea) glänzend

[glentsent]
(person) großartig [grohss-artish]
bring bringen
I'll bring it back later ich
bringe es später zurück [bring-uh ess shpayter tsooroock]
Britain Großbritannien [grohss-britannee-en]
British britisch [breetish]
brochure die Broschüre
[broshoor-uh]
broken kaputt
bronchitis die Bronchitis [bron-sheetis]
brooch die Brosche [brosh-uh]
broom der Besen [bayzen]
brother der Bruder [brooder]
brother-in-law der Schwager
[shvahger]
brown braun [brown]
bruise der blaue Fleck [blow-uh]
brush die Bürste [boorst-uh]
(artist's) der Pinsel [pinzel]
Brussels Brüssel [broossel]
bucket der Eimer [ime-er]
buffet car der Speisewagen
[shpize-uh-vahgen]
buggy (for child) der
Sportwagen [shport-vahgen]
building das Gebäude [geboyd-uh]
bulb (light bulb) die Birne [beern-uh]
bumper die Stoßstange
[shtohss-shtang-uh]
bunk das Bett
bureau de change die
Wechselstube [veksel-shtoob-uh]

burglary der Einbruch [ine-brooKH]
burn die Verbrennung [fair-brennoong]
(verb) brennen
burnt: this is burnt das ist
angebrannt [an-gebrannt]
burst: a burst pipe ein
geplatztes Rohr
bus der Bus [booss]
what number bus is it to ...?
welcher Bus fährt nach ...?
[velsher booss fairt naKH]
when is the next bus to ...?
wann fährt der nächste Bus
nach ...? [naykst-uh]
what time is the last bus?
wann fährt der letzte Bus?
[letst-uh]
could you let me know when
we get there? können Sie mir
Bescheid sagen, wenn wir da
sind? [kurnen zee meer beshite
zahgen]

dialogue

does this bus go to ...?
fährt dieser Bus nach ...?
[fairt]
no, you need a number ...
nein, Sie müssen mit der
... fahren
where does it leave from?
wo fährt er ab? [vo]

business das Geschäft [gesheft]
bus station der Busbahnhof
[booss-bahnhohf]

bus stop die Bushaltestelle [**booss**-halt-uh-shtell-uh]

bust der Busen [**boo**zen]

busy (restaurant etc) voll [foll] (telephone) besetzt [be**zetst**]

I'm busy tomorrow morgen bin ich beschäftigt [be**shef**-tisht]

but aber [**ah**ber]

butcher's der Metzger [**metsger**]

butter die Butter [**boo**tter]

button der Knopf [k-nopf]

buy kaufen [**kow**fen]

where can I buy ...? wo kann ich ... bekommen? [voh]

by: by bus/car mit dem Bus/ Auto [daym]

written by ... geschrieben von

by the window am Fenster

by the sea am Meer

by Thursday bis Donnerstag

bye auf Wiedersehen [owf-**vee**derzayn]

C

cabbage der Kohl

cable car die Drahtseilbahn [**draht**zile-bahn]

café das Café [kaf**fay**]

cagoule das Windhemd [**vint**-hemt]

cake der Kuchen [**koo**KHen]

cake shop die Konditorei [kondeetor-**ī**]

call (verb) rufen [**roo**fen] (to phone) anrufen [**an**roofen]

what's it called? wie heißt das? [vee hyst dass]

he/she is called ... er/sie heißt ...

please call a doctor bitte rufen Sie einen Arzt

please give me a call at 7.30 a.m. tomorrow morning könnten Sie mich morgen früh um sieben Uhr dreißig wecken? [**kur**nten zee mish morgen froo – **ve**cken]

please ask him to call me sagen Sie ihm bitte, er möchte mich anrufen [**mur**sht-uh]

call back: I'll call back later ich komme später noch einmal wieder [ish **komm**-uh shp**ay**ter noKH **ine**-mahl **vee**der] (phone back) ich rufe später noch einmal an [**roof**-uh]

call round: I'll call round tomorrow ich komme morgen vorbei [**komm**-uh – for-by]

camcorder der Camcorder

camera die Kamera

camera shop der Fotoladen [**foto**-lahden]

camp (verb) zelten [**tse**lten]

camping gas das Campinggas [**kemping**-gahss]

campsite der Campingplatz [**kemping**plats]

can (tin) die Dose [**dohz**-uh] **a can of beer** eine Dose Bier

can*: can you ...? kannst du/ können Sie ...? [doo/**kur**nen zee]

can I have ...? kann ich ...

haben? [**hah**ben]

I can't ... ich kann nicht...
[nisht]

Canada Kanada

Canadian (adj) kanadisch
[ka**nah**dish]

I'm Canadian (man/woman) ich
bin Kanadier [kan**ah**dee-er]/
Kanadierin

canal der Kanal [ka**nahl**]

cancel (reservation) rückgängig
machen [**rOO**ck-gengish
ma**KH**en]

candle die Kerze [**kairts**-uh]

candy (US) die Süßigkeiten
[**zOO**ssish-kyten]

canoe das Kanu [kah**nOO**]

canoeing das Kanufahren
[kah**nOO**-fahren]

can-opener der Dosenöffner
[**dohz**en-urfner]

cap (hat) eine Mütze [**mOOts**-uh]
(of bottle) der Deckel

car das Auto [**ow**to]
by car mit dem Auto

carafe die Karaffe [ka**raff**-uh]
a carafe of house white,
please eine Karaffe wei**ß**en
Tafelwein, bitte

caravan der Wohnwagen
[**vohn**vahgen]

caravan site der
Wohnwagenplatz [**vohn**vahgen-
plats]

carburettor der Vergaser [fair-
gahzer]

card (birthday etc) die Karte
[**kart**-uh]
here's my (business) card

hier ist meine Karte

cardigan die Strickjacke
[**shtrick**-yack-uh]

cardphone das Kartentelefon

careful vorsichtig [**for**-zishtish]
be careful! seien Sie
vorsichtig! [**zy**-en zee]

caretaker der Hausmeister
[**howss**-myster]

car ferry die Autofähre [**ow**to-
fair-uh]

car hire die Autovermietung
[**ow**to-fairmeetoong]

carnival der Karneval [**karn**-
uh-val]

car park der Parkplatz
[**park**plats]

carpet der Teppich [**tepp**ish]

carriage (of train) der Wagen
[**vah**gen]

carrier bag die Tragetasche
[**trahg**-uh-tash-uh]

carrot die Möhre [**mur**-uh]

carry tragen [**trahg**en]

carry-cot die
Säuglingstragetasche
[**zoyg**lings-trahg-uh-tash-uh]

carton (of orange juice etc) die
Packung [**pack**oong]

carwash (place) die
Autowaschanlage [**ow**to-vash-
anlahg-uh]

case (suitcase) der Koffer

cash das Bargeld [**bahr**gelt]
(verb) einlösen [**ine**-lurzen]
will you cash this for me?
können Sie das für mich
einlösen? [**kur**nen]

cash desk die Kasse [**kass**-uh]

cash dispenser der Geldautomat [**ge**lt-owtomaht]

cassette die Kassette [kassett-uh]

cassette recorder der Kassettenrecorder

castle das Schloss [shloss]

casualty department die Unfallstation [**oo**nfal-shtats-yohn]

cat die Katze [**ka**ts-uh]

catch fangen

where do we catch the bus to ...? wo k**ö**nnen wir den Bus nach ... bek**o**mmen?

cathedral der Dom [dohm]

Catholic (adj) katholisch [kat**oh**lish]

cauliflower der Blumenkohl [bl**oo**menkohl]

cave die Höhle [**hur**l-uh]

CD die CD [tsay-d**ay**]

ceiling die Decke [**de**ck-uh]

celery der Sellerie [**ze**lleree]

cellar (for wine) der Weinkeller [**vine**-keller]

cemetery der Friedhof [freet-hohf]

Centigrade* Celsius [ts**el**zee-oos]

centimetre* der Zentimeter [ts**e**ntimayter]

central zentral [tsentr**ah**l]

central heating die Zentralheizung [tsentr**ah**l-hytsoong]

centre das Zentrum [ts**e**ntroom]

how do we get to the city centre? wie kommt man zum Stadtzentrum? [tsoom sht**a**t-tsentroom]

cereal die Zerealien [tsairay-**ah**lee-en]

certainly sicher [**zi**sher]

certainly not ganz bestimmt nicht [gants besht**i**mmt nisht]

chair der Stuhl [sht**oo**l]

chairlift der Sessellift [**ze**ssel-lift]

champagne der Champagner [shamp**a**n-yer]

change (noun: money) das Wechselgeld [**ve**ksel-gelt]

to change (money) wechseln [**we**kseln]

to change a reservation umbuchen [**oo**mb**oo**кнen]

can I change this for ...? kann ich das gegen ... umtauschen? [g**ay**gen ... **oo**m-towshen]

I don't have any change ich habe kein Kleingeld [h**ah**b-uh kine kl**ine**-gelt]

can you give me change for a 50 euro note? können Sie einen 50-Euro-Schein wechseln? [k**ur**nen zee **ine**-en – **oy**ro-shine]

dialogue

do we have to change (trains/buses)? müssen wir umsteigen? [m**oo**ssen veer **oo**m-shtygen]

yes, change at Düsseldorf ja, Sie müssen in Düsseldorf umsteigen

no, it's direct nein, das ist eine Dir**e**ktverbindung

changed: to get changed sich umziehen [zish **oo**m-tsee-en]

chapel die Kapelle [kapell-uh]

charge der Preis [price]

charge (verb) verlangen [**fair**langen]

charge card die Kreditkarte [kray**deet**-kart-uh]

cheap billig [**bill**ish]

do you have anything cheaper? haben Sie etwas billigeres? [**hah**ben zee **et**vass billigeress]

check (verb) überprüfen [**oo**ber-pr**oo**fen]

could you check the ... please? könnten Sie die ... überprüfen, bitte? [**kurn**ten] (US) der Scheck [sheck] (in restaurant etc) die Rechnung [**resh**noong]

check-in der Check-in

check in (at hotel) sich anmelden [zish **a**nmelden] (at airport) einchecken [**ine**-checken]

where do we have to check in? wo müssen wir einchecken?

cheek (of face) die Backe [**back**-uh]

cheerio! (bye-bye) tschüs! [ch**oo**ss]

cheers! (toast) Prost! [prohst] (thanks) danke [**dan**kuh]

cheese der Käse [**kayz**-uh]

chemist's die Apotheke [apo**tayk**-uh]

cheque der Scheck [sheck]

do you take cheques? nehmen Sie Schecks? [**nay**men zee shecks]

cheque book das Scheckheft [**sheck**-heft]

cheque card die Scheckkarte [**sheck**-kart-uh]

cherry die Kirsche [**keersh**-uh]

chess Schach [shakH]

chest (body) die Brust [broost]

chewing gum der Kaugummi [**kow**-goommee]

chicken (as food) das Hähnchen [**hayn**shen]

chickenpox die Windpocken [**vint**pocken]

child das Kind [kint]

children die Kinder

child minder die Tagesmutter [**tah**gess-mootter]

children's pool das Kinderschwimmbecken [**kinder**-shvimmbecken]

children's portion der Kinderteller [**kinder**-teller]

chin das Kinn

china (noun) das Porzellan [portsell**ahn**]

Chinese (adj) chinesisch [shin**ay**zish]

chips die Pommes frites [pom frit] (US) die Chips

chocolate die Schokolade [shoko**lahd**-uh]

milk chocolate die Milchschokolade [**milsh**-]

plain chocolate die Bitterschokolade

chocolates die Pralinen [praleenen]

hot chocolate der Kakao [kakow]

choose wählen [vaylen]

Christian name der Vorname [fornahm-uh]

Christmas Weihnachten [vynakHten]

Christmas Eve der Heiligabend [hylish-ahbent]

merry Christmas! frohe Weihnachten [froh-uh]

church die Kirche [keersh-uh]

cider der Apfelwein [apfel-vine]

cigar die Zigarre [tsigarr-uh]

cigarette die Zigarette [tsigarett-uh]

cigarette lighter das Feuerzeug [foyer-tsoyk]

cinema das Kino [keeno]

circle der Kreis [krice]
(in theatre) der Balkon [balkohn]

city die Stadt [shtatt]

city centre die Innenstadt [innenshtatt]

clean (adj) sauber [zowber]

can you clean this for me? können Sie dies für mich reinigen? [kurnen zee deess foor mish rynigen]

cleaning solution (for contact lenses) die Reinigungslösung [rynigoongs-lurzoong]

cleansing lotion (cosmetic) die Reinigungscreme [rynigoongs-kraym]

clear klar

clever klug [klook]

cliff die Klippe [klipp-uh]

climbing das Bergsteigen [bairk-shtygen]

cling film die Frischhaltefolie [frish-halt-uh-fohlee-uh]

clinic die Klinik [kleenik]

cloakroom (for coats) die Garderobe [garderohb-uh]

clock die Uhr [oor]

close schließen [shleessen]

dialogue

> what time do you close? wann schließen Sie?
>
> we close at 8 p.m. on weekdays and 6 p.m. on Saturdays wir schließen wochentags um zwanzig Uhr und samstags um achtzehn Uhr [voKHen-tahks oom – zams-tahks oom]
>
> do you close for lunch? haben Sie mittags geschlossen? [geshlossen]
>
> yes, between 1 and 2.30 p.m. ja, von dreizehn Uhr bis vierzehn Uhr dreißig

closed geschlossen [geshlossen]

cloth (fabric) der Stoff [shtoff]
(for cleaning etc) der Lappen

clothes die Kleider [klyder]

clothes line die Wäscheleine [vesh-uh-line-uh]

clothes peg die Wäscheklammer [vesh-uh-klammer]

cloud die Wolke [volk-uh]

cloudy wolkig [**vo**lkish]

clutch (of car) die Kupplung [**koo**ploong]

coach (bus) der Bus [booss]
(on train) der Wagen [**vah**gen]

coach station der Busbahnhof [**boo**ssbahnhohf]

coach trip die Busreise [booss-rize-uh]

coast die Küste [**koo**st-uh]
on the coast an der Küste

coat (long coat) der Mantel
(jacket) die Jacke [**ya**ck-uh]

coathanger der Kleiderbügel [**kly**derboogel]

cockroach die Küchenschabe [**koo**shen-shahb-uh]

cocoa der Kakao [kak**ow**]

code (for phoning) die Vorwahl [**fo**rvahl]
what's the (dialling) code for Berlin? was ist die Vorwahl für Berlin?

coffee der Kaffee [**ka**ffay]
two coffees, please zwei Kaffee bitte

coin die Münze [m**oo**nts-uh]

Coke® die Cola [**koh**la]

cold (adj) kalt
I'm cold mir ist kalt [meer]
I have a cold ich bin erkältet [ish bin air**ke**ltet]

collapse: he's collapsed er ist zusammengebrochen [air ist tsooz**a**mmengebrokнen]

collar der Kragen [kr**ah**gen]

collect sammeln
I've come to collect ... ich komme, um ... abzuholen [ish komm-uh oom ... ap-tsoo-hohlen]

collect call das R-Gespräch [**air**-geshpraysh]

college das College

Cologne Köln [kurln]

colour die Farbe [**far**b-uh]
do you have this in other colours? haben Sie dies noch in anderen Farben? [**hah**ben zee deess noкн in **a**nder-en **far**ben]

colour film der Farbfilm [**far**p-film]

comb (noun) der Kamm

come kommen

dialogue

where do you come from? woher kommen Sie? [voh**air**]
I come from Edinburgh ich komme aus Edinburgh [ish komm-uh owss]

come back zurückkommen [tsoor**oo**ck-kommen]
I'll come back tomorrow ich komme morgen zurück [komm-uh]

come in hereinkommen [hair-**ine**-kommen]

comfortable (hotel etc) komfortabel [komfor**ah**bel]

compact disc die Compact-Disc

company (business) die Firma [**fee**rma]

compartment (on train) das Abteil [ap**tile**]

compass der Kompass [ko**mpass**]

complain sich beschweren [zish beshv**ai**ren]

complaint die Beschwerde [beshv**ai**rd-uh]

I have a complaint ich möchte mich beschweren [m**u**rsht-uh mish beshv**ai**ren]

completely völlig [f**u**rlish]

computer der Computer ['computer']

concert das Konzert [konts**ai**rt]

concussion die Gehirnerschütterung [geh**ee**rn-airsh**oo**tteroong]

conditioner (for hair) der Festiger

condom das Kondom [kond**oh**m]

conference die Konferenz [konfair**e**nts]

confirm bestätigen [besht**ay**tigen]

congratulations! herzlichen Glückwunsch! [h**ai**rtslishen gl**oo**ckvoonsh]

connecting flight der Anschlussflug [**a**nshlooss-flook]

connection (in travelling) die Verbindung [fairb**i**ndoong]

conscious (medically) bei Bewusstsein [by bev**oo**st-zine]

constipation die Verstopfung [fair-sht**o**pfoong]

consulate das Konsulat [konzool**aht**]

contact: where can I contact him? wo kann ich ihn

erreichen? [vo – een air-r**y**shen]

contact lenses die Kontaktlinsen [kont**a**kt-linzen]

contraceptive das Verhütungsmittel [fairh**oo**toongs-mittel]

convenient (time, location) günstig [g**oo**nstish]

that's not convenient das ist nicht sehr günstig [nisht zair]

cook kochen [ko**KH**en]

not cooked (underdone) nicht gar [nisht gahr]

cooker der Herd [hairt]

cookie (US) das Plätzchen [pl**e**ts-shen]

cooking utensils die Küchengeräte [k**oo**shen-gerayt-uh]

cool kühl [k**oo**l]

cork der Korken

corkscrew der Korkenzieher [k**o**rken-tsee-er]

corner: on the corner an der Ecke [**e**ck-uh]

in the corner in der Ecke

cornflakes die Corn-flakes

correct (right) richtig [r**i**shtish]

corridor der Gang

cosmetics die Kosmetika [kosm**ay**tika]

cost (verb) kosten

how much does it cost? was kostet das? [vass k**o**stet dass]

cot (for baby) das Kinderbett

cotton die Baumwolle [b**ow**mvoll-uh]

cotton wool die Watte [v**a**t-uh]

couch (sofa) die Couch

couchette der Liegewagen [leeg-uh-vahgen]

cough (noun) der Husten [hoosten]

cough medicine das Hustenmittel [hoosten-mittel]

could: could you ...? könnten Sie...? [kurnten zee]

could I have ...? könnte ich ... haben? [kurnt-uh ish ... hahben]

I couldn't ... (wasn't able to) ich konnte nicht... [ish konnt-uh nisht]

country das Land [lant]

countryside die Landschaft [lant-shafft]

couple (man and woman) das Paar [pahr]

a couple of ... ein paar... [ine pahr]

courier der Reiseleiter [rize-uh-lyter]

course (of meal) der Gang

of course natürlich [natoorlish]

of course not natürlich nicht [nisht]

cousin (male) der Vetter [fetter] (female) die Kusine [koozeen-uh]

cow die Kuh [koo]

crab die Krebs [krayps]

cracker (biscuit) der Kräcker [krecker]

craft shop der Handwerksladen [hantvairks-lahden]

crash (noun) der Zusammenstoß [tsoo-zammen-shtohss]

I've had a crash ich hatte einen Unfall [ish hatt-uh ine-en oonfal]

crazy verrückt [fair-rookt]

cream (on milk, in cake) die Sahne [zahn-uh] (lotion) die Creme [kraym] (colour) cremefarben [kraym-farben]

creche (for babies) die Kinderkrippe [kinderkripp-uh]

credit card die Kreditkarte [kredeet-kart-uh]

dialogue

can I pay by credit card? kann ich mit Kreditkarte bezahlen? [betsahlen]
which card do you want to use? mit welcher Karte möchten Sie bezahlen? [velsher]
what's the number? was ist die Nummer? [noommer]
and the expiry date? und das Ablaufdatum? [aplowf-dahtoom]

crisps die Chips [chips]

crockery das Geschirr [gesheer]

crossing (by sea) die Überfahrt [ooberfahrt]

crossroads die Kreuzung [kroytsoong]

crowd die Menge [meng-uh]

crowded (streets, bars) voll [foll]

crown (on tooth) die Krone [krohn-uh]

cruise (by ship) die Kreuzfahrt [kroyts-fahrt]

crutches die Krücken [kroock-en]

cry weinen [vynen]

cucumber die Gurke [goork-uh]

cup die Tasse [tass-uh]

a cup of ... please eine Tasse ..., bitte [ine-uh]

cupboard der Schrank [shrank]

curly (hair) kraus [krowss]

current (electrical, in water) der Strom [shtrohm]
(in sea) die Strömung [shtrurmoong]

curtains die Vorhänge [forheng-uh]

cushion das Kissen

custom der Brauch [browKH]

Customs der Zoll [tsoll]

cut der Schnitt [shnitt]

cut (verb) schneiden [shnyden]
I've cut myself ich habe mich geschnitten [ish hahb-uh mish geshnitten]

cutlery das Besteck [beshteck]

cycling das Radfahren [rahtfahren]

cyclist (man/woman) der Radfahrer [rahtfahrer]/die Radfahrerin

Czech (adj) tschechisch [cheshish]
(language) Tschechisch

Czech Republic die Tschechische Republik [cheshish-uh repoo-bleek]

D

dad der Vater [fahter]

daily täglich [tayglish]

damage (verb) beschädigen [beshaydigen]
I'm sorry, I've damaged this tut mir leid, ich habe es beschädigt [toot meer lite]

damaged beschädigt [beshaydisht]

damn! verdammt! [fairdamt]

damp feucht [foysht]

dance (noun) der Tanz [tants]

dance (verb) tanzen [tantsen]
would you like to dance? möchtest du/möchten Sie tanzen? [murshtest doo/murshten zee]

dangerous gefährlich [gefairlish]

Danish dänisch [daynish]

Danube die Donau [dohnow]

dark dunkel [doonkel]
it's getting dark es wird dunkel [veert]

date*: what's the date today? der Wievielte ist heute? [dair veefeelt-uh ist hoyt-uh]
let's make a date for next Monday wir sollten einen Termin für nächsten Montag vereinbaren [ine-en tairmeen foor – fair-ine-bahren]

dates (fruit) die Datteln fpl

daughter die Tochter [toKHter]

daughter-in-law die Schwiegertochter [shveegertoKHter]

dawn das Morgengrauen
[morgen-growen]

at dawn bei Tagesanbruch [by
tahgess-anbrooKH]

day der Tag [tahk]

the day after am Tag danach
[danaKH]

the day after tomorrow
übermorgen [**oo**bermorgen]

the day before am Tag zuvor
[ts**oo**for]

the day before yesterday
vorgestern [**for**gestern]

every day jeden Tag [**yay**den]

all day den ganzen Tag [dayn
gantsen]

in two days' time in zwei
Tagen [**tah**gen]

have a nice day schönen Tag
noch [sh**ur**nen – noKH]

day trip der Tagesausflug
[**tah**gess-owssfl**oo**k]

dead tot [toht]

deaf taub [towp]

deal (business) das Geschäft
[gesheft]

it's a deal abgemacht [**ap**-
gemaKHt]

death der Tod [toht]

decaffeinated coffee
koffeinfreier Kaffee [koffay-
een-fry-er kaffay]

December der Dezember
[dayts**e**mber]

decide entscheiden [ent-
sh**y**den]

we haven't decided yet
wir haben uns noch nicht

entschieden [veer h**ah**ben oonss
noKH nisht ent-sh**ee**den]

decision die Entscheidung
[ent-sh**y**doong]

deck (on ship) das Deck

deckchair der Liegestuhl [l**ee**g-
uh-sht**oo**l]

deduct abziehen [**ap**-tsee-en]

deep tief [teef]

definitely bestimmt [besht**i**mmt]

definitely not ganz bestimmt
nicht [gants]

degree (qualification) der
Abschluss [**ap**shlooss]

delay die Verzögerung [fair-
ts**u**rgeroong]

deliberately absichtlich
[**ap**zishtlish]

delicatessen der
Feinkostladen [**fine**-kost-
lahden]

delicious köstlich [k**ur**stlish]

deliver liefern [**lee**fern]

delivery (of mail) die Zustellung
[ts**oo**-shtelloong]

Denmark Dänemark [**dayn**-
uh-mark]

dental floss die Zahnseide
[ts**ahn**zide-uh]

dentist der Zahnarzt [ts**ahn**-
artst]

dialogue

it's this one here es ist
dieser hier [**dee**zer heer]
this one? dieser?
no that one nein, dieser
[nine]

here? hier? [heer]
yes ja [yah]

dentures das Gebiss
deodorant das Deodorant
department die Abteilung
[ap-**ty**loong]
department store das
Kaufhaus [**kow**fhowss]
departure die Abreise [ap-
rize-uh]
(of plane) der Abflug [**apf**look]
departure lounge die
Abflughalle [**apf**look-hal-uh]
depend: it depends es kommt
darauf an [ess kommt dar**ow**f an]
it depends on ... es hängt von
... ab [hengt fon ... ap]
deposit (as security) die Kaution
[kowts-**yohn**]
(as part payment) die Anzahlung
[**ant**sahloong]
description die Beschreibung
[beshr**y**boong]
dessert der Nachtisch
[**na**KHtish]
destination das Reiseziel [rize-
uh-tseel]
develop entwickeln [entv**ick**eln]

dialogue

could you develop these
films? können Sie diese
Filme entwickeln? [**kur**nen
zee d**ee**z-uh film-uh]
when will they be ready?
wann sind sie fertig?
[**fair**tish]

tomorrow afternoon
morgen nachmittag
how much is the four-hour
service? was kostet der
Vier-Stunden-Service?
[sht**oo**nden]

diabetic (man/woman) der
Diabetiker [dee-ab**ay**tiker]/die
Diabetikerin
diabetic foods diabetische
Kost [dee-ab**ay**tish-uh]
dial (verb) wählen [**vay**len]
dialling code die Vorwahl
[**for**vahl]
diamond der Diamant [dee-
amant]
diaper (US) die Windel [vindel]
diarrhoea der Durchfall
[**doo**rshfal]
diary (business etc) der
Terminkalender [tairmeen-
kalender]
(for personal experiences) das
Tagebuch [**tah**g-uh-booKH]
dictionary das Wörterbuch
[**vur**terbooKH]
didn't*
see not
die sterben [sht**air**ben]
diesel der Diesel
diet die Diät [dee-**ayt**]
I'm on a diet ich mache eine
Diät [ish ma**KH**-uh **ine**-uh]
I have to follow a special
diet ich muss nach einer
Diät leben [mooss na**KH** **ine**-er
– **lay**ben]
difference der Unterschied

[**oo**ntersheet]

what's the difference? was ist der Unterschied?

different verschieden [fairsh**ee**den]

this one is different dieses ist anders

a different table ein anderer Tisch

difficult schwer [shvair]

difficulty die Schwierigkeit [shv**ee**rish-kite]

dinghy (rubber) das Schlauchboot [shl**ow**KHboht] (sailing) das Dingi [ding-gee]

dining room das Speisezimmer [shp**ize**-uh-tsimmer]

dinner (evening meal) das Abendessen [**ah**bentessen]

to have dinner zu Abend essen [ts**oo**]

direct (adj) direkt [deer**ekt**]

is there a direct train? gibt es eine direkte Zugverbindung? [ts**oo**k-fairbindoong]

direction die Richtung [r**i**shtoong]

which direction is it? in welcher Richtung ist es? [v**el**sher]

is it in this direction? ist es in dieser Richtung? [d**ee**zer]

directory enquiries die Auskunft [**ow**sskoonft]

dirt der Schmutz [shmoots]

dirty schmutzig [shm**oo**tsish]

disabled behindert

is there access for the disabled? gibt es Zugang für

Behinderte? [geept ess ts**oo**gang foor behindert-uh]

disappear verschwinden [fairshv**i**nden]

it's disappeared es ist verschwunden [fairshv**oo**nden]

disappointed enttäuscht [entt**oy**sht]

disappointing enttäuschend [ent-t**oy**shent]

disaster die Katastrophe [katastr**oh**f-uh]

disco die Diskothek [diskot**ayk**]

discount der Rabatt [rabbat]

is there a discount? gibt es einen Rabatt? [geept ess **ine**-en]

disease die Krankheit [krankhite]

disgusting widerlich [v**ee**derlish]

dish (meal) das Gericht [ger**i**sht] (bowl) der Teller

dishcloth das Spültuch [shp**oo**lt**oo**KH]

disinfectant das Desinfektionsmittel [dezinfekts-y**oh**ns-mittel]

disk (for computer) die Diskette [disk**ett**-uh]

disposable diapers (US) die Papierwindeln [pap**ee**r-vindeln]

disposable nappies die Papierwindeln

distance die Entfernung [entf**air**noong]

in the distance weit weg [vite vek]

distilled water destilliertes Wasser [destilleertess vasser]

district das Gebiet [gebeet]

disturb stören [shtur-ren]

diversion (detour) die Umleitung [oom-lytoong]

diving board das Sprungbrett [shproongbrett]

divorced geschieden [gesheeden]

dizzy: I feel dizzy mir ist schwindlig [meer ist shvintlish]

do tun [toon]

 what shall we do? was sollen wir tun? [vass zollen veer]

 how do you do it? wie machen Sie das? [vee maKHen zee]

 will you do it for me? können Sie das für mich tun? [kurnen]

dialogues

 how do you do? guten Tag [gooten tahk]
 nice to meet you freut mich [froyt mish]
 what do you do? (work) was machst du/machen Sie beruflich? [vass maKHst doo/maKHen zee beroOflish]
 I'm a teacher, and you? ich bin Lehrer, und Sie?
 I'm a student ich bin Student
 what are you doing this evening? was machst du/machen Sie heute abend?

[maKHst doo/maKHen zee hoyt-uh ahbent]
 we're going out for a drink, do you want to join us? wir gehen einen trinken, möchtest du/möchten Sie mitkommen? [murshtest doo/murshten zee]

 do you want cream? möchtest du/möchten Sie Sahne?
 I do, but she doesn't ich ja, aber sie nicht [yah]

doctor der Arzt [artst]
 we need a doctor wir brauchen einen Arzt [veer browKHen ine-en]
 please call a doctor bitte rufen Sie einen Arzt [bitt-uh roofen zee]

dialogue

 where does it hurt? wo tut es weh? [vo toot ess vay]
 right here genau hier [genow heer]
 does that hurt now? tut es jetzt weh? [yetst]
 yes ja
 take this to the pharmacist gehen Sie hiermit zur Apotheke [gay-en zee heermit tsoor apotayk-uh]

document das Dokument [dokooment]

dog der Hund [hoont]

doll die Puppe [poop-uh]

domestic flight der Inlandflug [inlant-flook]

don't* see not

don't do that! tu das/tun Sie das nicht! [too dass/toon zee dass nisht]

door die Tür [toor]

doorman der Portier [portyay]

double doppelt

double bed das Doppelbett

double room das Doppelzimmer [doppel-tsimmer]

doughnut der Berliner [bairleener]

down: down here hier unten [heer oonten]

put it down over there setzen Sie es hier ab [zetsen zee ess heer ap]

it's down there on the right es ist hier unten rechts

it's further down the road es ist weiter die Straße entlang [vyter dee shtrahss-uh entlang]

downhill skiing der Abfahrtslauf [apfahrts-lowf]

downmarket (restaurant etc) weniger anspruchsvoll [vayniger anshprookнsfoll]

downstairs unten [oonten]

dozen das Dutzend [dootsent]

half a dozen sechs Stück [zeks shtöck]

drain (in sink, street) der Abfluss [ap-flooss]

draught beer das Fassbier [fassbeer]

draughty: it's draughty es zieht [ess tseet]

drawer die Schublade [shooplahd-uh]

drawing die Zeichnung [tsyshnoong]

dreadful furchtbar [foorshtbar]

dream der Traum [trowm]

dress das Kleid [klite]

dressed: to get dressed sich anziehen [zish antsee-en]

dressing (for cut) der Verband [fairbant]

salad dressing die Salatsoße [zalahtzohss-uh]

dressing gown der Bademantel [bahd-uh-mantel]

drink (alcoholic) der Drink (non-alcoholic) das Getränk [getrenk]

drink (verb) trinken

a cold drink ein kaltes Getränk

can I get you a drink? kann ich Ihnen etwas zu trinken besorgen? [etvass tsoo – bezorgen]

what would you like to drink? was möchtest du/möchten Sie zu trinken? [murshtest doo/murshten zee]

no thanks, I don't drink nein danke, ich trinke nicht [trink-uh nisht]

I'll just have a drink of water ich möchte nur etwas Wasser

drinking water das Trinkwasser [trinkvasser]

is this drinking water? ist das
Trinkwasser?

drive (verb) fahren

we drove here wir sind mit
dem Auto gekommen [veer
zint mit daym **ow**to gek**o**mmen]

I'll drive you home ich fahre
Sie nach Hause [ish f**ah**r-uh zee
naKH h**ow**z-uh]

driver (man/woman) der Fahrer/
die Fahrerin

driving licence der
Führerschein [f**oo**rer-shine]

drop: just a drop please (of
drink) nur einen Tropfen [noor
ine-en]

drug (medical) das Medikament

drugs (narcotics) die Drogen fpl
[dr**oh**gen]

drunk (adj) betrunken
[betr**oo**nken]

drunken driving Trunkenheit
am Steuer [tr**oo**nken-hite am
sht**oy**er]

dry (adj) trocken

dry-cleaner die chemische
Reinigung [sh**ay**mish-uh
rynigoong]

duck die Ente [**ent**-uh]

**due: he was due to arrive
yesterday** er sollte gestern
ankommen [air z**o**llt-uh]

when is the train due? wann
kommt der Zug an?

dull (pain) dumpf [doompf]
(weather) trüb [tr**oo**p]

dummy (baby's) der Schnuller
[shn**oo**ller]

during während [v**air**ent]

dust der Staub [shtowp]

dusty staubig [sht**ow**bish]

dustbin die Mülltonne
[m**oo**lltonn-uh]

Dutch (adj) holländisch
[h**o**llendish]
(language) Holländisch

duty-free (goods) zollfreie
Waren [ts**o**llfry-uh v**ah**ren]

duty-free shop der Duty-free-
Shop

duvet das Federbett [f**ay**derbet]

E

each (every) jeder [y**ay**der]

how much are they each?
was kosten sie pro Stück?
[vass k**o**sten zee pro sht**oo**k]

ear das Ohr

earache Ohrenschmerzen
[**oh**ren-shmairtsen]

early früh [fr**oo**]

early in the morning früh am
Morgen

I called by earlier ich war
schon einmal hier [shohn ine-
mahl heer]

earring der Ohrring

east der Osten

in the east im Osten

Easter Ostern [**oh**stern]

easy leicht [lysht]

eat essen

we've already eaten, thanks
danke, wir haben schon
gegessen [h**ah**ben shohn]

eau de toilette das Eau de

toilette
EC die EG [ay-g**ay**]
economy class die Touristen-
klasse [t**oo**risten-klass-uh]
egg das Ei [**i**]
Eire Irland [**ee**rlant]
either: either ... or ...
entweder... oder... [**e**ntvayder
... **oh**der]
either, I don't mind egal
welcher [ayg**ah**l v**e**lsher]
elastic der Gummi [g**oo**mmee]
elastic band das Gummiband
[g**oo**mmeebant]
elbow der **E**llbogen
electric elektrisch [ayl**e**ktrish]
electric fire das elektrische
Heizgerät [ayl**e**ktrish-uh h**i**tes-
gerayt]
electrician der Elektriker
[ayl**e**ktriker]
electricity der Strom [shtr**oh**m]
elevator (US) der Aufzug [**owf**-
ts**oo**k]
else: something else etwas
anderes [**e**tvass **a**nderess]
somewhere else woanders
[vo-**a**nders]

dialogue

**would you like anything
else?** möchten Sie noch
etwas? [m**ur**shten]
no, nothing else, thanks
danke, das ist alles [d**a**nk-uh
dass ist **a**l-ess]
e-mail die E-Mail
embassy die Botschaft [b**o**ht-

shafft]
emergency der Notfall [n**oh**t-
fal]
this is an emergency! dies ist
ein Notfall! [deess ist **i**ne]
emergency exit der
Notausgang [n**oh**t-owssgang]
empty leer [l**ai**r]
end das Ende [**e**nd-uh]
at the end of the street am
Ende der Straße
end (verb) **e**nden
when does it end? wann ist
es zu Ende? [vann ist ess ts**oo**
end-uh]
engaged (toilet, telephone)
besetzt [bez**e**tst]
(to be married) verlobt [fairl**oh**pt]
engine der Motor [m**oh**tohr]
England England [**e**ng-lant]
English englisch [**e**ng-lish]
I'm English (man/woman) ich
bin Engländer [**e**ng-lender]/
Engländerin
do you speak English?
sprichst du/sprechen Sie
Englisch? [shprisht d**oo**/
shpr**e**shen zee]
enjoy: to enjoy oneself sich
amüsieren [zish am**oo**z**ee**ren]

dialogue

how did you like the film?
wie hat dir/Ihnen der Film
gefallen? [vee hat deer/**ee**nen
dair]
**I enjoyed it very much
– did you?** er hat mir sehr

gut gefallen – dir/Ihnen auch? [meer zair goot – deer/**ee**nen owkH]

enjoyable unterhaltsam [oonter-halt-zahm]
(meal) angenehm [**a**n-genaym]
enlargement (of photo) die Vergrößerung [fairgr**u**rsseroong]
enormous enorm [ayn**o**rm]
enough genug [gen**oo**k]
  there's not enough ... es ist nicht genug ... da [ess ist nisht]
  it's not big enough es ist nicht groß genug
  that's enough das genügt [dass gen**oo**kt]
entrance der Eingang [**i**ne-gang]
envelope der Umschlag [**oo**mshlahk]
epileptic (man/woman) der Epil**e**ptiker/die Epil**e**ptikerin
equipment (for climbing etc) die Ausrüstung [**o**wss-r**oo**stoong]
error der Fehler [**fay**ler]
especially besonders [bez**o**nders]
essential wesentlich [**vay**zentlish]
  it is essential that ... es ist unbedingt notwendig, dass ... [**oo**nbedingt n**oh**tvendish]
Estonia Estland [**e**stlant]
EU die EU [ay-**oo**]
euro der Euro [**oy**ro]
Eurocheque der Euroscheck

[**oy**ro-sheck]
Eurocheque card die Euroscheckkarte [**oy**ro-sheck-kart-uh]
Europe Europa [oyr**oh**pa]
European europäisch [oyroh**pay**ish]
even sogar [zog**ah**r], selbst [**ze**lpst]
  even if ... selbst wenn ... [ven]
evening der Abend [**ah**bent]
  this evening heute abend [h**oy**t-uh]
  in the evening am Abend
evening meal das Abendessen [**ah**bent-essen]
eventually schließlich [shl**ee**sslish]
ever jemals [**yay**mahls]

dialogue

have you ever been to Heidelberg? waren Sie schon einmal in Heidelberg? [**vah**ren zee shohn **i**ne-mahl]
yes, I was there two years ago ja, ich war vor zwei Jahren da [for – **yah**ren]

every jeder [**yay**der]
  every day jeden Tag [**yay**den tahk]
everyone jeder [**yay**der]
everything alles [**a**l-ess]
everywhere überall [**oo**ber-al]
exactly! genau! [gen**ow**]
exam die Prüfung [pr**oo**foong]

example das Beispiel [byshpeel]
for example zum Beispiel [tsoom]
excellent hervorragend [hairforrahgent]
excellent ausgezeichnet [owssgetsyshnet]
except außer [owsser]
excess baggage das Übergewicht [oobergevisht]
exchange rate der Wechselkurs [veckselkoorss]
exciting (day, holiday) aufregend [owf-raygent]
(film) spannend [shpannent]
excuse me (to get past) entschuldigen Sie! [entshooldigen zee]
(to get attention) Entschuldigung! [ent-shooldigoong]
(to say sorry) Verzeihung [fairtsy-oong]
exhaust (pipe) der Auspuff [owsspooff]
exhausted erschöpft [airshurpft]
exhibition die Ausstellung [owss-shtelloong]
exit der Ausgang [owsssgang]
where's the nearest exit? wo ist der nächste Ausgang? [dair naykst-uh]
expect erwarten [airvarten]
expensive teuer [toyer]
experienced erfahren [airfahren]
explain erklären [airklairen]
can you explain that? könnten Sie mir das erklären? [kurnten zee meer]

express (mail) per Express [pair]
(train) der Schnellzug [shnelltsook]
extension (telephone) der Anschluss [anshlooss]
extension 21, please Anschluss einundzwanzig bitte [bitt-uh]
extension lead die Verlängerungsschnur [fairlengeroongs-shnoor]
extra: can we have an extra one? können wir noch eins haben? [kurnen veer noKH ine-ss hahben]
do you charge extra for that? kostet das extra?
extraordinary außergewöhnlich [owsser-gevurnlish]
extremely äußerst [oysserst]
eye das Auge [owg-uh]
will you keep an eye on my suitcase for me? könnten Sie auf meinen Koffer aufpassen? [kurnten zee – owfpassen]
eyebrow pencil der Augenbrauenstift [owgenbrowen-shtift]
eye drops die Augentropfen [owgen-tropfen]
eyeglasses (US) die Brille [brill-uh]
eyeliner der Eyeliner
eye make-up remover der Augen-Make-up-Entferner [owgen-'make-up'-entfairner]

eye shadow der Lidschatten [leet-shatten]

F

face das Gesicht [gezisht]
factory die Fabrik [fabreek]
Fahrenheit* Fahrenheit
faint (verb) ohnmächtig werden [ohnmeshtish vairden]
she's fainted sie ist ohnmächtig geworden [zee ist – gevorden]
I feel faint mir ist ganz schwach [meer ist gants shvaKH]
fair (funfair) der Jahrmarkt [yahrmarkt]
(trade) die Messe [mess-uh]
fair (adj) fair
fairly ziemlich [tseemlish]
fake die Fälschung [felshoong]
fall (verb) fallen [fal-en]
she's had a fall sie ist hingefallen [zee ist hin-gefal-en]
(US: autumn) der Herbst [hairpst]
false falsch [falsh]
family die Familie [fameelee-uh]
famous berühmt [beroomt]
fan (electrical) der Ventilator [ventilah-tor]
(hand held) der Fächer [fesher]
(sports) der Fan [fen]
fan belt der Keilriemen [kile-reemen]
fantastic fantastisch
far weit [vite]

dialogue

is it far from here? ist es weit von hier? [fon heer]
no, not very far nein, nicht sehr weit [nisht zair]
well how far? wie weit denn? [vee]
it's about 10 kilometres es sind etwa zehn Kilometer [etvah]

fare der Fahrpreis [fahrprice]
farm der Bauernhof [bowernhohf]
fashionable modisch [mohdish]
fast schnell
fat (person) dick
(on meat) das Fett
father der Vater [fahter]
father-in-law der Schwieger-vater [shveeger-fahter]
faucet (US) der Wasserhahn [vasserhahn]
fault der Fehler [fayler]
sorry, it was my fault tut mir leid, es war mein Fehler [mine]
it's not my fault es ist nicht meine Schuld [nisht mine-uh shoolt]
faulty defekt [dayfekt]
favourite Lieblings- [leeplings]
fax das Fax [faks]
fax (verb) (person) per Fax benachrichtigen [pair faks benaKH-rishtigen]
(document) faxen
February der Februar [faybrooar]

feel fühlen [**foo**len]

I feel hot mir ist heiß [meer ist hice]

I feel unwell mir ist nicht gut [nisht goot]

I feel like going for a walk mir ist nach einem Spaziergang [na**kH**]

how are you feeling? wie fühlen Sie sich? [vee **foo**len zee zish]

I'm feeling better es geht mir besser [ess gayt meer]

felt-tip (pen) der Filzstift [**filts**-shtift]

fence der Zaun [tsown]

fender (US) die Stoßstange [sht**oh**ss-shtang-uh]

ferry die Fähre [**fair**-uh]

festival das Festival [**festivahl**]

fetch holen [**hoh**len]

I'll fetch him ich hole ihn [**hohl**-uh]

will you come and fetch me later? können Sie mich später abholen? [**kur**nen zee mish sh**payter** ap-hohlen]

feverish: she's still feverish sie hat noch immer Fieber [zee hat no**kH** immer **fee**ber]

few: a few ein paar [ine pahr]

a few days ein paar Tage

fiancé: my fiancé mein Verlobter [mine fairl**oh**pter]

fiancée: my fiancée meine Verlobte [**mine**-uh fairl**oh**pt-uh]

field das Feld [felt]

fight der Kampf

fill füllen [**foo**llen]

fill in ausfüllen [**ow**ssf**oo**llen]

do I have to fill this in? muss ich das ausfüllen? [mooss]

fill up voll machen [foll ma**kH**en]

fill it up, please volltanken bitte [**foll**tanken **bitt**-uh]

filling (in sandwich) der Belag [bel**ah**k]

(in cake, tooth) die Füllung [**foo**lloong]

film der Film

dialogue

> do you have this kind of film? haben Sie diesen Film? [**hah**ben zee **dee**zen]
> yes, how many exposures? ja, wie viele Aufnahmen? [vee **veel**-uh **ow**fnahmen]
> 36 sechsunddreißig [seksoont-dr**ys**sish]

film processing die Filmentwicklung [film-entvickloong]

filter coffee der Filterkaffee [**filter**-kaffay]

filter papers das Filterpapier [**filter**-papeer]

filthy dreckig [dr**e**ckish]

find finden

I can't find it ich kann es nicht finden [ish kann ess nisht]

I've found it ich habe es gefunden [gef**oo**nden]

find out herausfinden [her**ow**ss-finden]

could you find out for me?
könnten Sie das für mich
herausfinden? [**kur**nten zee dass
foor mish]
fine (weather) schön [shurn]
(punishment) die Geldstrafe
[**g**elt-shtrahf-uh]

dialogues

how are you? wie geht's?
[vee gayts]
I'm fine thanks danke, gut
[goot]

is that OK? ist das okay?
that's fine thanks in
Ordnung, danke [**o**rtnoong]

finger der Finger [**fi**ng-er]
finish (verb) beenden [buh-
enden]
I haven't finished yet ich bin
noch nicht fertig [ish bin noKH
nisht f**ai**rtish]
when does it finish? wann
ist es zu Ende? [van ist ess tsoo
end-uh]
fire das Feuer [**foy**-er]
can we light a fire here?
können wir hier ein Feuer
machen? [**kur**nen veer heer
– ma**KH**en]
it's on fire es brennt
fire alarm der Feueralarm [**foy**-
er-alarm]
fire brigade die Feuerwehr
[**foy**-er-vair]
fire escape die Feuertreppe

[**foy**-er-trepp-uh], die
Feuerleiter [**foy**-er-lyter]
fire extinguisher der
Feuerlöscher [**foy**-er-lursher]
first erster [**ai**rster]
I was first ich war der/die
erste [dair/dee **ai**rst-uh]
at first zuerst [tsoo-**ai**rst]
the first time das erste Mal
first on the left die erste
Straße links
first aid die Erste Hilfe [**ai**rst-uh
h**i**lf-uh]
first aid kit die Erste-Hilfe-
Ausrüstung [**ai**rst-uh h**i**lf-uh
owssrOOstoong]
first class erster Klasse [**ai**rster
kl**a**ss-uh]
first floor der erste Stock [**ai**rst-
uh sht**o**ck]
(US) das Erdgeschoss [**ai**rt-
geshoss]
first name der Vorname
[**fo**rnahm-uh]
fish der Fisch [fish]
fishmonger's der Fischhändler
[fish-hentler]
fit (attack) der Anfall [**a**n-fal]
it doesn't fit me es passt mir
nicht [meer nisht]
fitting room der Anproberaum
[**a**nprohb-uh-rowm]
fix (arrange, sort out) regeln
[**ray**geln]
can you fix this? (repair)
können Sie das reparieren?
[**kur**nen zee dass repar**ee**ren]
fizzy sprudelnd [shprOOdelnt]
flag die Fahne [**fah**n-uh]

F

flannel der Waschlappen [vashlappen]
flash (for camera) der Blitz
flat (apartment) die Wohnung [vohnoong]
(adj) flach [flakH]
I've got a flat tyre ich habe einen Platten [ish hahb-uh ine-en]
flavour der Geschmack [geshmack]
flea der Floh
flight der Flug [flook]
flight number die Flugnummer [flook-noommer]
flippers die Schwimmflossen [shvimflossen]
flood die Flut [floot]
floor (of room) der Fußboden [foossbohden]
(storey) das Stockwerk [shtockvairk]
on the floor auf dem Boden [owf daym bohden]
on the third floor im dritten Stock
florist der Blumenhändler [bloomen-hentler]
flour das Mehl [mayl]
flower die Blume [bloom-uh]
flu die Grippe [gripp-uh]
fluent: he speaks fluent German er spricht fließend Deutsch [air shprisht fleessent doytch]
fly (insect) die Fliege [fleeg-uh]
fly (verb) fliegen [fleegen]
fly in einfliegen [ine-fleegen]
fly out abfliegen [apfleegen]

fog der Nebel [naybel]
foggy: it's foggy es ist neblig [nayblish]
folk dancing der Volkstanz [follks-tants]
folk music die Volksmusik [follks-moozeek]
follow folgen
follow me folgen Sie mir [zee meer]
food das Essen
food poisoning die Lebensmittelvergiftung [laybensmittel-fairgiftoong]
food shop/store das Lebensmittelgeschäft [laybensmittel-gesheft]
foot* der Fuß [fooss]
on foot zu Fuß [tsoo]
football der Fußball [foossbal]
football match das Fußballspiel [foossbal-shpeel]
for für [foor]
do you have something for ...? (headaches/diarrhoea etc) haben Sie etwas gegen ...? [hahben zee etvass gaygen]

dialogues

who's the bratwurst for?
für wen ist die Bratwurst? [vayn]
that's for me das ist für mich [mish]
and this one? und das hier?
that's for her das ist für sie [zee]

where do I get the bus for Stuttgart? wo fährt der Bus nach Stuttgart ab? [vo fairt – naКН]
the bus for Stuttgart leaves from Schillerstraße der Bus nach Stuttgart fährt von der Schillerstraße

how long have you been here for? wie lange sind Sie schon hier? [vee lang-uh zint zee shohn heer]
I've been here for two days, how about you? ich bin seit zwei Tagen hier, und Sie? [zite]
I've been here for a week ich bin seit einer Woche hier

forehead die Stirn [shteern]
foreign ausländisch [owsslendish]
foreigner (man/woman) der Ausländer [owsslender]/die Ausländerin
forest der Wald [vallt]
forget vergessen [fairgessen]
I forget, I've forgotten ich habe es vergessen [ish hahb-uh ess]
fork (for eating) die Gabel [gahbel]
(in road) die Abzweigung [ap-tsvygoong]
form (document) das Formular [formoolahr]
formal (dress) formell

fortnight zwei Wochen [tsvy voКНen]
fortress die Festung [festoong]
fortunately glücklicherweise [glOOck-lisher-vize-uh]
forward: could you forward my mail? könnten Sie meine Post nachsenden? [kurnten zee mine-uh posst naКН-zenden]
forwarding address die Nachsendeadresse [naКНzend-uh-adress-uh]
foundation cream die Grundierungscreme [groondeeroongs-kraym]
fountain der Brunnen [broonnen]
foyer das Foyer [foy-yay]
fracture der Bruch [brooКН]
France Frankreich [frank-rysh]
free frei [fry]
(no charge) kostenlos [kostenlohss], gratis [grahtiss]
is it free (of charge)? ist es gratis?
freeway (US) die Autobahn [owtobahn]
freezer die Gefriertruhe [gefreertroo-uh]
French (adj) französisch [frantsurzish]
(language) Französisch
French fries die Pommes frites [pom frit]
frequent häufig [hoyfish]
how frequent is the bus to Kiel? wie oft fährt der Bus

Fr

63

nach Kiel? [vee oft fairt]
fresh frisch [frish]
fresh orange juice der
natürliche Orangensaft
[natoorlish-uh oronJenzaft]
Friday Freitag [frytahk]
fridge der Kühlschrank
[koolshrank]
fried gebraten [gebrahten]
fried egg das Spiegelei
[shpeegel-ī]
friend (man/woman) der Freund
[froynt]/die Freundin [froyndin]
friendly freundlich [froyntlish]
from von [fon]
when does the next train from
Bremen arrive? wann kommt
der nächste Zug aus Bremen
an? [der naykst-uh tsook owss]
from Monday to Friday von
Montag bis Freitag
from next Thursday ab
nächsten Donnerstag

dialogue

where are you from?
woher kommst du/
kommen Sie? [vohair kommst
doo/kommen zee]
I'm from Slough ich bin aus
Slough [ish bin owss]

front die Vorderseite [forderzite-uh]
in front vorn [forn]
in front of the hotel vor dem
Hotel [for]
at the front vorn [forn]

frost der Frost
frozen gefroren
frozen food die Tiefkühlkost
[teefkoolkost]
fruit das Obst [ohpst]
fruit juice der Fruchtsaft
[frookHtzaft]
fry braten [brahten]
frying pan die Bratpfanne
[braht-pfan-uh]
full voll [foll]
it's full of ... es ist voller...
I'm full ich bin satt [ish bin zatt]
full board die Vollpension
[follpangz-yohn]
fun: it was fun es hat Spaß
gemacht [ess hat shpahss
gemaкht]
funfair das Volksfest [follks-fest]
funicular railway die Seilbahn
[zile-bahn]
funny (strange) seltsam
[zeltzahm]
(amusing) komisch [kohmish]
furniture die Möbel [murbel]
further weiter [vyter]
it's further down the road es
ist weiter die Straße entlang

dialogue

how much further is it to
the castle? wie weit ist es
noch bis zum Schloss? [vee
vite ist ess noкн bis tsoom]
about 3 kilometres etwa
drei Kilometer [etvah]

fuse (noun) die Sicherung
[zisheroong]

the lights have fused die
Sicherung ist durchgebrannt
[doorsh-gebrannt]

fuse box der Sicherungskasten
[zisheroongs-kasten]

fuse wire der Schmelzdraht
[shmelts-draht]

future die Zukunft [tsookoonft]

in future in Zukunft

G

gallon* die Gallone [galohn-uh]

game das Spiel [shpeel]

(meat) das Wild [vilt]

garage (fuel) die Tankstelle
[tank-shtell-uh]

(repairs) die Werkstatt
[vairkshtatt]

(parking) die Garage [garahj uh]

garden der Garten

garlic der Knoblauch
[k-nohblowkH]

gas das Gas [gahss]

(US: gasoline) das Benzin
[bentseen]

gas cylinder (camping gas) die
Gasflasche [gahss-flash-uh]

gasoline (US) das Benzin
[bentseen]

gas permeable lenses
luftdurchlässige
Kontaktlinsen [looft-doorsh-
lessig-uh kontakt-linzen]

gas station (US) die Tankstelle
[tank-shtell-uh]

gate das Tor [tohr]

(at airport) der Flugsteig [flook-
shtike]

gay schwul [shvool]

gay bar die Schwulenkneipe
[shvoolen-k-nipe-uh]

gear (in car etc) der Gang

gearbox das Getriebe [getreeb-
uh]

gear lever der Schaltknüppel
[shalt-k-nooppel]

general allgemein [al-gemine]

Geneva Genf

gents' (toilet) die
Herrentoilette [hairen-twalett-
uh]

genuine echt [esht]

German (man/woman) der/die
Deutsche [doytch-uh]

(adj) deutsch [doytch]

(language) Deutsch

the Germans die Deutschen

German measles die Röteln
[rurteln]

Germany Deutschland [doytch-
lant]

get (obtain) bekommen

(fetch) holen [hohlen]

(become) werden [vairden]

will you get me another one,
please? bringen Sie mir bitte
noch eins [nokH ine-ss]

do you know where I can get
them? wissen Sie, wo ich sie
bekommen kann?

how do I get to ...? wie
komme ich nach...? [vee
komm-uh ish nakH]

to get old alt werden [vairden]

dialogue

can I get you a drink?
möchtest du/möchten Sie
etwas trinken? [**mur**shtest
d**oo**/**mur**shten zee **e**tvass]
**no, I'll get this one, what
would you like?** nein, das
ich meine Runde, was
möchten Sie? [**mine**-uh
r**oo**nd-uh]
a glass of red wine ein
Glas R**o**twein

get back (return)
zurückkommen [ts**oor**oock-
kommen]
get in (arrive) ankommen [**an**-
kommen]
get off aussteigen [**ow**ss-
shtygen]
where do I get off? wo muss
ich aussteigen? [vo mooss
ish]
get on (to train etc) einsteigen
[**ine**-shtygen]
get out (of car etc) aussteigen
[**ow**ss-shtygen]
get up (in the morning) aufstehen
[**owf**-shtay-en]
gift das Geschenk [ge**shenk**]
gift shop der Geschenkladen
[ge**shenk**-lahden]
gin der Gin
a gin and tonic, please einen
Gin Tonic, bitte [**ine**-en]
girl das Mädchen [**may**dshen]
girlfriend die Freundin
[**froyn**din]

give geben [**gay**ben]
I gave it to him ich habe es
ihm gegeben [ish h**ah**b-uh ess
eem ge**gay**ben]
will you give this to ...? bitte
geben Sie dies ...
give back zurückgeben
[ts**oor**oock-gayben]
glad froh
glass das Glas [glahss]
a glass of wine ein Glas Wein
glasses (spectacles) die Brille
[**brill**-uh]
gloves die Handschuhe [hant-
sh**oo**-uh]
glue der Klebstoff [**klayp**-shtoff]
go gehen [**gay**-en]
(by car, train etc) fahren
**we'd like to go to the Black
Forest** wir möchten zum
Schwarzwald fahren [veer
m**ur**shten tsoom]
where are you going? wohin
gehen/fahren Sie? [vo**hin**]
where does this bus go?
wohin fährt dieser Bus? [fairt]
let's go gehen wir
she's gone (left) sie ist
geg**a**ngen
where has he gone? wohin
ist er geg**a**ngen?
I went there last week ich
war l**e**tzte W**o**che da
hamburger to go Hamburger
zum M**i**tnehmen [tsoom]
go away weggehen [**vek**-gay-en]
go away! gehen Sie weg!
go back (return) zurückgehen
[ts**oor**oock-gay-en]

go down (the stairs etc)
hinuntergehen [hin**oo**nter-gay-en]

go in hineingehen [hin-**ine**-gay-en]

go out (in the evening) ausgehen [**ow**ss-gay-en]

do you want to go out tonight? möchten Sie heute abend ausgehen? [**mur**shten zee h**oy**t-uh **ah**bent]

go through gehen durch [g**ay**-en doorsh]

go up (the stairs etc) hinaufgehen [hin**owf**-gay-en]

goat die Ziege [ts**ee**g-uh]

God Gott

goggles (ski) die Skibrille [sheebrill-uh]

gold das Gold [gollt]

golf Golf

golf course der Golfplatz [golf-plats]

good gut [g**oo**t]

good! gut!

it's no good es hat keinen Zweck [ess hat k**ine**-en tsveck]

goodbye auf Wiedersehen [owf-v**ee**derzayn]

good evening guten Abend [g**oo**ten **ah**bent]

Good Friday der Karfreitag [kar-fr**y**tahk]

good morning guten Morgen [g**oo**ten morgen]

good night gute Nacht [g**oo**t-uh nakнt]

goose die Gans [ganss]

got: we've got to ... wir

müssen ... [veer m**oo**ssen]

I've got to ... ich muss ... [mooss]

have you got any ...? haben Sie ...? [**hah**ben zee]

government die Regierung [reg**ee**roong]

gradually allmählich [al-m**ay**lish]

grammar die Grammatik

gram(me) das Gramm

granddaughter die Enkelin [enk-uh-lin]

grandfather der Großvater [gr**oh**ssfahter]

grandmother die Großmutter [gr**oh**ssmootter]

grandson der Enkel

grapefruit die Grapefruit

grapefruit juice der Grapefruitsaft [-zaft]

grapes die Trauben [tr**ow**ben]

grass das Gras [grahss]

grateful dankbar

gravy die Soße [z**oh**ss-uh]

great (excellent) großartig [gr**oh**ss-artish]

that's great! das ist toll! [tol]

a great success ein großer Erfolg [gr**oh**ss-er]

Great Britain Großbritannien [grohss-brit**a**nnee-en]

Greece Griechenland [gr**ee**shenlant]

greedy gefräßig [gefr**ay**ssish]

Greek griechisch [gr**ee**shish]

green grün [gr**oo**n]

green card (car insurance) die grüne Karte [gr**oo**n-uh kart-uh]

greengrocer's der Gemüse-
händler [gem**oo**z-uh-hentler]

grey grau [grow]

grill (on cooker) der Grill

grilled gegrillt

grocer's der
Lebensmittelhändler
[**lay**bensmittel-hentler]

ground der Boden [**boh**den]
on the ground auf dem
Boden

ground floor das Erdgeschoss
[**air**t-geshoss]

group die Gruppe
[gr**oo**p-uh]

guarantee die Garantie
[garant**ee**]
is it guaranteed? ist darauf
Garantie? [dar**ow**f]

guest der Gast

guesthouse die Pension
[pangz-**yohn**]

guide (person) der Reiseleiter
[**ry**-zuh-lyter]

guidebook der Reiseführer
[**ry**-zuh-f**oo**rer]

guided tour die Rundfahrt
[**roo**ntfahrt]
(on foot) der Rundgang
[**roo**ntgang]

guitar die Gitarre [git**arr**-uh]

gum (in mouth) das Zahnfleisch
[ts**ahn**-flysh]

gun das Gewehr [gev**air**]

gym das Fitness-Studio
[**fit**ness-sht**oo**dee-oh]

H

hair das Haar [hahr]

hairbrush die Haarbürste
[**hahr**b**oo**rst-uh]

haircut der Haarschnitt
[**hahr**shnit]

hairdresser der Frisör [friz**ur**]

hairdryer der Fön® [furn]

hair gel das Haargel [**hahr**-gayl]

hairgrip die Haarklemme
[**hahr**klem-uh]

hair spray das Haarspray [**hahr**-
shpray]

half* halb [halp]
half an hour eine halbe
Stunde [**ine**-uh halb-uh sht**oo**nd-
uh]
half a litre ein halber Liter
[**hal**ber **lee**ter]
about half that etwa die
Hälfte [**et**vah dee **helf**t-uh]

half board die Halbpension
[halp-pangz-yohn]

half-bottle die halbe Flasche
[**halb**-uh **flash**-uh]

half fare der halbe Fahrpreis
[**halb**-uh **fahr**-price]

half price: at half price zum
halben Preis [ts**oo**m **halb**en price]

hall (in house) die Diele [**deel**-uh]

ham der Schinken [**shin**ken]

hamburger der Hamburger
[**hem**burger]

hammer der Hammer

hand die Hand [hant]

handbag die Handtasche
[**hant**-tash-uh]

handbrake die Handbremse
[hantbremz-uh]

handkerchief das Taschentuch
[tashen-tooKH]

handle (on door) die Klinke
[klink-uh]
(on suitcase etc) der Griff

hand luggage das Handgepäck
[hant-gepeck]

hang-gliding das Drachen-
fliegen [draKHen-fleegen]

hangover der Kater [kahter]
I've got a hangover ich habe
einen Kater [ish hahb-uh ine-en]

happen geschehen [geshay-en]
what's happening? was ist
los? [lohss]
what has happened? was ist
passiert? [passeert]

happy glücklich [glOOcklish]
I'm not happy about this ich
bin damit nicht zufrieden [ish
bin dahmit nisht tsOOfreeden]

harbour der Hafen [hahfen]

hard hart
(difficult) schwer [shvair]

hard-boiled egg ein
hartgekochtes Ei
[hartgekoKHtess ī]

hard lenses harte
Kontaktlinsen [hart-uh kontakt-
linzen]

hardly kaum [kowm]
hardly ever fast nie [fasst nee]

hardware shop die
Eisenwarenhandlung
[īzenvahren-hantloong]

hat der Hut [hoot]

hate (verb) hassen

have* haben [hahben]
can I have a ...? kann ich ein
... haben? [kan ish]
can we have some ...?
können wir etwas ... haben?
[kurnen veer etvass]
do you have ...? hast du/
haben Sie...? [dOO/... zee]
what'll you have? (drink) was
möchtest du/möchten Sie?
[vass murshtest dOO/murshten
zee]
I have to leave now ich muss
jetzt gehen [mooss yetst gay-en]
do I have to ...? muss ich ...?

hayfever der Heuschnupfen
[hoy-shnoopfen]

hazelnuts die Haselnüsse
[hahzel-nOOss-uh]

he* er [air]

head der Kopf

headache die Kopfschmerzen
[kopf-shmairtsen]

headlights die Scheinwerfer
[shine-vairfer]

headphones die Kopfhörer
[kopf-hur-rer]

health food shop der Bioladen
[bee-oh-lahden]

healthy gesund [gezoont]

hear hören [hur-ren]

dialogue

can you hear me? können
Sie mich hören? [kurnen
zee mish]
I can't hear you ich kann
Sie nicht hören [ish kan zee

He

nisht]

hearing aid das Hörgerät [**hur**-gerayt]

heart das Herz [hairts]

heart attack der Herzinfarkt [**hairts**-infarkt]

heat die Hitze [**hits**-uh]

heater (in room) der Ofen [**oh**fen]

(in car) die Heizung [**hy**tsoong]

heating die Heizung [**hy**tsoong]

heavy schwer [shvair]

heel (of foot) die Ferse [**fairz**-uh]

(of shoe) der Absatz [**ap**zats]

could you heel these? können Sie mir hier die Absätze erneuern? [**kur**nen zee meer heer dee **ap**sets-uh airn**oy**ern]

heelbar die Absatzbar [**ap**zatsbar]

height (of mountain) die Höhe [**hur**-uh]

(of person) die Größe [**grurss**-uh]

helicopter der Hubschrauber [**hoo**p-shrowber]

hello hallo

helmet (for motorcycle) der Helm

help die Hilfe [**hilf**-uh]

(verb) helfen

help! Hilfe!

can you help me? können Sie mir helfen? [**kur**nen zee meer]

thank you very much for your help vielen Dank für Ihre Hilfe [**fee**len dank foor **eer**-uh]

helpful hilfreich [**hilf**-rysh]

hepatitis die Hepatitis [hepat**ee**tiss]

her*: **I haven't seen her** ich habe sie nicht gesehen [zee]

give it to her geben Sie es ihr [eer]

with her mit ihr

for her für sie

that's her das ist sie

that's her towel das ist ihr Handtuch

herbal tea der Kräutertee [**kroy**ter-tay]

herbs die Kräuter [**kroy**ter]

here hier [heer]

here is/are ... hier ist/sind [zint]

here you are (offering) bitte [**bitt**-uh]

hers*: **that's hers** das gehört ihr [dass geh**ur**t eer]

hey! he! [hay]

hi! hallo!

hide verstecken [fairsht**ecken**]

high hoch [hohKH]

highchair der Hochstuhl [**hoh**KH-shtool]

highway (US) die Autobahn [**ow**tobahn]

hill der Berg [bairk]

him*: **I haven't seen him** ich habe ihn nicht gesehen [een]

give it to him geben Sie es ihm [eem]

with him mit ihm

for him für ihn

that's him das ist er [air]

hip die Hüfte [**hooft**-uh]

hire: for hire zu vermieten [tsoo fairm**ee**ten]

(verb) mieten [**mee**ten]

where can I hire a bike? wo
kann ich ein Fahrrad mieten?
[vo kan ish ine **fahr**-raht]

his*: it's his car es ist sein Auto
[zine]

that's his das ist seins [zine-ss]

hit (verb) schlagen [**shlah**gen]

hitch-hike trampen [**trempen**]

hobby das Hobby

hold (verb) halten

hole das Loch [loKH]

holiday der Urlaub [**oor**lowp]

on holiday im Urlaub

Holland Holland [**hol**-lant]

home das Zuhause [ts00**howz**-
uh]

at home (in my house etc) zu
Hause

(in my country) bei uns [by oonss]

we go home tomorrow wir
fahren morgen nach Hause
[veer **fah**ren **mor**gen naKH]

honest ehrlich [**air**lish]

honey der Honig [**hoh**nish]

honeymoon die Flitterwochen
[**flitt**ervoKHen]

hood (US: of car) die Haube
[**howb**-uh]

hope hoffen

I hope so hoffentlich
[**hoffentlish**]

I hope not hoffentlich nicht
[nisht]

hopefully hoffentlich
[**hoffentlish**]

horn (of car) die Hupe [**h00p**-uh]

horrible schrecklich

horse das Pferd [pfairt]

horse riding Reiten [**ryten**]

hospital das Krankenhaus
[**kranken**-howss]

hospitality die Gastfreundschaft [**gast**-froynt-shafft]

thank you for your hospitality
vielen Dank für Ihre
Gastfreundschaft [**feelen** dank
f00r **eer**-uh]

hot heiß [hice]

(spicy) scharf [sharf]

I'm hot mir ist heiß [meer]

it's hot today es ist heiß heute
[**hoyt**-uh]

hotel das Hotel

hotel room: in my hotel room
in meinem Hotelzimmer
[**mine**-em hotel-tsimmer]

hot spring die Thermalquelle
[tairm**ah**l-kvell-uh]

hour die Stunde [**sht00nd**-uh]

house das Haus [howss]

house wine der Tafelwein
[**tah**fel-vine]

hovercraft das Luftkissenboot
[**looft**-kissenboht]

how wie [vee]

how many? wie viele? [**feel**-uh]

how do you do? guten Tag!
[**g00ten** tahk]

dialogues

how are you? wie geht es
dir/Ihnen? [gayt ess deer/
eenen]

fine, thanks, and you?
danke, gut, und dir/Ihnen?
[**dank**-uh g00t]

how much is it? was kostet

das?
75 euros fünfundsiebzig Euro
I'll take it ich nehme es [ish naym-uh ess]

humid feucht [foysht]
humour der Humor [hoom**oh**r]
Hungarian ungarisch [**oo**ngahrish]
Hungary Ungarn [**oo**ngarn]
hungry hungrig [h**oo**ngrish]
I'm hungry ich habe Hunger [ish hahbuh hoong-er]
are you hungry? hast du/ haben Sie Hunger? [doo/ hahben zee]
hurry (verb) sich beeilen [zish buh-**i**len]
I'm in a hurry ich habe es eilig [ish hahb-uh ess **i**lish]
there's no hurry es eilt nicht [ilt nisht]
hurry up! beeilen Sie sich!
hurt (verb) weh tun [vay toon]
it really hurts es tut echt weh [toot esht vay]
husband der Mann
hydrofoil das Tragflächenboot [tra**h**kfleshenboht]
hypermarket der Verbrauchermarkt [fair-bro**w**kHer-markt]

I

I ich [ish]
ice das Eis [ice]

with ice mit Eis
no ice, thanks kein Eis, danke [kine ice, d**a**nk-uh]
ice cream das Eis [ice]
ice-cream cone die Tüte Eiskrem [t**oo**t-uh **ice**-kraym]
ice lolly das Eis am Stiel [ice am shteel]
ice rink die Schlittschuhbahn [shli**tt**-shoo-bahn]
ice skates die Schlittschuhe [shli**tt**-shoo-uh]
idea die Idee [eed**ay**]
idiot der Idiot [eedee-**oh**t]
if wenn [ven]
ignition die Zündung [ts**oo**ndoong]
ill krank
I feel ill ich fühle mich krank [ish f**oo**l-uh mish]
illness die Krankheit [kra**n**khite]
imitation (leather etc) nachgemacht [na**kH**-gemakHt]
immediately sofort [zof**o**rt]
important wichtig [v**i**shtish]
it's very important es ist sehr wichtig [ist zair]
it's not important es ist nicht wichtig [nisht]
impossible unmöglich [oon-m**ur**glish]
impressive beeindruckend [be-**ine**-droockent]
improve verbessern [fair-b**e**ssern]
I want to improve my German ich möchte mein Deutsch aufbessern [ish m**ur**sht-uh mine doytch **ow**f-bessern]

in: it's in the centre es ist im Zentrum

in my car in meinem Auto

in Munich in München

in two days from now in zwei Tagen [**tah**gen]

in May im Mai

in English auf Englisch [owf **eng**-lish]

in German auf Deutsch [doytch]

is he in? ist er da?

in five minutes in fünf Minuten [min**oo**ten]

inch* der Zoll [tsoll]

include enthalten [ent-**hal**ten]

does that include meals? ist das einschließlich der Mahlzeiten? [**ine**-shleeslish dair ma**hl**-tsyten]

is that included? ist das im Preis enthalten? [price]

inconvenient ungünstig [**oo**ng**oo**nstish]

incredible (very good, amazing) unglaublich [**oo**n-gl**ow**plish]

Indian indisch [**in**dish]

indicator (on car) der Blinker

indigestion die Magenverstimmung [**mah**gen-fair-shtimmoong]

indoor pool das Hallenbad [**hal**lenbaht]

indoors drinnen

inexpensive billig [**bil**lish]

infection die Infektion [infekts-**yohn**]

infectious ansteckend [**an**shteckent]

inflammation die Entzündung [ent-ts**oo**ndoong]

informal (clothes, occasion, meeting) zwanglos [**tsv**ang-lohss]

information die Information [informats-**yohn**]

do you have any information about ...? haben Sie Informationen über ...? [**hah**ben zee informats-**yoh**nen **oo**ber]

information desk der Informationsschalter [informats-**yoh**ns-shalter]

injection die Spritze [shprits-uh]

injured verletzt [**fair**letst]

she's been injured sie ist verletzt [zee]

in-laws die Schwiegereltern [shv**ee**ger-eltern]

inner tube der Schlauch [shl**ow**KH]

innocent unschuldig [**oo**n-shooldish]

insect das Insekt [**in**zekt]

insect bite der Insektenstich [**in**zekten-shtish]

do you have anything for insect bites? haben Sie etwas für Insektenstiche? [**hah**ben zee etvass f**oo**r]

insect repellent das Insektenbekämpfungsmittel [**in**zekten-bek**em**pfoongs-mittel]

inside **i**nnen

inside the hotel im Hot**e**l

let's sit inside setzen wir uns nach dr**i**nnen [**ze**tsen veer oonss naKH] insist: I insist ich bestehe darauf [ish beshtay-uh darowff]

insomnia die Schlaflosigkeit [shlahf-lohzish-kite]

instant coffee der Pulverkaffee [poolver-kaffay]

instead statt dessen [shtatt]

instead of ... anstelle von ... [anshtell-uh fon]

give me that one instead geben Sie mir statt dessen das [gayben zee meer shtatt dessen dass]

insulin das Insulin [inzooleen]

insurance die Versicherung [fairzisheroong]

intelligent intelligent [intelligent]

interested: I'm interested in ... ich interessiere mich für... [ish interesseer-uh mish foor]

interesting interessant

that's very interesting das ist sehr interessant [zair]

international international [internats-yonahl]

Internet das Internet

interpret dolmetschen [dolmetchen]

interpreter (man/woman) der Dolmetscher [dolmetcher]/die Dolmetscherin

intersection (US) die Kreuzung [kroytsoong]

interval (at theatre) die Pause [powz-uh]

into

I'm not into ... ich stehe nicht auf ... [ish shtay-uh nisht owf]

introduce vorstellen [for-shtellen]

may I introduce ...? darf ich Ihnen ... vorstellen? [ish eenen]

invitation die Einladung [ine-lahdoong]

invite einladen [ine-lahden]

Ireland Irland [eerlant]

Irish irisch [eerish]

I'm Irish (man/woman) ich bin Ire/Irin [ish bin eer-uh/eerin]

iron (for ironing) das Bügeleisen [boogel-īzen]

can you iron these for me? könnten Sie diese Sachen für mich bügeln? [kurnten zee deez-uh zakHen foor mish boogeln]

is* ist

island die Insel [inzel]

it* es; er; sie [ess, air, zee]

it is ... es ist ...

is it ...? ist es...?

where is it? wo ist es? [vo]

it's him er ist es

it was ... es war... [var]

Italian (adj) italienisch [ital-yaynish]

(language) Italienisch

Italy Italien [itahlee-en]

itch: it itches es juckt [ess yoockt]

J

jack (for car) der Wagenheber [vahgen-hayber]

jacket die Jacke [yackuh]

jam die Marmelade [marm-uhlahd-uh]

jammed: it's jammed es klemmt

January der Januar [yanooar]

jar das Glas [glahss]

jaw der Kiefer [keefer]

jazz der Jazz

jealous eifersüchtig [iferzooshtish]

jeans die Jeans

jellyfish die Qualle [kvall-uh]

jersey der Pullover [poollohver]

jetty der Steg [shtayk]

Jewish jüdisch [yoodish]

jeweller's das Juweliergeschäft [yoov-uh-leer-gesheft]

jewellery der Schmuck [shmoock]

job die Arbeit [arbite]

jogging das Joggen

I'm going jogging ich gehe joggen [ish gay-uh]

joke der Witz [vits]

journey die Reise [rize-uh]

have a good journey! gute Reise! [goot-uh]

jug die Kanne [kann-uh]

a jug of water ein Krug mit Wasser [krook mit vasser]

juice der Saft [zaft]

July der Juli [yoolee]

jump (verb) springen [shpringen]

jumper der Pullover [poollohver]

jump leads das Starthilfekabel [shtart-hilf-uh-kahbel]

junction die Kreuzung [kroytsoong]

June der Juni [yoonee]

just (only) nur [noor]

just two nur zwei

just for me nur für mich [foor mish]

just here genau hier [genow heer]

not just now nicht jetzt [nisht yetst]

we've just arrived wir sind gerade angekommen [veer zint gerahd-uh an-gekommen]

K

keep behalten

keep the change der Rest ist für Sie [dair rest ist foor zee]

can I keep it? kann ich es behalten?

please keep it bitte behalten Sie es

ketchup der Ketchup

kettle der Wasserkessel [vasser-kessel]

key der Schlüssel [shloossel]

the key for room 201, please den Schlüssel für Zimmer zweihunderteins, bitte [dayn – foor tsimmer]

key ring der Schlüsselring [shloossel-ring]

kidneys die Nieren [neeren]

kill töten [turten]

kilo* das Kilo [keelo]

kilometre* der Kilometer [keelo-mayter]

how many kilometres is it to ...? wieviel Kilometer sind

es nach ...? [veefeel]
kind (generous) nett
that's very kind das ist sehr nett [zair]

dialogue

which kind do you want?
welche möchtest du/
möchten Sie? [velsh-uh
murshtest doo/murshten zee]
I want this/that kind ich
möchte diese hier/die da
[ish mursht-uh deez-uh heer/
dee da]

king der König [kurnish]
kiosk der Kiosk
kiss der Kuss [kooss]
(verb) küssen [koossen]
kitchen die Küche [koosh-uh]
kitchenette die Kochnische
[koKHneesh-uh]
Kleenex® die Papiertücher
[papeer-toosher]
knee das Knie [k-nee]
knickers das Höschen [hurss-
shen]
knife das Messer
knitwear die Strickwaren
[shtrick-vahren]
knock (verb) klopfen
knock down anfahren
he's been knocked down er
ist angefahren worden [air ist
an-gefahren vorden]
knock over (object) umstoßen
[oom-shtohssen]
(pedestrian) anfahren

know (somebody, a place) kennen
(something) wissen [vissen]
I don't know ich weiß nicht
[ish vice nisht]
I didn't know that das wusste
ich nicht [voost-uh]
do you know where I can
find ...? wissen Sie, wo ich ...
finden kann?

L

label das Etikett
ladies' (toilets) die
Damentoilette [dahmen-
twalett-uh]
ladies' wear die
Damenkleidung [dahmen-
klydoong]
lady die Dame [dahm-uh]
lager das helle Bier [hell-uh
beer]
lake der See [zay]
Lake Constance der Bodensee
[bohdenzay]
Lake Lucerne der
Vierwaldstätter See [feervalt-
shtetter zay]
lamb das Lamm
lamp die Lampe [lamp-uh]
lane (on motorway) die Spur
[shpoor]
(small road) die Gasse [gass-uh]
language die Sprache
[shprahKH-uh]
language course der
Sprachkurs [shprahKH-koors]
large groß [grohss]

last letzter [**let**ster]

last week letzte Woche [**l**etst-uh **vo**KH-uh]

last Friday letzten Freitag [**l**etsten]

last night gestern abend [**g**estern **ah**bent]

what time is the last train to Hamburg? wann fährt der letzte Zug nach Hamburg? [vann fairt]

late spät [shpayt]

sorry I'm late tut mir leid, dass ich zu spät komme [toot meer lite dass ish ts00 shpayt komm-uh]

the train was late der Zug hatte Verspätung [dair ts00k hatt-uh fairshp**ay**toong]

we must go, we'll be late wir müssen gehen, sonst kommen wir zu spät [veer m00ssen g**ay**-en zonst kommen veer ts00]

it's getting late es wird spät [ess veert]

later später [shp**ay**ter]

I'll come back later ich komme später wieder [ish komm-uh – v**ee**der]

see you later bis später

later on nachher [naKH-h**air**]

latest spätester [shp**ay**tester]

by Wednesday at the latest spätestens bis Mittwoch [shp**ay**testens biss]

Latvia Lettland [**l**ettlant]

laugh (verb) lachen [**l**akHen]

launderette der Waschsalon

[**v**ash-zall**ong**]

laundromat (US) der Waschsalon

laundry (clothes) die Wäsche [**v**esh-uh]

(place) die Wäscherei [vesher**ī**]

lavatory die Toilette [twal**e**tt-uh]

law das Gesetz [gezets]

lawn der Rasen [**rah**zen]

lawyer der Rechtsanwalt [**r**eshts-anvallt]

laxative das Abführmittel [**a**pf00r-mittel]

lazy faul [**f**owl]

lead (electrical) das Kabel [**kah**bel]

lead (verb) führen [**f00**ren]

where does this road lead to? wohin führt diese Straße? [vohin f00rt d**ee**z-uh shtr**ah**ss-uh]

leaf das Blatt

leaflet der Prospekt

leak die undichte Stelle [**oo**ndisht-uh sht**e**ll-uh]

(verb) lecken

the roof leaks das Dach ist undicht

learn lernen [**l**airnen]

least: not in the least nicht im mindesten [nisht]

at least mindestens

leather das Leder [**l**ayder]

leave verlassen [fair**l**assen]

I am leaving tomorrow ich reise morgen ab [ish **r**ize-uh morgen ap]

he left yesterday er ist gestern abgereist [**a**p-geryst]

may I leave this here? kann

ich das hierlassen? [**heer**lassen]

I left my coat in the bar ich habe meinen Mantel in der Bar gelassen [**hahb**-uh **mine**-en]

when does the bus for Saarbrücken leave? wann fährt der Bus nach Saarbrücken? [vann fairt dair booss nakH]

leek der Lauch [lowkH]

left links

on the left links

to the left nach links [nakH]

turn left biegen Sie links ab [**bee**gen zee – ap]

there's none left es ist alle [**al**uh]

left-handed linkshändig [**links**-hendish]

left luggage (office) die Gepäckaufbewahrung [ge**peck**-owfbevahroong]

leg das Bein [bine]

lemon die Zitrone [tsit**rohn**-uh]

lemonade die Limonade [limon**ahd**-uh]

lemon tea der Zitronentee [tsit**rohn**entay]

lend leihen [**ly**-en]

will you lend me your ...? könnten Sie mir Ihr ... leihen? [**kurn**ten zee meer eer – **ly**-en]

lens (of camera) das Objektiv [ob-yek**teef**]

lesbian die Lesbierin [**les**bee-erin]

less weniger [**vay**niger]

less than weniger als

less expensive nicht so teuer [nisht zoh]

lesson die Stunde [**shtoond**-uh]

let (allow) lassen

will you let me know? können Sie mir Bescheid sagen? [**kur**nen zee meer be**shite** zahgen]

I'll let you know ich werde Ihnen Bescheid sagen [ish vaird-uh **een**en]

let's go for something to eat gehen wir etwas essen [**gay**-en veer **et**vass]

let off absetzen [**ap**zetsen]

will you let me off at ...? können Sie mich in ... absetzen? [**kur**nen zee mish – **ap**setsen]

letter der Brief [breef]

do you have any letters for me? ist ein Brief für mich angekommen? [ine breef foor mish **an**-gekommen]

letterbox der Briefkasten [**breef**kasten]

lettuce der Kopfsalat [**kopf**zalaht]

lever der Hebel [**hay**bel]

library die Bücherei [boo**sheri**]

licence die Genehmigung [ge**nay**migoong]

(driving) der Führerschein [**foo**rer-shine]

lid der Deckel

lie (tell untruth) lügen [**loo**gen]

lie down sich hinlegen [zish **hin**laygen]

life das Leben [**lay**ben]

lifebelt der Rettungsgürtel [**ret**toongs-g**oo**rtel]

lifeguard (on beach) der Rettungsschwimmer [**ret**toongs-shvimmer]

life jacket die Schwimmweste [shv**i**mm-vest-uh]

lift (in building) der Aufzug [**ow**f-tsook]

could you give me a lift? könnten Sie mich mitnehmen? [**kur**nten zee mish **mit**naymen]

would you like a lift? kann ich Sie mitnehmen?

lift pass (for ski lift) der Liftpass [**lift**pas]

a daily/weekly lift pass ein Liftpass für einen Tag/eine Woche [f**oo**r **ine**-en tahk/**ine**-uh v**o**KH-uh]

light das Licht [lisht]

(not heavy) leicht [lysht]

do you have a light? (for cigarette) haben Sie Feuer? [**hah**ben zee f**oy**er]

light green hellgrün [**hell**gr**oo**n]

light bulb die Glühbirne [gl**oo**beern-uh]

I need a new light bulb ich brauche eine neue Birne [**noy**-uh]

lighter (cigarette) das Feuerzeug [**foy**er-tsoyk]

lightning der Blitz [blits]

like mögen [**mur**gen]

I like it es gefällt mir [ess gef**e**lt meer]

I don't like it es gefällt mir nicht [nisht]

I like going for walks ich gehe gern spazieren [ish g**ay**-uh gairn]

I like you ich mag dich [ish mahk dish]

do you like ...? magst du/mögen Sie...? [**mah**kst doo/**mur**gen zee]

I'd like a beer ich möchte gern ein Bier [**mur**sht-uh gairn]

I'd like to go swimming ich würde gern schwimmen gehen [v**oo**rd-uh]

would you like a drink? möchtest du/möchten Sie etwas trinken?

would you like to go for a walk? möchtest du/möchten Sie einen Spaziergang machen?

what's it like? wie ist es? [vee]

I want one like this ich möchte so eins [zoh **ine**-ss]

lime die Limone [lim**oh**n-uh]

lime cordial der Limonensaft [lim**oh**nenzaft]

line (on paper) die Linie [**lee**nee-uh]

(telephone) die Leitung [**ly**toong]

could you give me an outside line? könnten Sie mir ein Amt geben? [**kur**nten zee meer ine amt **gay**ben]

lips die Lippen

lip salve der Lippen-Fettstift [**fett**-shtift]

lipstick der Lippenstift [**lippen**-shtift]

liqueur der Likör [likur]
listen zuhören [tsoo-hur-ren]
Lithuania Litauen [litowen]
litre* der Liter [leeter]
  a litre of white wine ein Liter Weißwein
little klein [kline]
  just a little, thanks danke, nur ein bisschen [dank-uh noor ine biss-shen]
  a little milk etwas Milch [etvass]
  a little bit more ein bisschen mehr [mair]
live leben [layben]
  we live together wir wohnen zusammen [veer vohnen tsoozammen]

dialogue

  where do you live? wo wohnen Sie? [vo vohnen zee]
  I live in London ich wohne in London

lively lebhaft [layp-haft]
liver die Leber [layber]
loaf das Brot [broht]
lobby (in hotel) das Foyer [foy-yay]
lobster der Hummer [hoommer]
local örtlich [urtlish]
  can you recommend a local restaurant? können Sie ein Restaurant am Ort empfehlen? [kurnen zee ine restorong am ort empfaylen]

lock das Schloss [shloss]
  (verb) abschließen [ap-shleessen]
  it's locked es ist abgeschlossen [ap-geshlossen]
lock in einschließen [ine-shleessen]
lock out ausschließen [owss-shleessen]
  I've locked myself out ich habe mich ausgesperrt [ish hahb-uh mish owss-geshpairt]
locker (for luggage etc) das Schließfach [shleessfakH]
lollipop der Lutscher [lootcher]
London London [lon-don]
long lang
  how long will it/does it take? wie lange dauert es? [vee lang-uh dowert ess]
  a long time eine lange Zeit [ine-uh lang-uh tsite]
  one day/two days longer ein Tag/zwei Tage länger [leng-er]
long distance call das Ferngespräch [fairn-geshpraysh]
look: I'm just looking, thanks danke, ich sehe mich nur um [dank-uh, ish zay-uh mish noor oom]
  you don't look well du siehst nicht gut aus [doo zeest nisht goot owss]
  look out! passen Sie auf! [passen zee owf]
  can I have a look? kann ich mal sehen? [kann ish mahl zay-en]

look after sich kümmern um [zish k00mmern oom]

look at ansehen [anzay-en]

look for suchen [z00KHen]

I'm looking for ... ich suche... [ish z00KH-uh]

look forward to sich freuen auf [zish froyen owf]

I'm looking forward to it ich freue mich darauf [ish froy-uh mish darowf]

loose (handle etc) lose [lohz-uh]

lorry der Lastwagen [lasst-vahgen]

lose verlieren [fairleeren]

I've lost my way ich habe mich verlaufen [ish hahb-uh mish fairlowfen]

I'm lost, I want to get to ... ich weiß nicht, wo ich bin, ich möchte nach ... [vice nisht vo ish bin ish mursht-uh naKH]

I've lost my handbag ich habe meine Handtasche verloren [fairlohren]

lost property (office) das Fundbüro [foont-b00roh]

lot: a lot, lots viel [feel]

not a lot nicht sehr viel [nisht zair]

a lot of people viele Leute [feel-uh]

a lot bigger viel größer

I like it a lot ich mag es sehr [ish mahk ess zair]

lotion die Lotion [lohts-yohn]

loud laut [lowt]

lounge (in house) das Wohnzimmer [vohn-tsimmer]

(in hotel) die Lounge

(in airport) der Warteraum [vart-uh-rowm]

love die Liebe [leeb-uh]

(verb) lieben [leeben]

I love Germany ich liebe Deutschland

lovely herrlich [hairlish]

low (prices, bridge) niedrig [needrish]

luck das Glück [gl00ck]

good luck! viel Glück [feel]

luggage das Gepäck [gepeck]

luggage trolley der Kofferkuli [koffer-k00li]

lump (on body) die Beule [boyl-uh]

lunch das Mittagessen [mittahkessen]

lungs die Lungen [loong-en]

Luxembourg Luxemburg [l00ksemboork]

luxurious luxuriös [looksooree-urss]

luxury der Luxus [l00ksooss]

M

machine die Maschine [masheen-uh]

mad (insane) verrückt [fair-r00ckt]

(angry) böse [burz-uh]

made: what is it made of? woraus ist es? [vohrowss]

(food) was ist da drin? [vass]

magazine die Zeitschrift [tsite-shrift]

maid (in hotel) das Zimmermädchen [tsimmer-maydshen]

maiden name der Mädchenname [maydshen-nahm-uh]

mail die Post

is there any mail for me? ist Post für mich da? [foor mish]

mailbox der Briefkasten [breefkasten]

main Haupt- [howpt]

main course das Hauptgericht [howpt-gerisht]

main post office die Hauptpost [howpt-posst]

main road die Hauptstraße [howpt-shtrahss-uh]

mains switch der Hauptschalter [howpt-shalter]

make (brand name) die Marke [mark-uh]

(verb) machen [maкнen]

I make it 200 euros nach meiner Rechnung sind das zweihundert Euro [naкн mine-er reshnoong zint dass]

make-up das Make-up

man der Mann

manager der Geschäftsführer [geshefts-foorer]

can I see the manager? kann ich den Geschäftsführer sprechen? [dayn – shpreshen]

manageress die Geschäftsführerin [geshefts-foorerin]

manual (car) ein Auto mit Handschaltung [owto mit hant-shaltoong]

many viele [feel-uh]

not many nicht viele [nisht]

map (of city) der Stadtplan [shtat-plahn]

(road map) die Straßenkarte [shtrahssen-kart-uh]

(geographical) die Landkarte [lantkart-uh]

March der März [mairts]

margarine die Margarine [margareen-uh]

market der Markt

marmalade die Orangenmarmelade [oronjen-marmelahd-uh]

married: I'm married ich bin verheiratet [ish bin fairhyrahtet]

are you married? sind Sie verheiratet? [zint zee]

mascara die Wimperntusche [vimpern-toosh-uh]

match (football etc) das Spiel [shpeel]

matches die Streichhölzer [shtrysh-hurltser]

material (fabric) der Stoff [shtoff]

matter: it doesn't matter das macht nichts [maкнt nishts]

what's the matter? was ist los? [vass ist lohss]

mattress die Matratze [matrats-uh]

May der Mai [my]

may: may I have another one? kann ich noch eins haben? [ish noкн ine-ss hahben] may I come in? darf ich hereinkommen? [hair**ine**-kommen]

may I see it? kann ich es sehen? [**zay**-en]

maybe vielleicht [feel**y**sht]

mayonnaise die Mayonnaise [my-oh-n**ayz**-uh]

me* mich [mish]

that's for me das ist für mich

send it to me schicken Sie es mir [meer]

me too ich auch [ish owKH]

meal die Mahlzeit [**mah**ltsite]

dialogue

did you enjoy your meal? hat es Ihnen geschmeckt? [**ee**nen geshm**e**ckt]

it was excellent, thank you es war ausgezeichnet, danke [var owss-gets**y**shnet, d**a**nk-uh]

mean (verb) bedeuten [bed**oy**ten]

what do you mean? was meinen Sie damit? [vass m**ine**-en zee]

dialogue

what does this word mean? was bedeutet dieses Wort? [vass bed**oy**tet d**ee**zess vort]

it means ... in English auf Englisch bedeutet es ... [owf **e**ng-lish]

measles die Masern [m**ah**zern]

meat das Fleisch [flysh]

mechanic der Mechaniker [mesh**ah**niker]

medicine die Medizin [med**itse**en]

medium (size) mittlerer

medium-dry (wine) halbtrocken [h**a**lp-trocken]

medium-rare (steak) medium [m**ay**dee-oom]

medium-sized mittelgroß [m**i**ttelgrohss]

meet treffen

nice to meet you freut mich [froyt mish]

where shall I meet you? wo treffen wir uns? [vo – veer oonss]

meeting die Besprechung [beshpr**e**shoong]

meeting place der Treffpunkt [tr**e**ff-poonkt]

melon die Melone [mel**oh**n-uh]

men die Männer [m**e**nner]

mend reparieren [repar**ee**ren]

could you mend this for me? können Sie das reparieren? [k**u**rnen zee]

menswear die Herrenkleidung [h**ai**ren-klydoong]

mention erwähnen [airv**ay**nen]

don't mention it gern geschehen [gairn gesh**ay**-en]

menu die Speisekarte [shp**i**ze-uh-kart-uh]

may I see the menu, please? kann ich bitte die Speisekarte

haben? [bitt-uh]
see **Menu Reader** on page 214
message die Nachricht
[naKHrisht]
are there any messages for
me? ist eine Nachricht für
mich hinterlassen worden?
[ine-uh – foor mish]
I want to leave a message
for ... ich möchte eine
Nachricht für ... hinterlassen
[ish mursht-uh]
metal das Metall
metre* der Meter [mayter]
microwave (oven) der
Mikrowellenherd
[meekrovellen-hairt]
midday der Mittag
at midday mittags [mittahgs]
middle: in the middle in der
Mitte [dair mitt-uh]
in the middle of the night
mitten in der Nacht
the middle one der mittlere
[mittler-uh]
midnight die Mitternacht
[mitter-naKHt]
at midnight um Mitternacht
[oom]
might: I might vielleicht
[feelysht]
I might not vielleicht nicht
[nisht]
I might want to stay another
day vielleicht bleibe ich noch
einen Tag länger [blibe-uh ish
noKH ine-en tahk leng-er]
migraine die Migräne [migrayn-
uh]

mild (taste, weather) mild [milt]
mile* die Meile [mile-uh]
milk die Milch [milsh]
milkshake der Milchshake
millimetre* der Millimeter
[millimayter]
minced meat das Hackfleisch
[hackflysh]
mind: never mind macht
nichts [maKHt nishts]
I've changed my mind ich
habe es mir anders überlegt
[ish hahb-uh ess meer anders
ooberlaykt]

dialogue

do you mind if I open the
window? macht es Ihnen
etwas aus, wenn ich das
Fenster öffne? [maKHt ess
eenen etvass owss venn ish]
no, I don't mind nein, das
ist mir gleich [meer glysh]

mine*: it's mine es gehört mir
[gehurt meer]
mineral water das Mineralwasser [minerahlvasser]
mint (sweet) das Pfefferminz
[pfeffermints]
minute die Minute [minoot-uh]
in a minute gleich [glysh]
just a minute Moment mal
[mohment mahl]
mirror der Spiegel [shpeegel]
Miss Frau [frow]
Miss! (waitress etc) Fräulein
[froyline]

miss (bus, train) verpassen
[fairpassen]

(regret absence of) vermissen
[fairmissen]

I missed the bus ich habe den
Bus verpasst [ish hahb-uh dayn
booss fairpasst]

missing: to be missing fehlen
[faylen]

there's a suitcase missing ein
Koffer fehlt

mist der Nebel [naybel]

mistake der Fehler [fayler]

I think there's a mistake ich
glaube, da ist ein Fehler [ish
glowb-uh]

sorry, I've made a mistake
tut mir leid, ich habe einen
Fehler gemacht [toot meer lite
ish hahb-uh ine-en]

misunderstanding das
Missverständnis [miss-
fairshtentniss]

mix-up: sorry, there's been a
mix-up tut mir leid, etwas ist
schiefgelaufen [toot meer lite,
etvass ist sheef-gelowfen]

mobile phone das Handy
[hendi]

modern modern [modairn]

modern art gallery die Galerie
für moderne Kunst [gal-eree
foor modairn-uh koonst]

moisturizer die
Feuchtigkeitscreme
[foyshtishkites-kraym]

moment: I'll be back in a
moment ich bin gleich wieder
da [glysh veeder]

Monday Montag [mohntahk]

money das Geld [gelt]

month der Monat [mohnaht]

monument das Denkmal
[denkmahl]

moon der Mond [mohnt]

moped das Moped [mohpet]

more* mehr [mair]

can I have some more water,
please? kann ich bitte noch
etwas Wasser haben? [ish bitt-
uh noKH etvass]

more expensive/interesting
teurer/interessanter [toyrer]

more than 50 über fünfzig
[oober]

more than that mehr als das

a lot more viel mehr [feel]

dialogue

would you like some
more? möchten Sie noch
etwas? [murshten zee noKH
etvass]

no, no more for me, thanks
nein danke, das ist genug
[nine dank-uh dass ist genook]

how about you? und Sie?
[oont zee]

I don't want any more,
thanks ich möchte nichts
mehr, danke [nishts]

morning der Morgen

this morning heute morgen
[hoyt-uh]

in the morning am Morgen

most: I like this one most of

all dies gefällt mir am besten [deess gefellt meer]

most of the time die meiste Zeit [dee myst-uh tsite]

most tourists die meisten Touristen [mysten]

mostly meistens [mystens]

mother die Mutter [mootter]

motorbike das Motorrad [motohr-raht]

motorboat das Motorboot [motohr-boht]

motorway die Autobahn [owtobahn]

mountain der Berg [bairk]

in the mountains in den Bergen [dayn bairgen]

mountaineering das Bergsteigen [bairk-shtygen]

mouse die Maus [mowss]

moustache der Schnurrbart [shnoorr-bart]

mouth der Mund [moont]

mouth ulcer die Mundfäule [moont-foyl-uh]

move bewegen [bevaygen] (move house) umziehen [oomtsee-en]

he's moved to another room er ist in ein anderes Zimmer gezogen [air ist in ine anderess tsimmer getsohgen]

could you move your car? könnten Sie Ihr Auto wegfahren? [kurnten zee eer owto veckfahren]

could you move up a little? könnten Sie etwas aufrücken? [etvass owf-roocken]

where has it moved to? (shop, gallery) wo ist es jetzt? [vo]

movie der Film

movie theater (US) das Kino [keeno]

Mr Herr [hair]

Mrs Frau [frow]

Ms Frau [frow]

much viel [feel]

much better/worse viel besser/schlechter [shleshter]

much hotter viel heißer

not much nicht viel [nisht]

not very much nicht sehr viel [zair]

I don't want very much ich möchte nicht so viel

mud der Dreck

mug (for drinking) die Tasse [tass-uh]

I've been mugged ich bin überfallen worden [ish bin ooberfallen vorden]

mum die Mutter [mootter]

mumps der Mumps [moomps]

Munich München [moonshen]

museum das Museum [moozayoom]

mushrooms die Pilze [pilts-uh]

music die Musik [moozeek]

musician der Musiker [mooziker]

Muslim moslemisch [moslaymish]

mussels die Muscheln [moosheln]

must*: I must ich muss... [ish mooss]

I mustn't drink alcohol ich

darf keinen Alkohol trinken
[k**ine**-en]
mustard der Senf [zenf]
my*: my room mein Zimmer
[m**ine**]
my family meine Familie
[m**ine**-uh]
my parents meine Eltern
myself: I'll do it myself ich
mache es selbst [ish maкн-uh
ess z**e**lpst]
by myself allein [all**ine**]

N

nail (finger, metal) der Nagel
[**nah**gel]
nail varnish der Nagellack
[**nah**gel-lack]
name der Name [**nah**muh]
my name's John ich heiße
John [ish h**ice**-uh]
what's your name? wie
heißen Sie? [vee h**ice**-en zee]
what is the name of this
street? wie heißt diese
Straße? [vee hysst]
napkin die Serviette [zairvee-
ett-uh]
nappy die Windel [**vindel**]
narrow eng
nasty (person) gemein [gem**ine**]
(weather, accident) furchtbar
[**foo**rshtbar]
national national [nats-yohn**ahl**]
nationality die
Staatsangehörigkeit [sht**ahts**-
an-gehurishk**ite**]

natural natürlich [nat**oo**rlish]
nausea die Übelkeit [**oo**belkite]
navy (blue) marineblau
[mar**ee**n-uh-blow]
near nah
is it near the city centre? ist
es nahe dem Stadtzentrum?
[n**ah**-uh daym]
do you go near the
Brandenburg Gate?
fahren Sie in die Nähe des
Brandenburger Tores? [**fah**ren
zee in dee **nay**-uh]
where is the nearest ...? wo
ist der nächste ...? [vo ist dair
n**ay**kst-uh]
nearby in der Nähe [dair nay-
uh]
nearly fast [fasst]
necessary notwendig
[**noht**vendish]
neck der Hals [halss]
necklace die Halskette
[**hals**kett-uh]
necktie (US) die Krawatte
[krav**att**-uh]
need: I need ... ich brauche ...
[ish br**ow**кн-uh]
do I need to pay? muss ich
bezahlen? [mooss]
needle die Nadel [**nah**del]
negative (film) das Negativ
[**nay**gateef]
neither: neither (one) of them
keiner (von ihnen) [k**ine**-er
fon **ee**nen]
neither ... nor ... weder ...
noch ... [**vay**der ... noкн]
nephew der Neffe [neff-uh]

net (in sport) das Netz
Netherlands die Niederlande
[neederland-uh]
network map der
Nahverkehrsplan [nahfairkairs-plahn]
never nie [nee]

dialogue

have you ever been to
Mainz? waren Sie schon
einmal in Mainz? [vahren
zee shohn ine-mahl]
no, never, I've never been
there nein, ich war noch
nie da [noKH]

new neu [noy]
news (radio, TV etc) die
Nachrichten [naKHrishten]
newsagent's der
Zeitungshändler [tsytoongs-hentler]
newspaper die Zeitung
[tsytoong]
newspaper kiosk der
Zeitungskiosk [tsytoongs-kee-osk]
New Year Neujahr [noy-yahr]
Happy New Year! frohes
neues Jahr [froh-ess noyess yar]
New Year's Eve Silvester
[zilvester]
New Zealand Neuseeland
[noyzaylant]
New Zealander: I'm a New
Zealander (man/woman) ich bin
Neuseeländer [noyzaylender]/

Neeseeländerin
next nächster [naykster]
the next turning/street on the
left die nächste Abzweigung/
Straße links [naykst-uh]
at the next stop an der
nächsten Haltestelle
[nayksten]
next week nächste Woche
next to neben [nayben]
nice (food) gut [goot]
(looks, view etc) hübsch [hoopsh]
(person) nett
niece die Nichte [nisht-uh]
night die Nacht [naKHt]
at night nachts
good night gute Nacht [goot-uh]

dialogue

do you have a single room
for one night? haben Sie
ein Einzelzimmer für eine
Nacht? [hahben zee ine ine-tsel-tsimmer foor ine-uh]
yes ja [yah]
how much is it per night?
was kostet es pro Nacht?
it's 150 euros for one night
eine Übernachtung kostet
hundertfünfzig Euro
[oober-naKHtoong]
thank you, I'll take it
danke, ich nehme es
[naym-uh]

nightclub der Nachtklub
[naKHtkloob]

nightdress das Nachthemd
[naKHt-hemt]

night porter der Nachtportier
[naKHt-port-yay]

no nein [nine]

I've no change ich habe kein
Kleingeld [kine]

there's no ... left es ist kein ...
übrig [**oo**brish]

no way! auf keinen Fall [owf
kine-en fal]

oh no! (upset) nein!

nobody keiner [**kine**-er]

there's nobody there es ist
keiner da

noise der Lärm [lairm]

noisy: it's too noisy es ist zu
laut [ts00 lowt]

non-alcoholic alkoholfrei
[alkoho**ohl**fry]

none keiner [**kine**-er]

nonsmoking compartment
das Nichtraucherabteil
[nishtrowKHer-aptile]

noon der Mittag [**mit**tahk]

no-one keiner [**kine**-er]

nor: nor do I ich auch nicht
[owKH nisht]

normal normal [nor**mahl**]

north der Norden

in the north im Norden

north of Leipzig nördlich von
Leipzig [**nurt**lish fon]

northeast der Nordosten [nort-
osten]

northern nördlich [**nurt**lish]

North Sea die Nordsee
[**nort**zay]

northwest der Nordwesten

[nort**vest**en]

Northern Ireland Nordirland
[nort-**eer**lant]

Norway Norwegen [**nor**vaygen]

Norwegian (adj) norwegisch
[**nor**vaygish]

nose die Nase [**nah**z-uh]

nosebleed Nasenbluten
[**nah**zen-bl00ten]

not* nicht [nisht]

no, I'm not hungry nein, ich
habe keinen Hunger [**kine**-en]

I don't want any, thank you
ich möchte keine, danke
[**mursht**-uh **kine**-uh **dank**-uh]

it's not necessary es ist nicht
nötig

I didn't know that das wusste
ich nicht [**voo**st-uh]

not that one – this one nicht
den – diesen [dayn – **dee**zen]

note (banknote) der Geldschein
[**gelt**-shine]

notebook das Notizbuch
[noh**teets**-b00KH]

notepaper (for letters) das
Briefpapier [**breef**-papeer]

nothing nichts [nishts]

nothing for me, thanks nichts
für mich, danke

nothing else sonst nichts
[zonst]

novel der Roman [ro**mahn**]

November der November

now jetzt [yetst]

number die Nummer
[**noo**mmer]

I've got the wrong number
ich habe mich verwählt

[hahb-uh mish fairvaylt]
what is your phone number?
was ist Ihre Telefon-
nummer? [eer-uh telefohn-
noommer]
number plate das
Nummernschild [noommern-
shilt]
Nuremburg Nürnberg [noorn-
bairk]
nurse (female) die
Krankenschwester [kranken-
shvester]
(male) der Krankenpfleger
[kranken-pflayger]
nursery slope der
Anfängerhügel [anfenger-
hoogel]
nut (for bolt) die
Schraubenmutter
[shrowbenmootter]
nuts die Nüsse [nooss-uh]

O

occupied (toilet) besetzt
[bezetst]
o'clock*: it's nine o'clock es ist
neun Uhr [oor]
October der Oktober
odd (strange) merkwürdig
[mairk-voordish]
of* von (+dat) [fon]
the name of the hotel der
Name des Hotels
off (lights) aus [owss]
it's just off Goethestraße es
ist ganz in der Nähe der

Goethestraße [gants in dair nay-
uh]
we're off tomorrow wir reisen
morgen ab [veer ryzen]
offensive anstößig [an-
shturssish]
office das Büro [booroh]
often oft
not often nicht oft [nisht]
how often are the buses? wie
oft fahren die Busse? [vee]
oil (for car, for salad) das Öl [url]
ointment die Salbe [zalb-uh]
OK okay
are you OK? sind Sie okay?
is that OK with you? ist das in
Ordnung? [ortnoong]
is it OK if I ...? kann ich ... ?
that's OK thanks (it doesn't
matter) danke, das ist in
Ordnung
I'm OK (nothing for me, I've got
enough) nein, danke [nine]
(I feel OK) mir geht's gut [meer
gayts goot]
is this train OK for ...? fährt
dieser Zug nach ...?
I said I'm sorry, OK ich habe
doch gesagt, es tut mir leid
[hahb-uh dokH gezahkt]
old alt

dialogue

how old are you? wie alt
bist du/sind Sie? [vee alt bist
doo/zint zee]
I'm twenty-five ich bin
fünfundzwanzig

and you? und du/Sie? [oont]

old-fashioned altmodisch [altmohdish]

old town (old part of town) die Altstadt [alt-shtatt]

in the old town in der Altstadt

olive oil das Olivenöl [oleeven-url]

olives die Oliven [oleeven]

omelette das Omelette [omlett]

on* auf [owf]

on the street/beach auf der Straße/am Strand

is it on this road? ist es auf dieser Straße?

on the plane im Flugzeug

on Saturday am Samstag

on television im Fernsehen

I haven't got it on me ich habe es nicht bei mir [hahb-uh ess nisht by meer]

this one's on me (drink) diese Runde ist auf meine Rechnung [deez-uh roond-uh ist owf mine-uh reshnoong]

the light wasn't on das Licht war nicht an

what's on tonight? was gibt es heute abend? [vass geept ess]

once (one time) einmal [ine-mahl]

at once (immediately) sofort [zofort]

one* ein(e) [ine(-uh)]

(as figure) eins [ine-ss]

the white one der weiße [dair]

one-way ticket die einfache Fahrkarte [ine-faKH-uh fahr-kart-uh]

onion die Zwiebel [tsveebel]

only nur [noor]

only one nur einer

it's only 6 o'clock es ist erst sechs Uhr [airst]

I've only just got here ich bin gerade erst angekommen [gerahd-uh airst]

on/off switch der Ein/Aus-Schalter [ine-owss-shalter]

open (adj) offen

open (verb) öffnen [urfnen]

when do you open? wann machen Sie auf? [van maKHen zee owf]

I can't get it open ich bekomme es nicht auf [bekomm-uh]

in the open air im Freien [fry-en]

opening times die Öffnungszeiten [urfnoongs-tsyten]

open ticket die unbeschränkte Fahrkarte [oonbeshrenkt-uh fahrkart-uh]

opera die Oper [ohper]

operation (medical) die Operation [operats-yohn]

operator (telephone) die Vermittlung [fairmittloong]

opposite: the opposite direction die entgegengesetzte Richtung [entgaygen-gezetst-uh rishtoong]

the bar opposite die Kneipe

gegenüber [gaygen-**oo**ber]
opposite my hotel gegenüber meinem Hotel
optician der Augenarzt [**ow**genartst]
or oder [**oh**der]
orange (fruit) die Apfelsine [apfelz**ee**n-uh], die Orange [or**o**nJ-uh]
(colour) orange
orange juice der Orangensaft [or**o**nJen-zaft]
orchestra das Orchester [ork**e**ster]
order: can we order now? können wir jetzt bestellen? [k**u**rnen veer yetst besht**e**llen]
I've already ordered, thanks danke, ich habe schon bestellt [h**a**hb-uh shohn]
I didn't order this das habe ich nicht bestellt
out of order außer Betrieb [**ow**sser betr**ee**p]
ordinary normal [norm**ah**l]
other andere [**a**nder-uh]
the other one der andere
the other day (recently) neulich [n**oy**lish]
I'm waiting for the others ich warte auf die anderen [dee **a**nderen]
do you have any others? haben Sie noch andere? [h**ah**ben zee noKH]
otherwise sonst [zonst]
our* unser [**oo**nzer]
ours* unserer [**oo**nzerer]
out: he's out (not at home) er ist

nicht da [air ist nisht]
three kilometres out of town drei Kilometer außerhalb der Stadt [**ow**sserhalp dair shtatt]
outdoors draußen [dr**ow**ssen]
outside ... außerhalb ... (+gen) [**ow**sser-halp]
can we sit outside? können wir draußen sitzen? [dr**ow**ssen]
oven der Backofen [b**a**ck-ohfen]
over: over here hier [heer]
over there dort drüben [dr**oo**ben]
over 500 über fünfhundert [**oo**ber]
it's over (finished) es ist vorbei [for-b**y**]
overcharge: you've overcharged me Sie haben mir zuviel berechnet [zee h**ah**ben meer tso**of**eel ber**e**shnet]
overcoat der Mantel
overnight (travel) über Nacht [**oo**ber naKHt]
overtake überholen [**oo**berh**oh**len]
owe: how much do I owe you? was bin ich Ihnen schuldig? [vass bin ish **ee**nen sh**oo**ldish]
own: my own ... mein eigener ... [mine **ī**gener]
are you on your own? sind Sie allein hier? [zint zee all**ine** heer]
I'm on my own ich bin allein hier
owner (man/woman) der Besitzer [bez**i**tser]/die Besitzerin

P

pack (verb) packen
pack: a pack of ... (food, drink etc) eine Packung ... [**ine**-uh pack**oong**]
package das Paket [pak**ayt**]
package holiday die Pauschalreise [powsh**ahl**rize-uh]
packed lunch das Lunchpaket [-pak**ayt**]
packet: a packet of cigarettes eine Schachtel Zigaretten [shak**H**tel tsigar**e**tten]
padlock das Vorhängeschloss [**f**orheng-uh-shloss]
page (of book) die Seite [z**i**te-uh]
could you page Mr ...? können Sie Herrn ... ausrufen lassen? [**kur**nen zee hairn ... **ow**ssroofen]
pain der Schmerz [shm**ai**rts]
I have a pain here ich habe hier Schmerzen [ish h**ah**b-uh heer]
painful schmerzhaft [shm**ai**rts-haft]
painkillers das Schmerzmittel [shm**ai**rts-mittel]
paint die Farbe [**f**arb-uh]
painting (picture) das Gemälde [gem**e**ld-uh]
pair: a pair of ... ein Paar ... [ine pahr]
Pakistani (adj) pakistanisch [pakist**ah**nish]
palace der Palast
pale blass

pale blue zartblau [ts**a**rtblow]
pan die Pfanne [pfann-uh]
panties das Höschen [**hurs**-shen]
pants (underwear: men's) die Unterhose [**oo**nter-hohz-uh] (women's) das Höschen [**hurs**-shen] (US) die Hose [h**oh**z-uh]
pantyhose die Strumpfhose [shtr**oo**mpf-hohz-uh]
paper das Papier [pap**eer**] (newspaper) die Zeitung [ts**y**toong]
a piece of paper ein Stück Papier [ine sht**oo**ck]
paper handkerchiefs die Papiertaschentücher [pap**eer**-tashent**oo**sher]
parcel das Paket [pak**ayt**]
pardon?, (US) pardon me? (didn't understand) wie bitte? [vee **bi**tt-uh]
parents: my parents meine Eltern [**mine**-uh eltern]
parents-in-law die Schwiegereltern [shv**ee**ger-eltern]
park der Park (verb) parken
can I park here? kann man hier parken? [heer]
parking lot (US) der Parkplatz [**park**plats]
part ein Teil [tile]
partner (boyfriend, girlfriend) der Partner/die Partnerin
party (group) die Gruppe [gr**oo**pp-uh]

(celebration) die Fete [**fay**t-uh]

pass (in mountains) der Pass [pas]

passenger der Passagier [passa**J**eer]

passport der Pass [pas]

past*: in the past in der Vergangenheit [dair fairgangen-hite]

just past the information office kurz hinter dem **Aus**kunftsbüro [koorts]

path der Weg [vayk]

pattern das Muster [**moo**ster]

pavement der Bürgersteig [**boo**rgershtike]

on the pavement auf dem Bürgersteig

pay (verb) zahlen [ts**ah**len]

can I pay, please? kann ich zahlen, bitte? [**bitt**-uh]

it's already paid for es ist schon bezahlt [shohn bets**ah**lt]

dialogue

who's paying? wer bezahlt? [vair bets**ah**lt]
I'll pay ich bezahle
no, you paid last time, I'll pay nein, du hast letztes Mal bezahlt, ich bezahle [**letstess** mahl]

pay phone der Münzfernsprecher [**moo**nts-fairnshpresher]

peaceful friedlich [**free**tlish]

peach der Pfirsich [**pfeer**zish]

peanuts die Erdnüsse [**air**tn**oo**ss-uh]

pear die Birne [**beer**n-uh]

peas die Erbsen [**air**psen]

peculiar eigenartig [**ī**gen-artish]

pedestrian crossing der Fußgängerüberweg [f**oo**ssgeng-er-**oo**bervayk]

pedestrian precinct die Fußgängerzone [f**oo**ssgeng-er-tsohn-uh]

peg (for washing) die Wäscheklammer [**vesh**-uh-klammer]

(for tent) der Hering [**hai**ring]

pen der Stift [shtift]

pencil der Bleistift [**bly**-shtift]

penfriend (boy/girl) der Brieffreund [**breef**-froynt]/die Brieffreundin

penicillin das Penizillin [penitsill**een**]

penknife das Taschenmesser [**tashen**-messer]

pensioner (man/woman) der Rentner/die Rentnerin

people die Leute [**loy**t-uh]

the other people in the hotel die anderen Leute im Hotel

too many people zu viele Leute [ts**oo** **fee**l-uh]

pepper (spice) der Pfeffer (vegetable) die Paprikaschote [**paprika**-shoht-uh]

peppermint (sweet) das Pfefferminz [**pfeffer**mints]

per: per night pro Nacht [na**KH**t]

how much per day? was kostet es pro Tag? [tahk]

per cent Prozent [protsent]

perfect perfekt [pairfekt]

perfume das Parfüm [parfoom]

perhaps vielleicht [feelysht]

perhaps not vielleicht nicht

period (of time) die Zeit [tsite]
(menstruation) die Periode
[pairee-ohd-uh]

perm die Dauerwelle
[dowervell-uh]

permit die Genehmigung
[genay-migoong]

person die Person [pairzohn]

personal stereo der
Walkman®

petrol das Benzin [bentseen]

petrol can der Reservekanister
[rezairv-uh-kanister]

petrol station die Tankstelle
[tank-shtell-uh]

pharmacy die Apotheke
[apotayk-uh]

phone das Telefon [telefohn]
(verb) anrufen [an-roofen]

phone book das Telefonbuch
[telefohn-booKH]

phonecard die Telefonkarte
[-kart-uh]

phone number die
Telefonnummer [-noommer]

photo das Foto

excuse me, could you take a
photo of us? entschuldigen
Sie, könnten Sie ein Foto von
uns machen? [kurnten zee ine]

phrase book der Sprachführer
[shprahKH-foorer]

piano das Klavier [klaveer]

pickpocket der Taschendieb
[tashen-deep]

pick up: will you be there to
pick me up? werden Sie da
sein, um mich abzuholen?
[oom mish aptsoo-hohlen]

picnic das Picknick

picture das Bild [bilt]

pie (meat) die Pastete [pastayt-
uh]
(fruit) der Kuchen [kooKHen]

piece das Stück [shtoock]
a piece of ... ein Stück ... [ine]

pill die Pille [pill-uh]
I'm on the pill ich nehme die
Pille [ish naym-uh dee]

pillow das Kopfkissen

pillow case der
Kopfkissenbezug [kopfkissen-
betsook]

pin die Nadel [nahdel]

pineapple die Ananas [ananas]

pineapple juice der Ananassaft
[ananas-zaft]

pink rosa [rohza]

pipe (for smoking) die Pfeife
[pfife-uh]
(for water) das Rohr

pipe cleaner der
Pfeifenreiniger [pfyfen-ryniger]

pity: it's a pity das ist schade
[shahd-uh]

pizza die Pizza [peetsa]

place der Platz [plats]
is this place taken? ist dieser
Platz besetzt? [deezer – bezetst]
at your place bei dir/Ihnen
[by deer/eenen]
at his place bei ihm [eem]

plain (not patterned) uni [oonee]

plane das Flugzeug [flooktsoyk]
 by plane mit dem Flugzeug [daym]
plant die Pflanze [pflants-uh]
plaster (for cut) das Heftpflaster
plaster cast der Gipsverband [gips-fairbant]
plastic das Plastik
 (credit cards) die Kreditkarten [kredeet-karten]
plastic bag die Plastiktüte [plastik-toot-uh]
plate der Teller
platform der Bahnsteig [bahnshtike]
 which platform is it, please?
 welches Gleis, bitte? [velshess glice bitt-uh]
play (verb) spielen [shpeelen]
 (noun: in theatre) das Stück [shtook]
playground der Spielplatz [shpeel-plats]
pleasant angenehm [an-genaym]
please bitte [bitt-uh]
 yes please ja bitte [yah]
 could you please ...? könnten Sie bitte ...? [kurnten zee]
 please don't bitte nicht [nisht]
 pleased to meet you! freut mich! [froyt mish]
pleasure die Freude [froyd-uh]
 my pleasure ganz meinerseits [gants mine-er-zites]
plenty: plenty of ... viel ... [feel]
 we've plenty of time wir haben viel Zeit
 that's plenty, thanks das

reicht, danke [rysht]
pliers die Zange [tsang-uh]
plug (electrical) der Stecker [shtecker]
 (for car) die Zündkerze [tsoontkairts-uh]
 (in sink) der Stöpsel [shturpsel]
plumber der Klempner
p.m.* (in the afternoon) nachmittags [naκκmittahks]
 (in the evening) abends [ahbents]
poached egg das pochierte Ei [posheert-uh ī]
pocket die Tasche [tash-uh]
point: two point five zwei Komma fünf
 there's no point es hat keinen Sinn [kine-en zin]
points (in car) die Kontakte [kontakt-uh]
poisonous giftig [giftish]
Poland Polen
Polish polnisch
police die Polizei [politsī]
 call the police! rufen Sie die Polizei! [roofen zee dee]
policeman der Polizist [politsist]
police station die Polizeiwache [politsī-vaκκ-uh]
policewoman die Polizistin [politsistin]
polish die Creme [kraym]
polite höflich [hurflish]
polluted verschmutzt [fairshmootst]
pony der Pony [ponnee]
pool (for swimming) das Schwimmbecken [shvimm-

becken]

poor (not rich) arm
(quality) schlecht [shlesht]

pop music die Popmusik [pop-moozeek]

pop singer (male/female) der
Popsänger [popzenger]/die
Popsängerin

population die Bevölkerung
[befurlkeroong]

pork das Schweinefleisch
[shvine-uh-flysh]

port (for boats) der Hafen
[hahfen]
(drink) der Portwein [portvine]

porter (in hotel) der Portier
[port-yay]

portrait das Porträt [portray]

posh (restaurant, people)
vornehm [fornaym]

possible möglich [murglish]
is it possible to ...? ist es
möglich, zu ...?
as ... as possible so ... wie
möglich [zo ... vee]

post (mail) die Post [posst]
(verb) absenden
could you post this for me?
könnten Sie das für mich
aufgeben? [kurnten zee dass foor
mish owf-gayben]

postbox der Briefkasten
[breefkasten]

postcard die Postkarte
[posstkart-uh]

poster das Plakat [plakaht]

post office die Post

poste restante postlagernd
[posst-lahgernt]

pots and pans das
Kochgeschirr [kokHgesheer]

potato die Kartoffel

potato chips (US) die Chips
[chips]

potato salad der Kartoffelsalat
[kartoffel-zalaht]

pottery (objects) die
Töpferwaren [turpfer-vahren]

pound* (money, weight) das
Pfund [pfoont]

power cut der Stromausfall
[shtrohm-owssfal]

power point die Steckdose
[shteck-dohz-uh]

practise: I want to practise
my German ich will mein
Deutsch üben [ish vill mine
doytch ooben]

prawns die Krabben

prefer: I prefer ... ich mag
lieber ... [ish mahk leeber]

pregnant schwanger [shvang-er]

prescription (for chemist) das
Rezept [raytsept]

present (gift) das Geschenk
[geshenk]

president der Präsident
[prezeedent]

pretty hübsch [hoopsh]
it's pretty expensive es ist
ganz schön teuer [gants shurn
toyer]

price der Preis [price]

priest der Geistliche [gystlish-uh]

prime minister der
Premierminister [premyay-minister]

printed matter die Drucksache [**droo**ck-zaKH-uh]

priority (in driving) die Vorfahrt [**for**fahrt]

prison das Gefängnis [gefeng-niss]

private privat [priv**aht**]

private bathroom das eigene Bad [**i**gen-uh baht]

private room das Einzelzimmer [**ine**-tseltsimmer]

probably wahrscheinlich [vahrsh**ine**-lish]

problem das Problem [probl**aym**]
no problem! kein Problem [kine]

program(me) das Programm [progr**a**mm]

promise: I promise ich verspreche es [fairshr**e**sh-uh]

pronounce: how is this pronounced? wie spricht man das aus? [vee shpr**i**sht man dass owss]

properly (repaired, locked etc) richtig [r**i**shtish]

protection factor der Lichtschutzfaktor [l**i**sht-shoots-faktor]

Protestant evangelisch [ayvang**ay**lish]

public convenience die öffentliche Toilette [**ur**fentlish-uh twal**ett**-uh]

public holiday der gesetzliche Feiertag [gez**e**tslish-uh f**i**re-tahk]

pudding (dessert) der Nachtisch [n**a**KHtish]

pull ziehen [ts**ee**-en]

pullover der Pullover [pooll**oh**ver]

puncture die Reifenpanne [r**y**fen-pann-uh]

purple violett [vee-oh-l**ett**]

purse (for money) das Portemonnaie [port-mon**ay**] (US) die Handtasche [h**a**nt-tash-uh]

push schieben [sh**ee**ben]

pushchair der Sportwagen [shp**or**t-vahgen]

put tun [t**oo**n]
where can I put ...? wo kann ich ... hinstellen? [h**i**n-shtellen]
could you put us up for the night? könnten Sie uns heute nacht unterbringen? [**oo**nss h**oy**t-uh naKHt **oo**nterbringen]

pyjamas der Schlafanzug [shl**ah**f-ants00k]

Q

quality die Qualität [kvalit**ayt**]

quarantine die Quarantäne [kvarant**ayn**-uh]

quarter das Viertel [f**ee**rtel]

quayside: on the quayside am Kai [ky]

question die Frage [fr**ah**g-uh]

queue die Schlange [shl**a**ng-uh]

quick schnell [shnell]
that was quick das war schnell [vahr]
what's the quickest way there? wie komme ich am schnellsten dorthin? [vee

komm-uh ish am shnellsten dort-
hin]

fancy a quick drink? wollen
wir schnell einen trinken
gehen? [vollen veer – ine-en
trinken gay-en]

quickly schnell [shnell]

quiet (place, hotel) ruhig [rooish]

quiet! Ruhe! [roo-uh]

quite (fairly) ziemlich [tseemlish]

(very) ganz [gants]

that's quite right ganz recht
[resht]

quite a lot eine ganze Menge
[ine-uh gants-uh meng-uh]

R

rabbit das Kaninchen
[kaneenshen]

race (for runners, cars) das
Rennen

racket (squash, tennis etc) der
Schläger [shlayger]

radiator (in room) der
Heizkörper [hites-kurper]
(of car) der Kühler [kooler]

radio das Radio [rahdee-oh]
on the radio im Radio

rail: by rail per Bahn [pair]

railway die Eisenbahn
[izenbahn]

rain der Regen [raygen]
in the rain im Regen
it's raining es regnet [raygnet]

raincoat der Regenmantel
[raygenmantel]

rape die Vergewaltigung

[fairgeval-tigoong]

rare (steak) englisch [eng-lish]

rash (on skin) der Ausschlag
[owss-shlahk]

raspberry die Himbeere
[himbair-uh]

rat die Ratte [ratt-uh]

rate (for changing money) der
Wechselkurs [veksel-koorss]

rather: it's rather good es ist
ganz gut [gants goot]
I'd rather ... ich würde lieber
... [ish voord-uh leeber]

razor (electric) der
Rasierapparat [razeer-apparaht]

razor blades die
Rasierklingen [razeer-klingen]

read lesen [layzen]

ready fertig [fairtish]
are you ready? bist du/sind
Sie fertig?
I'm not ready yet ich bin
noch nicht fertig [noKH nisht]

dialogue

when will it be ready?
wann ist es fertig? [vann]
it should be ready in a
couple of days es müßte in
ein paar Tagen fertig sein
[moosst-uh]

real echt [esht]

really wirklich [veerklish]
that's really great das ist echt
toll [esht tol]

rearview mirror der
Rückspiegel [roock-shpeegel]

reasonable (prices etc)
vernünftig [fairn**oo**nftish]

receipt die Quittung [kv**i**ttoong]

recently kürzlich [k**oo**rtslish]

reception (in hotel, for guests) der
Empfang

at reception am Empfang

reception desk die Rezeption
[retsepts-y**oh**n]

receptionist die
Empfangsperson [empf**a**ngs-
pairzohn]

recognize erkennen [air**ke**nnen]

recommend: could you
recommend ...? könnten Sie
... empfehlen? [k**ur**nten zee ...
empf**ay**len]

record (music) die Schallplatte
[sh**a**llplat-uh]

red rot [roht]

red wine der Rotwein
[r**oh**tvine]

refund (verb) erstatten [air-
sht**a**tten]

can I have a refund? kann ich
das Geld zurückbekommen?
[kan ish dass gelt tsoor**oo**ck-
bekommen]

region das Gebiet [geb**ee**t]

registered: by registered mail
per Einschreiben [pair **ine**-
shryben]

registration number die
Autonummer [**ow**to-noommer]

relative der/die Verwandte
[fairv**a**nt-uh]

religion die Religion [relig-
y**oh**n]

remember: I don't remember

ich kann mich nicht erinnern
[ish kan mish nisht air-**i**nnern]

I remember ich erinnere mich
[air-**i**nner-uh]

do you remember? erinnern
Sie sich? [zee zish]

rent die Miete [m**ee**t-uh]
(verb) mieten [m**ee**ten]

for rent zu vermieten [ts**oo**
fairm**ee**ten]

rented car das Mietauto [m**ee**t-
owto]

repair (verb) reparieren
[repar**ee**ren]

can you repair it? können Sie
es reparieren? [k**ur**nen zee]

repeat wiederholen
[veederh**oh**len]

could you repeat that?
können Sie das noch einmal
wiederholen? [k**ur**nen zee dass
noKH **ine**-mahl]

reservation die Reservierung
[rezairv**ee**roong]

I'd like to make a
reservation ich möchte eine
Reservierung vornehmen
[m**ur**sht-uh **ine**-uh – f**o**r-naymen]

dialogue

I have a reservation ich
habe eine Reservierung
[ish h**ah**b-uh]
yes sir, what name
please? auf welchen
Namen, bitte? [owf v**e**lshen
n**ah**men]

reserve reservieren
[rezairveeren]

dialogue

can I reserve a table for
tonight? kann ich für
heute abend einen Tisch
reservieren? [kan ish foor
hoyt-uh ahbent ine-en tish]
yes madam, for how many
people? ja, für wieviele
Personen? [foor vee veel-uh
pairzohnen]
for two für zwei [tsvy]
and for what time? und für
welche Zeit? [velsh-uh tsite]
for eight o'clock für acht
Uhr [oor]
and could I have your
name please? und kann
ich bitte Ihren Namen
haben? [eeren nahmen]
see alphabet

rest: I need a rest ich brauche
Erholung [ish browкн-uh
airhohloong]
the rest of the group der Rest
der Gruppe
restaurant das Restaurant
[restorong]
rest room (US) die Toilette
[twalett-uh]
retired: I'm retired ich bin im
Ruhestand [ish bin im roo-uh-
shtant]
return (ticket) die Rückfahrkarte [roock-fahrkart-uh]

dialogue

a return to Heilbronn
eine Rückfahrkarte nach
Heilbronn
coming back when? wann
soll die Rückfahrt sein?
[roock-fahrt]

reverse charge call das R-
Gespräch [air-geshpraysh]
reverse gear der
Rückwärtsgang
[roockvairtsgang]
revolting ekelhaft [aykelhaft]
Rhine der Rhein [rine]
rib die Rippe [ripp-uh]
rice der Reis [rice]
rich (person) reich [rysh]
(food) schwer [shvair]
ridiculous lächerlich [lesherlish]
right (correct) richtig [rishtish]
(not left) rechts [reshts]
you were right Sie hatten
recht [resht]
that's right das stimmt
[shtimmt]
this can't be right das kann
nicht stimmen [nisht shtimmen]
right! okay!
is this the right road for ...?
ist dies die Straße nach ...?
[deess]
on the right rechts
turn right biegen Sie rechts ab
[beegen zee – ap]
right-hand drive die
Rechtssteuerung [reshts-
shtoyeroong]

ring (on finger) der Ring

I'll ring you ich rufe Sie an [ish roof-uh zee]

ring back zurückrufen [tsooroock-roofen]

ripe (fruit) reif [rife]

rip-off: it's a rip-off das ist Wucher [vooKHer]

rip-off prices Wucherpreise [vooKHer-prize-uh]

risky riskant

river der Fluss [flooss]

road die Straße [shtrahss-uh]

is this the road for ...? ist dies die Straße nach ...? [deess dee – naKH]

down the road die Straße entlang

road accident der Verkehrs-unfall [fairkairss-oonfal]

road map die Straßenkarte [shtrahssen-kart-uh]

roadsign das Verkehrszeichen [fairkairs-tsyshen]

rob: I've been robbed ich bin bestohlen worden [ish bin beshtohlen vorden]

rock der Felsen [felzen]

(music) der Rock

on the rocks (with ice) mit Eis [ice]

roll (bread) das Brötchen [brurtchen]

roof das Dach [daKH]

roof rack der Dachgepäckträger [daKH-gepeck-trayger]

room das Zimmer [tsimmer]

in my room in meinem

Zimmer [mine-em]

room service der Zimmer-service [tsimmer'service']

rope das Seil [zile]

rosé (wine) der Roséwein [rohzay-vine]

roughly (approximately) ungefähr [oongefair]

round: it's my round das ist meine Runde [mine-uh roond-uh]

roundabout (for traffic) der Kreisverkehr [krice-fairkair]

round trip ticket die Rückfahrkarte [roock-fahrkart-uh]

route die Strecke [shtreck-uh]

what's the best route? welches ist der beste Weg? [velshess ist dair best-uh vayk]

rubber (material) das Gummi [goommee]

(eraser) der Radiergummi [radeer-goommee]

rubber band das Gummiband [goommee-bant]

rubbish (waste) der Abfall [ap-fal]

(poor quality goods) der Mist

rubbish! (nonsense) Quatsch! [kvatch]

rucksack der Rucksack [roockzack]

rude unhöflich [oon-hurflish]

ruins die Ruinen [roo-eenen]

rum der Rum [roomm]

rum and coke ein Rum mit Cola [kohla]

run (person) rennen, laufen

[**ow**fen]
how often do the buses run?
wie oft fahren die Busse? [vee
oft **fah**ren dee **boo**ss-uh]
I've run out of money ich
habe kein Geld mehr [ish
hahb-uh kine gelt mair]
rush hour die Rush-hour

S

sad traurig [**trow**rish]
saddle der Sattel [**zat**tel]
safe (not in danger) sicher [**zi**sher]
(not dangerous) ungefährlich
[**oon**-gefairlish]
safety pin die Sicherheitsnadel
[**zi**sher-hites-nahdel]
sail das Segel [**zay**gel]
sailboard das Windsurfbrett
[**vint**-surfbrett]
sailboarding das Windsurfen
[**vint**-surfen]
salad der Salat [zal**aht**]
salad dressing die Salatsoße
[zal**aht**-zohss-uh]
sale: for sale zu verkaufen
[tsoo fairk**ow**fen]
salmon der Lachs [lacks]
salt das Salz [zalts]
same: the same derselbe
[dair**zelb**-uh]
the same man/woman
derselbe Mann/dieselbe Frau
[dee**zelb**-uh]
the same as this dasselbe wie
das [dass**elb**-uh vee]
the same again, please

dasselbe nochmal, bitte
[noKH**mahl** bitt-uh]
it's all the same to me das
ist mir ganz egal [meer gants
ayg**ahl**]
sand der Sand [zant]
sandals die Sandalen
[zand**ahl**en]
sandwich das belegte Brot
[bel**ay**kt-uh broht]
sanitary napkin (US) die
Damenbinde [**dah**menbind-uh]
sanitary towel die
Damenbinde [**dah**menbind-uh]
sardines die Sardinen
[zard**ee**nen]
Saturday Samstag [**za**mstahk]
sauce die Soße [**zoh**ss-uh]
saucepan der Kochtopf
[**ko**KHtopf]
saucer die Untertasse [**oon**ter-
tass-uh]
sauna die Sauna [**zow**nah]
sausage die Wurst [voorst]
**say: how do you say ... in
German?** was heißt ... auf
Deutsch? [vass hyst ... owf
doytch]
what did he say? was hat er
gesagt? [gez**ah**kt]
I said ... ich sagte ... [**zah**kt-uh]
he said ... er sagte ...
**could you say that
again?** könnten Sie das
wiederholen? [**kur**nten zee dass
veeder-**hoh**len]
scarf (for neck) der Schal [shahl]
(for head) das Kopftuch
[**ko**pftOOKH]

scenery die Landschaft [lant-shafft]

schedule (US) der Fahrplan [fahrplahn]

scheduled flight der Linienflug [leen-yenflook]

school die Schule [shool-uh]

scissors: a pair of scissors eine Schere [shair-uh]

scotch der Scotch

Scotch tape der Tesafilm® [tayzahfilm]

Scotland Schottland [shottlant]

Scottish schottisch [shottish]

I'm Scottish (man/woman) ich bin Schotte [shott-uh]/Schottin

scrambled eggs die Rühreier [roor-ier]

scratch der Kratzer [kratser]

screw die Schraube [shrowb-uh]

screwdriver der Schraubenzieher [shrowben-tsee-er]

scrubbing brush (for hands) die Handbürste [hant-boorst-uh] (for floors) die Scheuerbürste [shoyer-boorst-uh]

sea das Meer [mair]

by the sea am Meer

seafood die Meeresfrüchte [mairess-froosht-uh]

seafood restaurant das Fischrestaurant [fish-restorong]

seafront die Strandpromenade [shtrant-promenahd-uh]

seagull die Möwe [murv-uh]

search (verb) suchen [zooкнen]

seashell die Muschel [mooshel]

seasick: I feel seasick ich bin seekrank [ish bin zaykrank]

I get seasick ich werde leicht seekrank [vaird-uh lysht]

seaside: by the seaside am Meer [mair]

seat der Sitzplatz [zitsplats]

is this anyone's seat? sitzt hier jemand? [zitst heer yaymant]

seat belt der Sicherheitsgurt [zisherhites-goort]

seaweed der Tang

secluded abgelegen [ap-gelaygen]

second (adj) zweiter [tsvyter] (of time) die Sekunde [zekoond-uh]

just a second! Moment mal! [mahl]

second class zweiter Klasse [tsvyter klass-uh]

second-hand gebraucht [gebrowкнt]

see sehen [zay-en]

can I see? kann ich mal sehen?

have you seen ...? haben Sie ... gesehen? [hahben zee ... gezay-en]

I saw him this morning ich habe ihn heute morgen gesehen

see you! bis später! [shpayter]

I see (I understand) ich verstehe [fairstay-uh]

self-catering apartment die Ferienwohnung [fayree-en-vohnoong] self-service die Selbstbedienung [**zelpst**-bedeenoong]

sell verkaufen [fairk**ow**fen]
  do you sell ...? haben Sie ...? [**hah**ben zee]

Sellotape® der Tesafilm® [**tay**zahfilm]

send senden [**zen**den]
  I want to send this to England ich möchte dies nach England senden [ish m**ur**sht-uh deess **zen**den]

senior citizen (man/woman) der Rentner/die Rentnerin

separate getrennt

separated: I'm separated ich lebe getrennt [ish l**ay**b-uh]

separately (pay, travel) getrennt

September der September [**zept**ember]

septic vereitert [fair-**i**tert]

serious ernst [airnst]

service charge (in restaurant) die Bedienung [bed**ee**noong]

service station die Tankstelle (mit Werkstatt) [**tank**shtell-uh mit v**air**kshtatt]

serviette die Serviette [zairvee-**ett**-uh]

set menu die Tageskarte [**tah**gess-kart-uh]

several mehrere [m**air**er-uh]

sew nähen [**nay**-en]
  could you sew this back on? können Sie das wieder annähen? [**kur**nen zee dass **v**eeder **an**-nay-en]

sex der Sex

sexy sexy

shade: in the shade im Schatten [**shatten**]

shake: let's shake hands geben wir uns die Hand [**gay**ben veer oonss dee hant]

shallow (water) seicht [zysht]

shame: what a shame! wie schade! [vee sh**ah**d-uh]

shampoo das Shampoo
  can I have a shampoo and set? können Sie mir die Haare waschen und legen? [**kur**nen zee meer dee h**ah**r-uh vashen oont l**ay**gen]

share (room, table etc) sich teilen [zish t**y**len]

sharp (knife, taste) scharf [sharf]
  (pain) stechend [sht**e**shent]

shattered (very tired) todmüde [**toh**tm**oo**d-uh]

shaver der Rasierapparat [raz**eer**-apparaht]

shaving foam die Rasierseife [raz**eer**-zife-uh]

shaving point die Steckdose für Rasierapparate [sht**e**ckdohz-uh foor raz**eer**-apparaht-uh]

she* sie [zee]
  is she here? ist sie hier? [heer]

sheet (for bed) das Laken [**lah**ken]

shelf das Brett

shellfish die Schaltiere [shahl-teer-uh]

sherry der Sherry

ship das Schiff [shiff]
  by ship mit dem Schiff

shirt das Hemd [hemt]

shit! Scheiße! [sh**ice**-uh]

shock der Schock [shock]

I got an electric shock from ... ich habe einen elektrischen Schlag von ... bekommen [ish hah**b**-uh **ine**-en aylektrishen shlahk fon]

shock-absorber der Stoßdämpfer [sht**oh**ss-dempfer]

shocking (behaviour, prices) skandalös [skandal**urss**] (custom etc) schockierend [shock**eer**ent]

shoe der Schuh [sh**00**]

a pair of shoes ein Paar Schuhe [pahr sh**00**-uh]

shoelaces die Schnürsenkel [shn**00**r-zenkel]

shoe polish die Schuhcreme [sh**00**-kraym]

shoe repairer der Schuhmacher [sh**00**-mak**H**er]

shop das Geschäft [gesh**eft**]

shopping: I'm going shopping ich gehe einkaufen [ish g**ay**-uh **ine**-kowfen]

shopping centre das Einkaufszentrum [**ine**-kowfss-tsentroom]

shop window das Schaufenster [sh**ow**fenster]

shore (of sea) der Strand [sht**rant**]

(of lake) das Ufer [**00**fer]

short (time, journey) kurz [k**oo**rts] (person) klein [kline]

shortcut die Abkürzung [ap-k**00**rtsoong]

shorts die Shorts

should: what should I do? was soll ich machen? [vass zoll ish mak**H**en]

he shouldn't be long er kommt sicher bald [air kommt zisher balt]

you should have told me das hätten Sie mir sagen sollen [**h**etten zee meer z**a**hgen zollen]

shoulder die Schulter [sh**oo**lter]

shout (verb) schreien [shry-en]

show (in theatre) die Vorstellung [for-shtelloong]

could you show me? könnten Sie mir das zeigen? [**kur**nten zee meer dass ts**y**gen]

shower (in bathroom) die Dusche [d**00**sh-uh]

with shower mit Dusche

shower gel das Duschgel [d**00**sh-gayl]

shut (verb) schließen [shl**ee**ssen]

when do you shut? wann machen Sie zu? [vann mak**H**en zee ts**00**]

when do they shut? wann machen sie zu?

they're shut sie sind geschlossen [gesh**lo**ssen]

I've shut myself out ich habe mich ausgesperrt [ish hah**b**-uh mish **ow**ss-geshpairt]

shut up! halt den Mund! [dayn moont]

shutter (on camera) der Verschluss [fairshl**00**ss]

shutters (on window) die Fensterläden [**fen**ster-layden]

shy (person) schüchtern
[sh**oo**shtern]
(animal) scheu [shoy]
sick (ill) krank
I'm going to be sick (vomit)
ich muss mich übergeben [ish
mooss mish ⲟⲟberg**ay**ben]
side die Seite [z**ite**-uh]
the other side of town das
andere Ende der Stadt [ander-
uh **e**nd-uh dair shtatt]
side lights das Standlicht
[sht**a**ntlisht]
side salad die Salatbeilage
[zal**ah**t-bylahg-uh]
side street die Seitenstraße
[z**y**ten-shtrass-uh]
sidewalk (US) der Bürgersteig
[b**oo**rgershtike]
sight: the sights of ... die
Sehenswürdigkeiten von ...
[z**ay**-ens-v**oo**rdish-kyten fon]
sightseeing: we're going
sightseeing wir machen eine
Rundfahrt [veer ma**кн**en **ine**-uh
r**oo**nt-fahrt]
(on foot) wir machen einen
Rundgang [**ine**-en r**oo**nt-gang]
sightseeing tour die
Rundfahrt [r**oo**nt-fahrt]
sign das Schild [shilt]
(roadsign) das Verkehrs-
zeichen [fairk**air**s-tsyshen]
signal: he didn't give a signal
(driver) er hat nicht geblinkt
(cyclist) er hat keine Richtung
angezeigt [k**ine**-uh rishtoong **an**-
getsykt]
signature die Unterschrift

[**oo**nter-shrift]
signpost der Wegweiser [v**ay**k-
vyzer]
silence die Ruhe [r**oo**-uh]
silk die Seide [z**y**duh]
silly (person) albern [**a**l-bairn]
(thing to do etc) dumm [doomm]
silver das Silber [z**i**lber]
silver foil die Alufolie [**ah**loo-
fohl-yuh]
similar ähnlich [**ay**nlish]
simple (easy) einfach [**ine**-faкн]
since: since yesterday seit
gestern [zite]
since I got here seit ich hier
bin [heer]
sing singen [z**i**ngen]
singer (man/woman) der Sänger
[z**e**nger]/die Sängerin
single (not married)
unverheiratet [**oo**n-fair-hyrahtet]
a single to ... eine einfache
Fahrt nach ... [**ine**-uh **ine**-faкн-
uh fahrt naкн]
single bed das Einzelbett [**ine**-
tsel-bett]
single room das Einzelzimmer
[**ine**-tsel-tsimmer]
sink (in kitchen) die Spüle
[shp**oo**l-uh]
sister die Schwester [shv**e**ster]
sister-in-law die Schwägerin
[shv**ay**gerin]
sit: can I sit here? kann ich
mich hinsetzen? [ish mish
heer h**i**nzetsen]
is anyone sitting here?
sitzt hier jemand? [zitst heer
yaymant]

sit down sich hinsetzen [zish hinzetsen]

do sit down nehmen Sie Platz [naymen zee plats]

size die Größe [grurss-uh]

ski der Ski [shee] (verb) skifahren [sheefahren]

a pair of skis ein Paar Skier [pahr shee-er]

ski boots die Skistiefel [shee-shteefel]

skiing das Skifahren [sheefahren]

we're going skiing wir gehen Skilaufen [veer gay-en shee-lowfen]

ski instructor (man/woman) der Skilehrer [shee-lairer]/die Skilehrerin

ski-lift der Skilift [sheelift]

skin die Haut [howt]

skinny dünn [dOOnn]

ski-pants die Skihose [shee-hohz-uh]

ski-pass der Skipass [sheepas]

ski pole der Skistock [sheeshtock]

skirt der Rock

ski run die Skipiste [shee-pist-uh]

ski slope die Skipiste [shee-pist-uh]

ski wax das Skiwachs [sheevacks]

sky der Himmel

sleep schlafen [shlahfen]

did you sleep well? haben Sie gut geschlafen? [hahben zee gOOt geshlahfen]

I need a good sleep ich muss mich mal richtig ausschlafen [rishtish owss-shlahfen]

sleeper (on train) der Schlafwagen [shlahfvahgen]

sleeping bag der Schlafsack [shlahfzack]

sleeping car der Schlafwagen [shlahfvahgen]

sleeping pill die Schlaftablette [shlahf-tablett-uh]

sleepy: I'm feeling sleepy ich bin müde [ish bin mOOd-uh]

sleeve der Ärmel [airmel]

slide (photographic) das Dia [dee-ah]

slip (under dress) der Unterrock [OOnter-rock]

slippery glatt

Slovak (adj) slowakisch [slovahkish]

Slovak Republic die Slowakische Republik [slovahkish-uh repOObleek]

slow langsam [langzahm]

slow down! etwas langsamer bitte [etvass]

slowly langsam [langzahm]

could you say it slowly? könnten Sie das etwas langsamer sagen? [kurnten zee dass etvass langzahmer zahgen]

very slowly ganz langsam [gants]

small klein [kline]

smell: it smells es stinkt [shtinkt]

smile (verb) lächeln [lesheln]

smoke der Rauch [rowкн]

do you mind if I smoke?
macht es Ihnen etwas aus,
wenn ich rauche? [maKHt
ess **een**-en **et**vass owss venn ish
row**KH**-uh]

I don't smoke ich bin
Nichtraucher [**nish**trowKHer]

do you smoke? rauchen Sie?
[**row**KHen zee]

snack: I'd just like a snack ich
möchte nur eine Kleinigkeit
[ish **mursh**t-uh n**oo**r **ine**-uh k**ly**nish-
kite]

sneeze (verb) niesen [**nee**zen]

snorkel der Schnorchel
[**shn**orshel]

snow der Schnee [shnay]

it's snowing es schneit [shnite]

so: it's so good es ist so gut
[zo g**oo**t]

not so fast nicht so schnell

so am I ich auch [ish owKH]

so do I ich auch

so-so einigermaßen [**ine**-iger-
mahssen]

soaking solution (for contact
lenses) die Aufbewahrungslösung [**owf**bevahroongs-
lurzoong]

soap die Seife [**zy**f-uh]

soap powder das Waschpulver
[**va**shpoolver]

sober nüchtern [n**oo**shtern]

sock die Socke [**zock**-uh]

socket (electrical) die Steckdose
[**shteck**-dohz-uh]

soda (water) das Sodawasser
[**zoh**da-vasser]

sofa das Sofa [**zoh**fa]

soft (material etc) weich [vysh]

soft-boiled egg das
weichgekochte Ei [**vysh**-
gekoKHt-uh ī]

soft drink das alkoholfreie
Getränk [alkoh**ohl**fry-uh
getrenk], der Soft drink

soft lenses die weichen
Kontaktlinsen [**vy**shen kont**ak**t-
linzen]

sole die Sohle [**zohl**-uh]

**could you put new soles
on these?** können Sie diese
Schuhe neu besohlen? [**kurn**en
zee d**ee**z-uh sh**oo**-uh noy bez**ohl**en]

**some: can I have some water/
rolls?** kann ich etwas Wasser/
ein paar Brötchen haben?
[**et**vass **va**sser/ine pahr br**urt**-shen
hahben]

can I have some of those?
kann ich ein paar davon
haben? [da-**fon**]

somebody, someone jemand
[**yay**mant]

something etwas [**et**vass]

something to drink etwas zu
trinken

sometimes manchmal
[**man**shmahl]

somewhere irgendwo
[**eer**gentvo]

son der Sohn [zohn]

song das Lied [leet]

son-in-law der Schwiegersohn
[**shvee**ger-zohn]

soon bald [balt]

I'll be back soon ich bin bald
zurück [ish bin balt tsoor**oo**ck]

as soon as possible so bald
wie möglich [vee **mur**glish]
sore: it's sore es tut weh [toot
vay]
sore throat die Halsschmerzen
pl [hals-shmairtsen]
sorry: (I'm) sorry tut mir leid
[toot meer lite]
sorry? (didn't understand) wie
bitte? [vee **bitt**-uh]
sort: what sort of ...? welche
Art von ...? [**velsh**-uh art fon]
soup die Suppe [**zoop**-uh]
sour (taste) sauer [**zow**er]
south der Süden [**zoo**den]
in the south im Süden
to the south nach Süden
South Africa Südafrika [zoot-
afrika]
South African (adj)
südafrikanisch [zoot-afrik**ah**nish]
I'm South African (man/woman)
ich bin Südafrikaner [zoot-
afrik**ah**ner]/Südafrikanerin
southeast der Südosten [zoot-
osten]
southwest der Südwesten
[zoot-**vesten**]
souvenir das Souvenir
spa der Kurort [**koo**r-ort]
spanner der
Schraubenschlüssel [shr**ow**ben-
shl**oo**sel]
spare part das Ersatzteil
[airz**a**ts-tile]
spare tyre der Ersatzreifen
[airz**a**ts-ryfen]
spark plug die Zündkerze
[ts**oo**nt-kairts-uh]

speak: do you speak English?
sprechen Sie Englisch?
[shpr**e**shen zee **eng**-lish]
I don't speak ... ich spreche
kein ... [ish shpr**e**sh-uh kine]

dialogue

can I speak to Wolfgang?
kann ich Wolfgang
sprechen?
who's calling? wer spricht
bitte? [vair shpr**i**sht **bitt**-uh]
it's Patricia Patricia
I'm sorry, he's not in, can
I take a message? tut mir
leid, er ist nicht da, kann
ich etwas ausrichten? [toot
meer lite, air ist nisht da, kann ish
etvass **ow**ss-rishten]
no thanks, I'll call back
later nein danke, ich rufe
später nochmal an [nine
dank-uh, ish r**oo**f-uh shp**ay**ter
no**k**Hmahl an]
please tell him I called
bitte sagen Sie ihm, dass
ich angerufen habe [zahgen
zee eem, dass ish an-ger**oo**fen
hahb-uh]

speciality die Spezialität
[shpets-yalit**ayt**]
spectacles die Brille [br**i**ll-uh]
speed die Geschwindigkeit
[geshv**i**ndish-kite]
speed limit die Geschwindigkeitsbeschränkung
[geshv**i**ndishkites-beshr**e**nkoong]

speedometer der Tachometer [takHom**ay**ter]

spell: how do you spell it? wie schreibt man das? [vee shrypt man dass]

see alphabet

spend ausgeben [**ow**ssgayben](time) verbringen [fairbring-en]

spider die Spinne [shp**inn**-uh]

spin-dryer die Schleuder [shl**oy**der]

splinter der Splitter [shpl**i**tter]

spoke (in wheel) die Speiche [shp**y**sh-uh]

spoon der Löffel [l**ur**fel]

sport der Sport [shport]

sprain: I've sprained my ... ich habe mein ... verstaucht [ish h**ah**b-uh mine ... fair-sht**ow**KHt]

spring (season) der Frühling [fr**oo**ling](of car, seat) die Feder [f**ay**der]

square (in town) der Platz [plats]

stairs die Treppe [tr**e**pp-uh]

stale (bread) alt(drink) abgestanden [**a**p-geshtanden]

stall: the engine keeps stalling der Motor geht dauernd aus [dair m**oh**tohr gayt d**ow**ernt owss]

stamp die Briefmarke [br**ee**fmark-uh]

dialogue

a stamp for England, please eine Marke nach England bitte [**ine**-uh mark-uh naKH]

what are you sending? was möchten Sie senden? [vass m**ur**shten zee z**e**nden]

this postcard diese Postkarte [d**ee**z-uh p**o**sstkart-uh]

standby: standby ticket das Standby-Ticket

star der Stern [shtairn](in film) der Star

start der Anfang [**a**nfang](verb) **a**nfangen

when does it start? wann fängt es an? [van fengt ess an]

the car won't start das Auto springt nicht an [dass **ow**to shpringt nisht an]

starter (of car) der **A**nlasser(food) die Vorspeise [f**o**r-shpize-uh]

state (in country) das Land [lant]

the States (USA) die USA [oo-ess-**ah**]

station der Bahnhof [b**ah**nhohf]

statue die Statue [sht**ah**-too-uh]

stay: where are you staying? wo wohnen Sie? [vo v**oh**nen zee]

I'm staying at ... ich wohne in ... [ish v**oh**n-uh]

I'd like to stay another two nights ich möchte gern noch zwei Tage bleiben [m**ur**sht-uh gairn noKH – t**ah**g-uh bl**y**ben]

steak das Steak

steal stehlen [sht**ay**len]

my bag has been stolen

meine Tasche ist gestohlen worden [geshtohlen vorden]
steep (hill) steil [shtile]
steering die Lenkung [lenkoong]
step: on the steps auf den Stufen [owf dayn shtoofen]
stereo die Stereoanlage [shtayray-oh-anlahg-uh]
sterling das Pfund Sterling [pfoont]
steward (on plane) der Steward
stewardess die Stewardess
sticking plaster das Heftpflaster
still: I'm still waiting ich warte immer noch [vart-uh – noкн]
is he still there? ist er noch da?
keep still! stillhalten! [shtill-halten]
sting: I've been stung ich bin gestochen worden [geshtoкнen vorden]
stockings die Strümpfe [shtroompf-uh]
stomach der Magen [mahgen]
stomach ache die Magenschmerzen [mahgen-shmairtsen]
stone (rock) der Stein [shtine]
stop (verb) anhalten
please, stop here (to taxi driver etc) bitte halten Sie hier [bitt-uh hal-ten zee heer]
do you stop near ...? halten Sie in der Nähe von ...? [nay-uh]
stop doing that! hören Sie auf

damit! [hur-ren zee owf damit]
stopover die Zwischenstation [tsvishen-shtats-yohn]
storm der Sturm [shtoorm]
straight: it's straight ahead es ist geradeaus [gerahd-uh-owss]
a straight whisky ein Whisky pur [poor]
straightaway sofort [zofort]
strange (odd) seltsam [zeltzahm]
stranger (man/woman) der/die Fremde [fremd-uh]
I'm a stranger here ich bin hier fremd [heer fremt]
strap (on watch) das Band [bant]
(on dress) der Träger [trayger]
(on suitcase) der Riemen [reemen]
strawberry die Erdbeere [airtbair-uh]
stream der Bach [baкн]
street die Straße [shtrahss-uh]
on the street auf der Straße [owf dair]
streetmap der Stadtplan [shtattplahn]
string die Schnur [shnoor]
strong (person, drink) stark [shtark]
(taste) kräftig [kreftish]
stuck: the key's stuck der Schlüssel steckt fest [shteckt]
student (male/female) der Student [shtoodent]/die Studentin
stupid dumm [doomm]
suburb die Vorstadt [for-shtatt]
subway (US) die U-Bahn [oo-bahn]

suddenly plötzlich [plurtslish]
suede das Wildleder [vilt-layder]
sugar der Zucker [tsoocker]
suit der Anzug [antsook]
 it doesn't suit me (jacket etc) es steht mir nicht [shtayt meer nisht]
 it suits you es steht Ihnen [eenen]
suitcase der Koffer
summer der Sommer [zommer]
 in the summer im Sommer
sun die Sonne [zonn-uh]
 in the sun in der Sonne
 out of the sun im Schatten [shatten]
sunbathe sonnenbaden [zonnen-bahden]
sunblock (cream) die Sun-Block-Creme [-kraym]
sunburn der Sonnenbrand [zonnen-brant]
sunburnt: to get sunburnt einen Sonnenbrand bekommen [ine-en zonnen-brant]
Sunday Sonntag [zonntahk]
sunglasses die Sonnenbrille [zonnen-brill-uh]
sun lounger der Ruhesessel [roo-uh-zessel]
sunny: it's sunny die Sonne scheint [dee zonn-uh shynt]
sun roof (in car) das Schiebedach [sheeb-uh-daKH]
sunset der Sonnenuntergang [zonnen-oontergang]
sunshade der Sonnenschirm [zonnen-sheerm]
sunshine der Sonnenschein [zonnen-shine]
sunstroke der Sonnenstich [zonnen-shtish]
suntan die Sonnenbräune [zonnen-broyn-uh]
suntan lotion die Sonnenmilch [zonnen-milsh]
suntanned braungebrannt [brown-gebrannt]
suntan oil das Sonnenöl [zonnen-url]
super fantastisch [fantastish]
supermarket der Supermarkt [zoopermarkt]
supper das Abendessen [ahbent-essen]
supplement (extra charge) der Zuschlag [tsooshlahk]
sure: are you sure? bist du/sind Sie sicher? [bist doo/zint zee zisher]
 sure! klar!
surname der Nachname [naKHnahm-uh]
swearword der Kraftausdruck [kraft-owssdroock]
sweater der Pullover [poolohver]
sweatshirt das Sweatshirt
Sweden Schweden [shvayden]
Swedish schwedisch [shvaydish]
sweet (taste) süß [zooss]
 (noun: dessert) der Nachtisch [naKHtish]
sweets die Süßigkeiten [zoossish-kyten]

swelling die Schwellung
[shvelloong]

swim (verb) schwimmen
[shvimmen]

I'm going for a swim ich gehe
schwimmen [gay-uh]

let's go for a swim gehen wir
schwimmen [gay-en veer]

swimming costume der
Badeanzug [bahd-uh-antsook]

swimming pool das
Schwimmbad [shvimmbaht]

swimming trunks die Badehose
[bahd-uh-hohz-uh]

Swiss (man/woman) der
Schweizer [shvytser]/die
Schweizerin
(adj) schweizerisch [shvytserish]

the Swiss die Schweizer

Swiss Alps die Schweizer
Alpen [shvytser]

switch der Schalter [shalter]

switch off (TV, lights) ausschalten
[owss-shalten]

(engine) abstellen [ap-shtellen]

switch on (TV, lights) einschalten
[ine-shalten]

(engine) anlassen

Switzerland die Schweiz
[shvites]

swollen geschwollen
[geshvollen]

T

table der Tisch [tish]

a table for two ein Tisch
für zwei Personen [foor tsvy

pairzohnen]

tablecloth das Tischtuch
[tishtOOKH]

table tennis das Tischtennis
[tishtennis]

table wine der Tafelwein
[tahfelvine]

tailback (of traffic) der Rückstau
[rOOck-shtow]

tailor der Schneider [shnyder]

take (lead) bringen
(accept) nehmen [naymen]

can you take me to the
airport? können Sie mich
zum Flughafen bringen?
[kurnen zee mish tsoom]

do you take credit cards?
nehmen Sie Kreditkarten?

fine, I'll take it gut, ich nehme
es [gOOt, ish naym-uh ess]

can I take this? (leaflet etc)
kann ich das mitnehmen?
[mitnaymen]

how long does it take? wie
lange dauert es? [vee lang-uh
dowert ess]

it takes three hours es dauert
drei Stunden

is this seat taken? ist dieser
Platz besetzt? [deezer plats
bezetst]

hamburger to take away
Hamburger zum Mitnehmen
[tsoom]

can you take a little off here?
(to hairdresser) können Sie hier
etwas kürzen? [kurnen zee heer
etvass kOOrtsen]

talcum powder der

Körperpuder [**ku**rper-p**oo**der]
talk (verb) sprechen [shpr**e**shen]
tall (person) groß [grohss]
(building) hoch [hohKH]
tampons die Tampons
tan die Bräune [br**oy**n-uh]
to get a tan braun werden
[brown v**ai**rden]
tank (of car) der Tank
tap der Wasserhahn
[**va**sserhahn]
tape (for cassette) das Band
[bant]
(sticky) das Klebeband [kl**ayb**-
uh-bant]
tape measure das Bandmaß
[**bant**mahss]
tape recorder der
Kass**e**ttenrecorder
taste der Geschmack
[gesh**mack**]
can I taste it? kann ich es
probieren? [prob**ee**ren]
taxi das T**a**xi
will you get me a taxi?
können Sie mir ein Taxi
bestellen? [**ku**rnen zee meer]
where can I find a taxi? wo
bekomme ich ein Taxi? [vo
bek**o**mm-uh ish]

dialogue

to the airport/to Hotel ...
please zum Flughafen/
zum Hotel ... bitte [tsoom]
how much will it be? was
kostet das?
thirty euros dreißig Euro

that's fine right here thanks
bis hierhin, d**a**nke [heer-hin]

taxi-driver der T**a**xifahrer
taxi rank der T**a**xistand [t**a**ksi-
shtant]
tea (drink) der Tee [tay]
tea for one/two please
Tee für eine Person/zwei
Personen bitte [f**oo**r **ine**-uh
pairz**ohn**/tsvy pairz**oh**nen
bitt-uh]
teabag der Teebeutel
[**tay**boytel]
teach: could you teach
me? könnten Sie es mir
beibringen? [**ku**rnten zee ess
meer b**y**bringen]
teacher (man/woman) der Lehrer
[**lai**rer]/die Lehrerin
team das Team
teaspoon der Teelöffel [**tay**-
lurfel]
tea towel das Geschirrtuch
[gesh**eer**-t**oo**KH]
teenager der Teenager
telephone das Telefon
[telef**ohn**]
television das Fernsehen [fairn-
zay-en]
tell: could you tell him ...?
können Sie ihm sagen ...?
[**ku**rnen zee eem z**ah**gen]
temperature (weather) die
Temperat**oor** [temperat**oor**]
(fever) das Fieber [f**ee**ber]
tennis das T**e**nnis
tennis ball der T**e**nnisball
[**t**ennis-bal]

tennis court der Tennisplatz
[tennis-plats]
tennis racket der Tennis-
schläger [tennis-shlayger]
tent das Zelt [tselt]
term (at school) das Halbjahr
[halp-yar]
(at university) das Semester
[zemester]
terminus (rail) die Endstation
[ent-shtats-yohn]
terrible furchtbar [foorshtbar]
terrific sagenhaft [zahgenhaft]
text (message) die SMS [ess-
em-ess]
than* als [alss]
smaller than kleiner als
thanks, thank you danke
[dank-uh]
thank you very much vielen
Dank [feelen]
thanks for the lift danke fürs
Mitnehmen [foors mitnaymen]
no thanks nein danke [nine]

dialogue

thanks danke
that's OK, don't mention it
bitte [bitt-uh]

that: that man dieser Mann
[deezer]
that woman diese Frau [deez-uh]
that one das da
I hope that ... ich hoffe, dass
... [dass]
that's nice das ist schön
is that ...? ist das ...?

that's it (that's right) genau
[genow]
the* (singular) der/die/das [dair/
dee/dass]
(plural) die [dee]
theatre das Theater [tayahter]
their* ihr/ihre [eer/eer-uh]
theirs* ihrer [eer-er]
them* sie [zee]
for them für sie [foor]
with them mit ihnen [een-en]
I gave it to them ich habe es
ihnen gegeben [hahb-uh]
then (at that time) damals
[dahmalss]
(after that) dann
there da, dort
over there dort drüben
[drooben]
up there da oben
is there ...? gibt es ...? [geept]
are there ...? gibt es ...?
there is ... es gibt ...
there are ... es gibt ...
there you are (giving something)
bitte [bitt-uh]
thermometer das
Thermometer [tairmo-mayter]
thermos flask die
Thermosflasche [tairmoss-
flash-uh]
these*: these men diese
Männer [deez-uh]
these women diese Frauen
can I have these? kann ich
diese hier haben? [heer]
they* sie [zee]
thick dick
(stupid) blöd [blurt]

thief der Dieb [deep]

thigh der Schenkel [shenkel]

thin dünn [dOOn]

thing das Ding

my things meine Sachen [mine-uh zakHen]

think denken

I think so ich glaube ja [glowb-uh ya]

I don't think so ich glaube nicht [nisht]

I'll think about it ich werde darüber nachdenken [vaird-uh darOOber nakHdenken]

third party insurance die Haftpflichtversicherung [haft-pflisht-fairzisheroong]

thirsty: I'm thirsty ich habe Durst [hahb-uh doorst]

this: this man dieser Mann [deezer]

this woman diese Frau [deez-uh]

this one dieser/diese/dieses [deezess]

this is my wife das ist meine Frau [mine-uh frow]

is this ...? ist das ...?

those: those men diese Männer [deez-uh]

those women diese Frauen [deez-uh]

which ones? – those welche? – diese [velsh-uh]

thread der Faden [fahden]

throat der Hals [halss]

throat pastilles die Halstabletten [halss-tabletten]

through durch [doorsh]

does it go through ...? (train, bus) fährt er über ...? [fairt air OOber]

throw (verb) werfen [vairfen]

throw away (verb) wegwerfen [vekvairfen]

thumb der Daumen [dowmen]

thunderstorm das Gewitter [gevitter]

Thursday Donnerstag [donnerstahk]

ticket (train, bus, boat) die Fahrkarte [fahrkart-uh] (plane) das Ticket (theatre, cinema) die Eintrittskarte [ine-trittskart-uh] (cloakroom) die Garderobenmarke [garderohben-mark-uh]

dialogue

a return ticket to Heidelberg eine Rückfahrkarte nach Heidelberg
coming back when? wann soll die Rückfahrt sein? [rOOck-fahrt]
today/next Tuesday heute/nächsten Dienstag
that will be ninety euros das macht neunzig Euro

ticket office (bus, rail) der Fahrkartenschalter [fahrkarten-shalter]

tide: high tide die Flut [flOOt]

low tide die Ebbe [ebb-uh]

tie (necktie) die Krawatte

117

[kravatt-uh]

tight (clothes etc) eng
it's too tight es ist zu eng [tsoo]

tights die Strumpfhose [shtroompf-hohz-uh]

till (cash desk) die Kasse [kass-uh]

time* die Zeit [tsite]
what's the time? wie spät ist es? [vee shpayt ist ess]
this time diesmal [deessmahl]
last time letztes Mal [letstess mahl]
next time nächstes Mal [naykstess]
four times viermal [feermahl]

timetable der Fahrplan [fahrplahn]

tin (can) die Dose [dohz-uh]

tinfoil die Alufolie [ahloo-fohl-yuh]

tin opener der Dosenöffner [dohzen-urfner]

tiny winzig [vintsish]

tip (to waiter etc) das Trinkgeld [trinkgelt]

tired müde [mood-uh]
I'm tired ich bin müde

tissues die Papiertücher [papeer-toosher]

to: to Freiburg/London nach Freiburg/London [naKH]
to Germany/England nach Deutschland/England
to the post office zum Postamt [tsoom]
to the bank zur Bank [tsoor]

toast (bread) der Toast

today heute [hoyt-uh]

toe der Zeh [tsay]

together zusammen [tsoozammen]
we're together (in shop etc) wir sind zusammen [veer zint]
can we pay together? können wir zusammen bezahlen? [kurnen veer – betsahlen]

toilet die Toilette [twalett-uh]
where is the toilet? wo ist die Toilette? [vo]
I have to go to the toilet ich muss zur Toilette [tsoor]

toilet paper das Toilettenpapier [twaletten-papeer]

tomato die Tomate [tomaht-uh]

tomato juice der Tomatensaft [tomahtenzaft]

tomato ketchup der Tomatenketchup

tomorrow morgen
tomorrow morning morgen früh [froo]
the day after tomorrow übermorgen [oobermorgen]

toner (cosmetic) die Tönungslotion [turnoongs-lohts-yohn]

tongue die Zunge [tsoong-uh]

tonic (water) das Tonic

tonight heute abend [hoyt-uh ahbent]

tonsillitis die Mandelentzündung [mandel-ent-tsoondoong]

too (excessively) zu [tsoo]
(also) auch [owKH]

118

too hot zu heiß [hice]
too much zuviel [tsoofeel]
me too ich auch [ish]
tooth der Zahn [tsahn]
toothache die Zahnschmerzen [tsahn-shmairtsen]
toothbrush die Zahnbürste [tsahn-boorst-uh]
toothpaste die Zahnpasta [tsahnpasta]
top: on top of ... oben auf... [ohben owf]
at the top oben
top floor der oberste Stock [ohberst-uh shtock]
topless oben ohne [ohben ohn-uh]
torch die Taschenlampe [tashenlamp-uh]
total die Endsumme [entzoom-uh]
what's the total? was macht das zusammen? [vass maKHt dass tsoozammen]
tour (journey) die Reise [rize-uh]
is there a tour of ...? gibt es eine Führung durch...? [geept ess ine-uh fooroong doorsh]
tour guide der Reiseleiter [rize-uh-lyter]
tourist (man/woman) der Tourist [toorist]/die Touristin
tourist information office das Fremdenverkehrsbüro [fremden-fairkairs-booroh]
tour operator der Reiseveranstalter [rize-uh-fairanshtalter]
towards nach [naKH]

towel das Handtuch [hant-tooKH]
town die Stadt [shtatt]
in town in der Stadt [dair]
just out of town am Stadtrand [shtattrant]
town centre die Innenstadt [innen-shtatt]
town hall das Rathaus [raht-howss]
toy das Spielzeug [shpeel-tsoyk]
track (US: at train station) der Bahnsteig [bahnshtike]
tracksuit der Trainingsanzug [trainings-antsook]
traditional traditionell [tradits-yohnell]
traffic der Verkehr [fairkair]
traffic jam der Stau [shtow]
traffic lights die Ampel
trailer (for carrying tent etc) der Anhänger [anheng-er] (US: caravan) der Wohnwagen [vohnvahgen]
trailer park (US) der Wohnwagenplatz [vohnvahgen-plats]
train der Zug [tsook]
by train mit dem Zug [daym]

dialogue

is this the train for ...? fährt dieser Zug nach ...? [fairt deezer tsook naKH]
sure ja [yah]
no, you want that platform there nein, gehen Sie zu dem Bahnsteig da

[nine, **gay**-en zee ts00 daym
bahnshtike]

trainers (shoes) die Turnschuhe
[**toorn**sh00-uh]

train station der Bahnhof
[**bahn**hohf]

tram die Straßenbahn
[**shtrah**ssen-bahn]

translate übersetzen [00ber-
zetsen]

could you translate that?
könnten Sie das übersetzen?
[**kurn**ten zee]

translation die Übersetzung
[00ber-zetsoong]

translator (man/woman) der
Übersetzer [00ber-**zetser**]/die
Übersetzerin

trash (waste) der Abfall [**ap**-fal]
(poor quality goods) der Mist

trashcan (US) die Mülltonne
[**m00ll**tonn-uh]

travel reisen [**ry**zen]

we're travelling around wir
machen eine Rundreise [veer
makHen **ine**-uh **roont**-rize-uh]

travel agent's das Reisebüro
[**rize**-uh-b00ro]

traveller's cheque der
Reisescheck [**rize**-uh-sheck]

tray das Tablett

tree der Baum [bowm]

tremendous fantastisch
[fan**tas**tish]

trendy schick [shick]

trim: just a trim please (to
hairdresser) nur etwas kürzen,
bitte [n00r **et**vass **k00r**tsen **bitt**-uh]

trip (excursion) der Ausflug
[**ows**sfl00k]

I'd like to go on a trip to ... ich
möchte gern eine Reise nach
... machen [**mur**sht-uh gairn **ine**-
uh **rize**-uh naKH ... **mak**Hen]

trolley (in supermarket) der
Einkaufswagen [**ine**-kowfs-
vahgen]
(in station) der Kofferkuli
[**koffer**-k00lee]

trouble die Schwierigkeiten
[**shveerish**-kyten]

I'm having trouble with ... ich
habe Schwierigkeiten mit ...
[**hahb**-uh]

sorry to trouble you tut mir
leid, Sie zu belästigen [**t00t**
meer lite zee ts00 be**les**tigen]

trousers die Hose [**hohz**-uh]

true wahr [vahr]

that's not true das stimmt
nicht [shtimmt nisht]

trunk (US: of car) der
Kofferraum [**koffer**-rowm]

trunks (swimming) die Badehose
[**bahd**-uh-hohz-uh]

try (verb) versuchen [fair**z00**KHen]

can I have a try? kann ich es
versuchen?

try on: can I try it on? kann ich
es anprobieren? [**an**-probeeren]

T-shirt das T-Shirt

Tuesday Dienstag [**deen**stahk]

tuna der Thunfisch [**t00n**fish]

tunnel der Tunnel [**t00**nnel]

Turkey die Türkei [t00rk-**ī**]

Turkish (adj) türkisch [**t00r**kish]
(language) Türkisch

turn: **turn left/right** biegen Sie links/rechts ab [**bee**gen zee links/reshts ap]

turn off: **where do I turn off?** wo muss ich abbiegen? [vo mooss ish **ap**-beegen]

can you turn the heating off? können Sie die Heizung abstellen? [**kur**nen zee dee hytsoong **ap**-shtellen]

turn on: **can you turn the heating on?** können Sie die Heizung anstellen? [**kur**nen zee dee hytsoong **an**-shtellen]

turning (in road) die Abzweigung [**ap**-tsvygoong]

TV das Fernsehen [**fair**nzay-en]

tweezers die Pinzette [pin-**tsett**-uh]

twice zweimal [tsv**y**mahl]

twice as much zweimal soviel [zof**ee**l]

twin beds zwei Einzelbetten [tsvy **ine**-tsel-betten]

twin room das Zweibettzimmer [tsv**y**bett-tsimmer]

twist: **I've twisted my ankle** ich habe mir den Fuß vertreten [ish h**ah**b-uh meer dayn fooss fairtr**ay**ten]

type die Art

a different type of ... eine andere Art von ... [**ine**-uh **ander**-uh]

typical typisch [t**oo**pish]

tyre der Reifen [r**y**fen]

ugly hässlich [**hess**lish]

UK das Vereinigte Königreich [fair-**ine**-isht-uh **kur**nish-rysh]

ulcer das Geschwür [geshv**oo**r]

umbrella der Schirm [sheerm]

uncle der **O**nkel

unconscious bewusstlos [bev**oo**st-lohss]

under unter [**oo**nter]

underdone (meat) nicht gar [nisht]

underground (railway) die U-Bahn [**oo**-bahn]

underpants die Unterhose [**oo**nter-hohz-uh]

understand: **I understand** ich verstehe [ish fairsht**ay**-uh]

I don't understand das verstehe ich nicht [nisht]

do you understand? verstehen Sie? [fairsht**ay**-en zee]

unemployed arbeitslos [**a**rbites-lohss]

United States die Vereinigten Staaten [fair-**ine**-ishten sht**ah**ten]

university die Universität [**oo**nivairzi-t**ay**t]

unleaded petrol das bleifreie Benzin [bl**y**-fry-uh bents**ee**n]

unlimited mileage ohne Kilometerbeschränkung [**oh**n-uh keelo-m**ay**ter-beshr**e**nkoong]

unlock aufschließen [**ow**f-shleessen]

unpack auspacken [**ow**ss-packen]

until bis [biss]
unusual ungewöhnlich [oon-gevurnlish]
up oben [ohben]
up there da oben
he's not up yet (not out of bed) er ist noch nicht auf [noKH nisht owf]
what's up? (what's wrong?) was ist los? [vass ist lohss]
upmarket (restaurant, hotel, goods etc) anspruchsvoll [anshprooKHsfoll]
upset stomach die Magenverstimmung [mahgen-fairshtimmoong]
upside down verkehrt herum [fairkairt hairoom]
upstairs oben [ohben]
urgent dringend [dring-ent]
us* uns [oonss]
with us mit uns
for us für uns [foor oonss]
USA die USA [oo-ess-ah]
use (verb) benutzen [benootsen]
may I use ...? kann ich ... benutzen?
useful nützlich [nootslish]
usual üblich [ooplish]
the usual (drink etc) dasselbe wie immer [dasselb-uh vee]

V

vacancy: do you have any vacancies? (hotel) haben Sie Zimmer frei? [hahben zee tsimmer fry]

vacation der Urlaub [oorlowp] (from university) die Semesterferien [zemester-fairee-en]
vaccination die Impfung [impfoong]
vacuum cleaner der Staubsauger [shtowp-zowger]
valid (ticket etc) gültig [gooltish]
how long is it valid for? wie lange ist es gültig? [vee lang-uh]
valley das Tal [tahl]
valuable (adj) wertvoll [vairtfol]
can I leave my valuables here? kann ich meine Wertsachen hierlassen? [mine-uh vairtzakHen heerlassen]
value der Wert [vairt]
van der Lieferwagen [leefervahgen]
vanilla die Vanille [vanill-uh]
a vanilla ice cream ein Vanilleeis [vanill-uh-ice]
vary: it varies es ist unterschiedlich [oonter-sheetlish]
vase die Vase [vahz-uh]
veal das Kalbfleisch [kalp-flysh]
vegetables das Gemüse [gemooz-uh]
vegetarian (man/woman) der Vegetarier [vegaytahree-er]/die Vegetarierin
vending machine der Automat [owtomaht]
very sehr [zair]
very little for me nur eine Kleinigkeit für mich [noor ine-

uh kl**ine**-ishkite f**oo**r mish]
I like it very much ich mag es
sehr gern [gairn]
vest (under shirt) das
Unterhemd [**oo**nterhemt]
via über [**oo**ber]
video (film) das Video
(recorder) der Videorecorder
Vienna Wien [veen]
view der Blick
villa die Villa
village das Dorf
vinegar der Essig [**e**ssish]
vineyard der Weinberg [**vine**-
bairk]
visa das Visum [**vee**zoom]
visit (verb) besuchen [bez**oo**KHen]
I'd like to visit ... ich möchte
... besuchen [m**ur**sht-uh]
vital: it's vital that ... es ist
unbedingt notwendig,
dass ... [**oo**n-bedingt n**oh**tvendish
dass]
vodka der Wodka [**vo**dka]
voice die Stimme [sht**i**mm-uh]
voltage die Spannung
[**shp**annoong]
vomit erbrechen [airb**r**eshen]

W

waist die Taille [t**al**-yuh]
waistcoat die Weste [**v**est-uh]
wait warten [**v**arten]
wait for me warten Sie auf
mich [zee owf mish]
don't wait for me warten Sie
nicht auf mich [nisht]

**can I wait until my wife/
partner gets here?** (eg as said
to waiter) kann ich warten,
bis meine Frau/Partnerin
kommt?
can you do it while I wait?
kann ich darauf warten?
[dar**owf**]
could you wait here for me?
(eg as said to taxi driver) können
Sie hier warten? [k**u**rnen zee
heer]
waiter der Ober [**oh**ber]
waiter! Herr Ober! [hair]
waitress die Kellnerin
waitress! Fräulein! [fr**oy**line]
**wake: can you wake me up at
5.30?** können Sie mich um
5.30 Uhr wecken? [k**u**rnen zee
mish oom – v**e**cken]
wake-up call der Weckanruf
[**v**eck-anr**oo**f]
Wales Wales
walk: is it a long walk? geht
man lange dorthin? [gayt man
lang-uh]
it's only a short walk es ist
nicht weit zu gehen [nisht vite
tsoo g**ay**-en]
I'll walk ich gehe zu Fuß [gay-
uh tsoo f**oo**ss]
I'm going for a walk ich gehe
spazieren [shpats**ee**ren]
Walkman® der Walkman
wall die Wand [vant]
(external) die Mauer [m**ow**er]
wallet die Brieftasche
[br**ee**ftash-uh]
wander: I like just wandering

around ich wandere gern
einfach so durch die Gegend
[ish vander-uh gairn **ine**-faKH zo
doorsh dee **gay**gent]
want: I want a ... ich möchte
ein(e)... [ish **mur**sht-uh **ine**(-uh)]
I don't want any ... ich
möchte keinen ... [**kine**-en]
I want to go home ich will
nach Hause [vill]
I don't want to ich will nicht
[nisht]
he wants to ... er will ...
what do you want? was
wollen Sie? [vass **vo**llen zee]
ward (in hospital) die Station
[shtats-**yohn**]
warm warm [varm]
I'm so warm mir ist so warm
[meer]
was*: it was ... es war ... [ess
vahr]
wash (verb) waschen [**va**shen]
can you wash these? können
Sie die für mich waschen?
[**kur**nen zee]
washer (for bolt etc) die
Dichtung [**di**shtoong]
washhand basin das
Handwaschbecken [**ha**ntvash-
becken]
washing (clothes) die Wäsche
[**ve**sh-uh]
washing machine die
Waschmaschine [**va**shmasheen-
uh]
washing powder das
Waschpulver [**va**shpoolver]
washing-up liquid das

Spülmittel [shp**oo**lmittel]
wasp die Wespe [**ve**sp-uh]
watch (wristwatch) die
Armbanduhr [**a**rmbant-oor]
**will you watch my things for
me?** könnten Sie auf meine
Sachen aufpassen? [**kur**nten zee
owf **mi**ne-uh zaKHen **owf**passen]
watch out! passen Sie auf!
watch strap das Uhrarmband
[**oo**r-armbant]
water das Wasser [**va**sser]
may I have some water?
kann ich etwas Wasser
haben? [**et**vass – ha**h**ben]
waterproof (adj) wasserfest
[**va**sserfest]
waterskiing Wasserskilaufen
[**va**ssershee-lowfen]
wave (in sea) die Welle [**ve**ll-uh]
way: it's this way es ist hier
entlang [heer]
it's that way es ist dort
entlang
is it a long way to ...? ist es
weit bis nach ...? [vite biss
naKH]
no way! auf keinen Fall! [owf
kine-en fal]

dialogue

**could you tell me the
way to ...?** können Sie
mir sagen, wie ich nach
... komme? [**kur**nen zee
meer **zah**gen vee ish naKH ...
komm-uh]
go straight on until you

reach the traffic lights fahren Sie geradeaus bis zur Ampel [gerahd-uh-owss]
turn left biegen Sie links ab [beegen]
take the first on the right nehmen Sie die erste Straße rechts [naymen zee dee airst-uh shtrahss-uh reshts]
see also where

we* wir [veer]
weak schwach [shvaKH]
weather das Wetter [vetter]

dialogue

what's the weather forecast? wie ist die Wettervorhersage? [vee ist dee vetter-forhairzahg-uh]
it's going to be fine es gibt schönes Wetter [geept shurness]
it's going to rain es gibt Regen [raygen]
it'll brighten up later es wird sich später aufklären [veert zish shpayter owf-klairen]

wedding die Hochzeit [hoKH-tsite]
wedding ring der Ehering [ay-uh-ring]
Wednesday Mittwoch [mittvoKH]
week die Woche [voKH-uh]
a week (from) today heute in einer Woche [hoyt-uh in ine-er]

a week (from) tomorrow morgen in einer Woche
weekend das Wochenende [voKHen-end-uh]
at the weekend am Wochenende
weight das Gewicht [gevisht]
weird seltsam [zeltzahm]
weirdo der Verrückte [fair-rOOckt-uh]
welcome: welcome to ... willkommen in ... [villkommen]
you're welcome (don't mention it) keine Ursache [kine-uh OOrzaKH-uh]
well: I don't feel well ich fühle mich nicht wohl [ish fOOl-uh mish nisht vohl]
she's not well sie fühlt sich nicht wohl [zee]
you speak English very well Sie sprechen sehr gut Englisch [shpreshen zair gOOt eng-lish]
well done! gut gemacht! [gemaKHt]
this one as well diesen auch [deezen owKH]
well well! (surprise) na so was! [zo vass]

dialogue

how are you? wie geht es dir? [vee gayt ess deer]
very well, thanks sehr gut, danke [zair gOOt dank-uh]
and you? und dir? [oont deer]

well-done (meat) gut durchgebraten [goot doorsh-gebrahten]

Welsh walisisch [val-**ee**zish]

I'm Welsh (man/woman) ich bin Waliser [vall**ee**zer]/Waliserin

were*: I/you were ich war [var]/du warst [varst]

we/they were wir/sie waren [v**ah**ren]

west der Westen [v**e**sten]

in the west im Westen

West Indian (adj) westindisch [vest**i**ndish]

wet nass

what? was? [vass]

what's that? was ist das?

what should I do? was soll ich tun? [zoll ish toon]

what a view! was für ein Blick! [vass foor ine]

what bus is it? welcher Bus ist das? [v**e**lsher]

wheel das Rad [raht]

wheelchair der Rollstuhl [rol-sht**oo**l]

when? wann? [van]

when's the train/ferry? wann fährt der Zug/die Fähre? [van fairt dair ts**oo**k/dee f**ai**r-uh]

when we get back wenn wir zurückkommen [ven veer tsoor**oo**ck-kommen]

when we got back als wir zurückkamen [alss]

where? wo? [vo]

I don't know where it is ich weiß nicht, wo es ist [vice nisht]

dialogue

where is the cathedral? wo ist der Dom?

it's over there er ist dort drüben [dr**oo**ben]

could you show me where it is on the map? können Sie ihn mir auf der Karte zeigen? [k**ur**nen zee een meer – ts**y**gen]

it's just here er ist da

see also way

which: which bus? welcher Bus? [v**e**lsher]

which house? welches Haus?

which bar? welche Bar?

dialogue

which one? welcher?

that one dieser [d**ee**zer]

this one? dieser?

no, that one nein, dieser [nine]

while: while I'm here während ich hier bin [v**ai**rent ish heer]

whisky der Whisky

white weiß [vice]

white wine der Weißwein [v**ice**-vine]

who? wer? [vair]

who is it? (reply to knock at door etc) wer ist da?

the man who ... der Mann, der ... [dair]

whole: the whole week die

ganze Woche [dee gants-uh voKH-uh]

the whole lot das Ganze

whose: whose is this? wem gehört das? [vaym gehurt]

why? warum? [vahroom]

why not? warum nicht? [nisht]

wide breit [brite]

wife: my wife meine Frau [mine-uh frow]

will*: will you do it for me? können Sie es für mich tun? [kurnen zee ess foor mish toon]

wind der Wind [vint]

window das Fenster

near the window am Fenster

in the window (of shop) im Schaufenster [show-fenster]

window seat der Fensterplatz

windscreen die Windschutzscheibe [vint-shoots-shybuh]

windscreen wiper der Scheibenwischer [shyben-visher]

windsurfing das Windsurfen [vintzurfen]

windy: it's so windy es ist so windig [zo vindish]

wine der Wein [vine]

can we have some more wine? können wir noch etwas Wein haben? [kurnen veer noKH etvass – hahben]

wine list die Weinkarte [vine-kart-uh]

winter der Winter [vinter]

in the winter im Winter

winter holiday der Winterurlaub [vinter-oorlowp]

wire die Draht

(electric) die Leitung [lytoong]

wish: best wishes mit besten Wünschen [voonshen]

with mit

I'm staying with ... ich wohne bei... [vohn-uh by]

without ohne [ohn-uh]

witness (man/woman) der Zeuge [tsoyg-uh]/die Zeugin

will you be a witness for me? würden Sie für mich als Zeuge zur Verfügung stehen? [voorden zee foor mish – tsoor fairfoogoong shtay-en]

woman die Frau [frow]

wonderful wundervoll [voonder-fol]

won't*: it won't start es will nicht anspringen [vill nisht an-shpringen]

wood (material) das Holz [holts]

woods (forest) der Wald [valt]

wool die Wolle [voll-uh]

word das Wort [vort]

work die Arbeit [arbite]

it's not working es funktioniert nicht [foonkts-yohneert nisht]

I work in ... ich arbeite in ... [arbite-uh]

world die Welt [velt]

worry: I'm worried ich mache mir Sorgen [ish maKH-uh meer zorgen]

worse: it's worse es ist schlimmer [shlimmer]

worst am schlimmsten [shlimmsten]

worth: is it worth a visit? lohnt sich ein Besuch dort? [zish ine bezooKH dort?]

would: would you give this to ...? könnten Sie dies ... geben? [kurnten zee – gayben]

wrap: could you wrap it up? können Sie es einpacken? [kurnen zee ess ine-packen]

wrapping paper das Packpapier [pack-papeer]

wrist das Handgelenk [hantgelenk]

write schreiben [shryben]

could you write it down? könnten Sie es aufschreiben? [kurnten zee ess owf-shryben]

how do you write it? wie schreibt man das? [vee shrypt]

writing paper das Schreibpapier [shripe-papeer]

wrong: it's the wrong key es ist der falsche Schlüssel [dair falsh-uh]

this is the wrong train dies ist der falsche Zug

the bill's wrong in der Rechnung ist ein Fehler [dair reshnoong ist ine fayler]

sorry, wrong number tut mir leid, falsch verbunden [toot meer lite falsh fairboonden]

sorry, wrong room tut mir leid, ich habe mich im Zimmer geirrt [ish hahb-uh mish im tsimmer guh-eerrt]

there's something wrong with ... mit ... stimmt etwas nicht [shtimmt etvass nisht]

what's wrong? was ist los? [vass ist lohss]

X

X-ray die Röntgenaufnahme [rurntgen-owfnahm-uh]

Y

yacht die Jacht [yaKHt]

yard* das Yard

year das Jahr [yahr]

yellow gelb [gelp]

yes ja [yah]

you don't smoke, do you? – yes Sie rauchen nicht, oder? – doch [zee rowKHen nisht ohder – doKH]

yesterday gestern

yesterday morning gestern morgen

the day before yesterday vorgestern [forgestern]

yet noch [noKH]

dialogue

is he here yet? ist er schon hier? [air shohn heer]

no, not yet nein, noch nicht [nine noKH nisht]

you'll have to wait a little longer yet Sie müssen noch etwas warten [zee moossen]

yoghurt der Joghurt [**yoh**g-
hoort]
you* (familiar: singular) du [doo]
(plural) ihr [eer]
(polite) Sie [zee]
this is for you das ist für dich/
euch [oych]/Sie
with you mit dir/euch/
Ihnen [**ee**nen]
young jung [yoong]
your* (familiar: singular) dein
[dine]
(plural) euer [**oy**er]
(polite) Ihr [eer]
your camera deine/Ihre
Kamera [**dine**-uh/**eer**-uh]
yours* (familiar: singular) deiner
[**dine**-er]
(plural) eurer [**oy**rer]
(polite) Ihrer [**ee**rer]
youth hostel die
Jugendherberge [**yoo**gent-
hairbairg-uh]

Z

zero null [nooll]
zip der Reißverschluß [**rice**-
fairshlooss]
could you put a new zip on?
könnten Sie einen neuen
Reißverschluß anbringen?
[**kur**nten zee **ine**-en **noy**-en]
zoo der Zoo [tsoh]

German → English

Colloquialisms

The following are words you might well hear. You shouldn't be tempted to use any of the stronger ones unless you are sure of your audience.

Arschloch **n** [arshloKH] arsehole
aufs Kreuz legen to screw, to lay; to take for a ride
blau [blow] pissed, smashed
Bulle **m** [bool-uh] cop
bumsen [boomss-en] to bonk
Bumslokal **n** [boomss-lohkahl] dive
das ist wie Jacke wie Hose [yack-uh vee hohz-uh] it doesn't make any difference
das ist mir scheißegal [meer sh**ice**-aygahl] I couldn't give a shit
du kannst mich mal fuck off, go to hell
du spinnst ja you're off your head
einen Scheißdreck werd' ich tun [**ine**-en sh**ice**-dreck vaird ish toon] no fucking way
ficken to fuck
geil [gile] brilliant; horny
kotzen to puke
leck mich am Arsch fuck off; fuck it
Mensch! [mensh] wow!, hey!
Mist **m** crap, rubbish
Nutte **f** [noot-uh] hooker, whore
Puff **m** [poof] brothel
Scheißdreck **m** [sh**ice**-dreck] shit
Scheiße **f** [sh**ice**-uh] shit
Scheißkerl **m** [sh**ice**-kairl] bastard, son-of-a-bitch
scheißvornehm [sh**ice**-fornaym] bloody posh, swanky
Spinner **m** [shp**inn**er] crazy guy, nutcase
stark [shtark] great
verdammte Scheiße [faird**a**mmt-uh sh**ice**-uh] bloody hell, fucking hell
verdammt noch mal bloody hell
verpiss dich [fairp**iss**] piss off, fuck off

A

ab [ap] from; off; down

abbiegen [ap-beegen] to turn off

Abblendlicht n [ap-blent-lisht] dipped/dimmed headlights

Abend m [ahbent] evening
zu Abend essen to have dinner

Abendessen n [ahbent-essen] dinner

Abendkleid n [ahbent-klite] evening dress

abends [ahbents] in the evening

aber [ahber] but

Abf. (Abfahrt) dept, departure

Abfahrt f [ap-fahrt] departure(s)

Abfall m [ap-fal] litter; rubbish, garbage

Abfälle litter

Abfalleimer m [apfal-ime-er] rubbish bin, trashcan

Abfertigung f [ap-fairtigoong] check-in

Abflug m [ap-flook] departure(s)

Abführmittel n [ap-foor-mittel] laxative

abgefüllt in ... bottled in ...

abgezähltes Geld [ap-getsayltess gelt] exact fare

abheben [ap-hayben] to take off; to withdraw

Abhebung f [ap-hayboong] withdrawal

abholen [ap-hohlen] to pick up

Abkürzung f [ap-koortsoong] abbreviation; shortcut

ablehnen [ap-laynen] to refuse

abnehmen [ap-naymen] to lift (the receiver); to remove; to lose weight

abreisen [ap-rize-en] to leave

abschließen [ap-shleessen] to lock

Absender m [ap-zender] sender

absichtlich [ap-zishtlish] deliberately

absolutes Halteverbot waiting strictly prohibited

absolutes Parkverbot parking strictly prohibited

absolutes Rauchverbot smoking strictly prohibited

Abstand m [ap-shtant] distance

Abtei f [ap-tī] abbey

Abteil n [ap-tile] compartment

Abteilung f [ap-tyloong] department

Abtreibung f [ap-tryboong] abortion

abtrocknen [ap-trocknen] to dry the dishes

Abwasch m [ap-vash] washing-up

abwaschen [ap-vashen] to do the dishes

Achse f [aks-uh] axle

ach so! [aKH zo] I see

acht [aKHt] eight

Achtung! [aKHtoong] look out!; attention

Achtung! Straßenbahn beware of trams

achtzehn [aKH-tsayn] eighteen

achtzig [aKH-tsish] eighty

ADAC (Allgemeiner Deutscher Automobil-Club) [ah-day-ah-ts**ay**] German motoring organization

Adressbuch n [adr**e**ssbOOKH] address book

Affe m [**a**ff-uh] monkey

Agentur f [agent**oo**r] agency

ähneln [**ay**neln] to look like

ähnlich [**ay**nlish] similar

Aktentasche f [**a**kten-tash-uh] briefcase

Aktie f [**a**ktsee-uh] share

Akzent m [akts**e**nt] accent

akzeptieren [aktsept**ee**ren] to accept

albern silly

alle [**a**l-uh] all; everybody; finished, all gone

allein [al**i**ne] alone

alle Kassen all health insurance schemes accepted

alle Rechte vorbehalten all rights reserved

Allergie f [al**ai**rg**ee**] allergy

allergisch gegen [al**ai**rgish g**ay**gen] allergic to

Allerheiligen n [allerh**y**ligen] All Saints' Day (1 November)

alles [**a**l-ess] everything

alles Gute [**a**l-ess g**oo**t-uh] best wishes; all the best

alles klar! [**a**l-ess klar] fine!, great!

allgemein [**a**l-gem**i**ne] general; generally

Alpen Alps

als [**a**lss] when; than; as

also [**a**lzo] therefore

als ob [alss op] as if

alt [alt] old

Altbau m [**a**ltbow] old building

Altenheim n [**a**lten-hime] old people's home

Alter n [**a**lter] age

Altersheim n [**a**lters-hime] old people's home

altmodisch [**a**lt-mohdish] old-fashioned

Altstadt f [**a**lt-shtatt] old (part of) town

Alufolie f [**a**hlOO-fohlee-uh] silver foil

a.M. (am Main) on the Main

am at the; on (the)

am schnellsten (the) fastest

am Apparat [am appar**a**ht] speaking

Ambulanz f [ambOOlants] out-patients

Ameise f [**a**hmize-uh] ant

Amerikaner m [amairee-k**a**hner], Amerikanerin f American

amerikanisch [amairee-k**a**hnish] American

Ampel f traffic lights

amüsieren: sich amüsieren [zish amOOz**ee**ren] to have fun

an at; to; on

anbieten [**a**nbeeten] to offer

Andenken n souvenir

andere [**a**nder-uh] other(s)

andere Orte other destinations

anderthalb [andert-h**a**lp] one and a half

Änderung f [**e**nderoong] change; alteration

Anfall m [**a**nfal] attack; fit

Anfang **m** beginning
anfangen to begin
Anfänger **m** [**anfenger**],
Anfängerin **f** beginner
Anfassen der Waren verboten
do not touch the merchandise
Angeklagte **m/f** [**an-geklahkt-uh**]
defendant
Angeln **m** [**ang-eln**] fishing
Angeln verboten no fishing
angenehm [**an-genaym**]
pleasant; pleased to meet you
Angestellte **m/f** [**an-geshtellt-uh**]
employee
Angst **f** fear
anhalten to stop
Anhalter: per Anhalter fahren
to hitchhike
Anhänger **m** [**anhenger**] trailer;
pendant; follower
Ank. (Ankunft) arr, arrival
Ankauf ... we buy ...
ankommen to arrive
ankreuzen [**ankroytsen**] to cross
Ankunft **f** [**ankoonft**] arrival(s)
Ankunftshalle **f** [**ankoonfts-hal-uh**] arrivals (area)
Anlieger frei residents only
Anmeldung **f** [**an-meldoong**]
reception
anprobieren [**anprobeeren**] to
try on
Anruf **m** [**anroof**] call
anrufen [**anroofen**] to phone,
to ring
ans [**anss**] to the
anschalten [**an-shalten**] to
switch on
Anschluss **m** [**an-shlooss**]

connection
Anschluss an ... connects
with ...
Anschrift **f** [**an-shrift**] address
ansehen [**anzay-en**] to look (at)
Ansicht **f** [**anzisht**] view;
opinion
Ansichtskarte **f** [**anzishts-kart-uh**]
picture postcard
anstatt [**an-shtatt**] instead of
ansteckend [**an-shteckent**]
contagious
Antenne **f** [**antenn-uh**] aerial;
antenna
Antiquitäten [**anti-kvitayten**]
antiques
Antwort **f** [**antvort**] answer
antworten [**antvorten**] to answer
Anwalt **m** [**anvalt**], Anwältin
[**anveltin**] **f** lawyer
Anwohner frei residents only
Anzahlung **f** [**an-tsahloong**]
deposit
anziehen [**antsee-en**] to dress
sich anziehen [**zish**] to get
dressed
Anzug **m** [**antsook**] suit
anzünden [**an-tsoonden**] to light
AOK (Allgemeine
Ortskrankenkasse) [**ah-oh-kah**]
German health insurance
scheme
Apotheke **f** [**apotayk-uh**]
chemist's, pharmacy
Apparat **m** [**apparaht**]
telephone; apparatus
Appetit **m** [**appeteet**] appetite
a.R. (am Rhein) on the Rhine
Arbeit **f** [**arbite**] work; job

arbeiten [arbite-en] to work

Arbeiter m [arbyter], Arbeiterin f worker

arbeitslos [arbites-lohss] unemployed

ARD (Arbeitsgemeinschaft der Rundfunkanstalten Deutschlands) [ah-air-day] first German television channel

Ärger m [airger] annoyance; trouble; hassle

ärgerlich [airgerlish] annoying

ärgern: sich ärgern [zish airgern] to be/get annoyed

arm poor

Arm m arm

Armaturenbrett n [armatooren-brett] dashboard

Armband n [armbant] bracelet

Armbanduhr f [armbant-oor] watch

Arschloch! [arshlokH] bastard!

Art f sort, kind

Arzt m [artst] doctor

Ärztin f [airtstin] doctor

Ärztlicher Notdienst m [airtst-lisher noht-deenst] emergency medical service

Asche f [ash-uh] ash

Aschenbecher m [ashenbesher] ashtray

Aschermittwoch m [asher-mittvokH] Ash Wednesday

aß [ahss], aßen [ahssen], aßt [ahsst] ate

atmen [aht-men] to breathe

Attentat n [atten-taht] assassination

Attest n certificate

auch [owkH] too, also

auf [owf] on; to; open

auf deutsch in German

Aufbewahrungslösung f [owf-bevahroongs-lurzoong] soaking solution

Aufenthalt m [owf-ent-halt] stay

Aufenthaltsraum m [owf-ent-halts-rowm] lounge

Aufführung f [owf-fooroong] performance

aufgeben [owf-gayben] to give up; to post, to mail

aufhören [owf-hur-ren] to stop

aufpassen [owf-passen] to pay attention

aufpassen auf [owf] to take care of; to watch out for

aufregend [owf-raygent] exciting

aufs [owfs] on the; onto the

Aufsicht f [owf-zisht] supervision

aufstehen [owf-shtay-en] to get up

aufwachen [owf-vakHen] to wake up

Aufzug m [owf-tsook] lift, elevator

Auge n [owg-uh] eye

Augenarzt m [owgen-artst] ophthalmologist, optician

Augenblick m [owgenblick] moment

Augenbraue f [owgen-brow-uh] eyebrow

Augenoptiker m [owgen-optiker] optician

Augenzeuge m [owgen-tsoyg-

uh], **Augenzeugin f** eye
witness

aus [owss] from; off; out; out
of; made of; finished

Ausfahrt f [owssfahrt] exit

Ausfahrt freihalten keep exit
clear

**Ausfahrt Tag und Nacht
freihalten** keep exit clear day
and night

Ausflug m [owssfl00k] trip

ausfüllen [owssf00llen] to fill in

Ausgang m [owssgang] exit,
way out; gate; departure

ausgeben [owssgayben] to
spend

ausgenommen [owss-
genommen] except

ausgezeichnet [owss-getsyshnet]
excellent

Auskunft f [owsskoonft]
information; information
desk; directory enquiries

Ausland n [owsslant]
international; overseas,
abroad

Ausländer m [owsslender],
Ausländerin f foreigner

ausländisch [owsslendish]
foreign

ausländisches Erzeugnis
foreign produce

ausländische Währungen fpl
[owsslendish-uh vairoongen]
foreign currencies

Ausland: im/ins Ausland
[owsslant] abroad

Auslandsflüge international
departures

Auslandsgespräche
international calls

Auslandsporto n [owsslants-
porto] overseas postage

Ausnahme f [owssnahm-uh]
exception

auspacken [owsspacken] to
unpack

Auspuff m [owsspooff] exhaust

ausruhen: sich ausruhen [zish
owssr00-en] to relax; to take
a rest

ausschalten [owss-shalten] to
switch off

ausschl. (ausschließlich) excl.,
exclusive

aussehen [owss-zay-en] to look

Aussehen n look; appearance

außen [owssen] outside

außer [owsser] except

außer Betrieb out of order

außerhalb [owsser-halp] outside
(of)

äußerlich anzuwenden not to
be taken internally

außer sonntags Sundays
excepted

Aussicht f [owss-zisht] view

Aussichtspunkt m [owss-zishts-
poonkt] viewpoint

aussprechen [owss-shpreshen]
to pronounce

aussteigen [owss-shtygen] to
get off

Ausstellung f [owss-shtelloong]
exhibition

Australien n [owstrahlee-en]
Australia

australisch [owstrahlish]

Australian

Ausverkauf m [owss-fairk**owf]** sale

ausverkauft [owss-fairk**owf**t] sold out

Auswahl f [owssvahl] choice; selection

Ausweis m [owssvice] pass, identity card; identification

Auszahlungen withdrawals; cash desk, cashier

ausziehen: sich ausziehen [zish **ow**ss-tsee-en] to undress

Auto n [owto] car
mit dem Auto by car

Autobahn f [owto-bahn] motorway, highway, freeway

Autobahndreieck motorway junction; motorways merge

Autobahnkreuz motorway junction

Autobahnraststätte service station

Autobus m [owtobooss] bus

Autofähre f [owto-fair-uh] car-ferry

Autofahrer m [owtofahrer], **Autofahrerin f** car driver, motorist

Automat m vending machine **dieser Automat nimmt folgende Banknoten an** this machine will accept the following banknotes/bills

automatisch [owtom**ah**tish] automatic

Autoradio n [owto-rahdee-o] car radio

Autoreparaturen auto repairs

Autotelefon n [owto-telef**ohn]** car phone

Autounfall m [owto-oonfal] car accident

Autovermietung f [owto-fairm**ee**toong] car rental

Autowäsche f [owtovesh-uh] car wash

B

Babyartikel babywear, items for babies

Bach m [baкн] stream

Bäcker m [becker] baker

Bäckerei f [becker-**ī]** baker's, bakery

Bad n [baht] bath; bathroom

Badeanzug m [bahd-uh-ants**oo**k] swimming costume

Badehose f [bahd-uh-hohz-uh] swimming trunks

Bademantel m [bahd-uh-mantel] dressing gown

baden [bah**d**en] to have a bath

Badesalz n [bahd-uh-zalts] bath salts

Badewanne f [bahd-uh-vann-uh] bathtub

Badezimmer n [bahd-uh-tsimmer] bathroom

Badezimmerartikel bathroom furniture and fittings

Badezimmerbedarf for the bathroom

Bahnhof m [bahn-hohf] station

Bahnhofsmission f [bahnhohfs-miss-**yoh**n] office providing help for travellers in difficulty

Bahnhofspolizei railway police

Bahnkilometer kilometres by rail

Bahnsteig m [bahn-shtike] platform, (US) track

Bahnsteigkarte f [bahn-shtike-kart-uh] platform ticket

Bahnübergang m [bahn-oobergang] level crossing

bald [balt] soon

Balkangrill m [balkahn-grill] restaurant serving dishes from Balkan countries

Balkon m [balkohn] balcony

Band n [bant] tape

Bank f bank; bench

Bankkonto n bank account

Bankleitzahl f [banklite-tsahl] sort code

Bankomat m [bankomaht] cash dispenser, automatic teller

bar zahlen [tsahlen] to pay cash

Bardame f [bardahm-uh] barmaid

Bargeld n [bargelt] cash

Barmann m [barmann] barkeeper

Bart m beard

Basel n [bahzel] Basle

bat [baht], **baten** [bahten] asked

Bauch m [bowKH] stomach; belly

Bauer m [bower] farmer

Bauernhof m [bowern-hohf] farm

Baum m [bowm] tree

Baumwolle f [bowmvoll-uh] cotton

Baustelle f building site; roadworks

Baustellenausfahrt works exit; building site exit

Bayern [by-ern] Bavaria

bayrisch [by-rish] Bavarian

Beamter m [buh-amter], **Beamtin f** civil servant; official

Bedarf m needs, requirements; demand

bedeuten [bedoyten] to mean

bedeutend [bedoytent] important

bedienen [bedeenen] to serve

bedienen Sie sich! [zee zish] help yourself

Bedienung f [bedeenoong] service (charge)

Bedienung inbegriffen service included

Bedienungsanleitung instructions for use

Bedingung f [bedingoong] condition

beeilen: sich beeilen [zish buh-Ilen] to hurry

beeilen Sie sich! [zee zish] hurry up!

beenden [buh-enden] to finish

Beerdigung f [buh-airdigoong] funeral

Beerdigungsunternehmen undertaker, mortician

befehlen [befaylen] to order

Beginn der Vorstellung um ... [dair forshtelloong oom] performance begins at ...

begleiten [begltyten] to accompany

behalten [behalten] to keep

behandeln to treat

Behandlung f [behantloong] treatment

behaupten [behowpten] to claim

Behauptung f [behowptoong] claim

behindert [behindert] disabled

Behinderte m/f [behindert-uh] handicapped person

bei [by] by; at; next to; near
bei Peter at Peter's

beide [bide-uh] both (of them)

Bei Frost Glatteisgefahr icy in cold weather

beim at the

Bein n [bine] leg

Beinbruch m [bine-brooкн] broken leg

Beispiel n [by-shpeel] example
zum Beispiel [tsoom] for example

Bei Störung Taste drücken press key in case of technical fault

bekannt known

Bekannte m/f [bekannt-uh] acquaintance

Bekleidung f [beklydoong] clothing

bekloppt [bekloppt] crazy

bekommen to get

belegt [belaykt] occupied, busy; no vacancies; full

beleidigen [belydigen] to offend

Beleuchtung f [beloyshtoong] lights

Beleuchtungsartikel lamps and lighting

Belgien n [belgee-en] Belgium

belgisch [belgish] Belgian

Belichtungsmesser m [belishtoongs-messer] light meter

bellen to bark

Belohnung f [belohnoong] reward

bemerken [bemairken] to notice; to remark

Bemerkung f [bemairkoong] remark

Benehmen n [benaymen] behaviour

benehmen: sich benehmen [zish benaymen] to behave

Benutzung f [benootsoong] use

Benutzung auf eigene Gefahr use at own risk

Benzin n [bentseen] petrol, gas(oline)

Benzinkanister m [bentseen-kanister] petrol/gasoline can

Benzinuhr f [bentseen-oor] fuel gauge

beobachten [buh-ohbaкнten] to watch

bequem [bekvaym] comfortable

bereit [berite] ready

Bereitschaftsdienst m [berite-shaftsdeenst] duty doctor; duty pharmacy

Berg m [bairk] mountain

Bergsteigen n [bairk-shtygen] mountaineering

Bergwacht f [bairk-vaкнt] mountain rescue

Bericht m [berisht] report

140

beruhigen: sich beruhigen [zish beroo-igen] to calm down

Beruhigungsmittel n [beroo-igoongs-mittel] tranquillizer

berühmt [beroomt] famous

berühren [berooren] to touch

Berühren der Waren verboten do not touch

Besatzung f [bezatsoong] crew

beschädigen [beshaydigen] to damage

Bescheid m [beshite] information

Bescheid sagen to tell

Bescheid wissen to know

Bescheinigung f [beshynigoong] certificate

bescheuert [beshoyert] crazy, daft

beschreiben [beshryben] to describe

Beschreibung f description

beschweren: sich beschweren [zish beshvairen] to complain

besetzt [bezetst] busy; engaged, occupied

Besetztzeichen n [besetst-tsyshen] engaged tone

Besichtigung f [bezishtigoong] tour

Besitzer m [bezitser] owner

besoffen [bezoffen] pissed, smashed

besonders [bezonders] especially

besorgt [bezorkt] worried

besser better

Bestandteile ingredients; component parts

bestätigen [beshtaytigen] to confirm

Bestattungen funeral director's

beste [best-uh] best

Bestechung f [beshteshoong] bribery

Besteck n [beshteck] cutlery

bestellen [beshtellen] to order

Bestellung f [beshtelloong] order

Bestimmungsort m [beshtim-moongs-ort] destination

bestrafen [beshtrahfen] to punish

Besuch m [bezooKH] visit

besuchen [bezooKHen] to visit

Besuchszeit f [bezooKHs-tsite] visiting time

Besuchszeiten fpl [bezooKHs-tsyten] visiting hours

Betäubung f [betoyboong] anaesthetic

Beton m [baytong] concrete

Betrag m [betrahk] amount

Betreten auf eigene Gefahr enter at own risk, keep off/out

Betreten der Baustelle verboten no admission to building site

Betreten der Eisfläche verboten keep off the ice

Betreten des Rasens nicht gestattet keep off the grass

Betreten verboten keep out

Betrieb m [betreep] company, firm; operation, running; bustle

außer Betrieb out of order

betriebsbereit ready to use

Betriebsferien [betreeps-fairee-en] works' holidays/vacation

Betrug m [betrook] fraud

betrunken [betroonken] drunk

Bett n bed

Bettdecken bedding

Betteln und Hausieren verboten no beggars, no hawkers

Bettwäsche f [bettvesh-uh] bed linen

Bettzeug n [bett-tsoyk] bedding

Be- und Entladen erlaubt loading and off-loading permitted

bevor [befor] before

bewegen: sich bewegen [zish be-vaygen] to move

Beweis m [bevice] proof

Bewohner m [bevohner], Bewohnerin f inhabitant

bewölkt [bevurlkt] cloudy

bezahlen [betsahlen] to pay

Bezahlung f [betsahloong] payment

Bezahlung mit Kreditkarte möglich credit cards welcome

beziehungsweise or

Bf. (Bahnhof) station

BH (Büstenhalter) m [bay-hah] bra

Bierkeller m [beer-keller] beer cellar

Bild n [bilt] picture

billig [billish] cheap, inexpensive

Billigpreise reduced prices

bin am

Bindemittel starch

Bio-Laden m [bee-oh-lahden] health food shop

biologisch abbaubar biodegradable

Birne f [beern-uh] light bulb; pear

bis until; by

bis morgen see you tomorrow

bis später [shpayter] see you later

Biss m [bis] bite

bisschen: ein bisschen [ine biss-shen] a little bit (of)

bist are

bitte [bittuh] please; you're welcome

bitte? pardon (me)?; can I help you?

bitte anschnallen fasten seat belt

bitte einordnen get in lane

bitte eintreten ohne zu läuten please enter without ringing

bitte einzeln eintreten please enter one at a time

bitte entwerten please stamp your ticket

bitte Karte einführen please insert card

bitte klingeln please ring

bitte klopfen please knock

bitten to ask

bitte nicht ... please do not ...

bitte nicht stören please do not disturb

bitte schließen please close the door

bitte schön/sehr [**bitt**-uh shurn/zair] here you are; you're welcome

bitte schön/sehr? what will it be?; can I help you?

bitte Schuhe abtreten please wipe your shoes

bitte warten please wait

Blase f [**blahz**-uh] bladder; blister

blass pale

Blatt n leaf

blau [blow] blue

blauer Fleck m [**blow**er] bruise

Blei n [bly] lead

bleiben [**bly**ben] to stay, to remain

bleiben Sie am Apparat [zee am appa**raht**] hold the line

Bleichmittel n [**blysh**-mittel] bleach

bleifrei [**bly**fry] unleaded

Bleistift m [**bly**-shtift] pencil

Blick m look; view

mit Blick auf ... [owf] overlooking ...

blieb [bleep], bliebst, blieben stayed

Blinddarmentzündung f [blint-darm-ent-ts**oo**ndoong] appendicitis

blinder Passagier m [**blinn**der passa**Jee**r] stowaway

Blinker m indicator

Blitz m [blits] flash; lightning

blockiert [block**eer**t] blocked

Blödmann m [**blurt**mann] twit

Blödsinn m [**blurt**-zinn] nonsense, rubbish

Blume f [**bloom**-uh] flower

Blumenhandlung f [bl**oo**men-hantloong] florist

Bluse f [bl**oo**z-uh] blouse

Blut n [bloot] blood

Blutdruck m [**bloot**-droock] blood pressure

bluten [**bloot**en] to bleed

Blutgruppe f [bloot-groopp-uh] blood group

Blutübertragung f [bloot-oobertr**ah**goong] blood transfusion

BLZ (Bankleitzahl) sort code

Boden m [**boh**den] bottom; floor

Bodenpersonal n [bohden-pairzon**ah**l] ground crew

Bodensee: der Bodensee [**boh**denzay] Lake Constance

Bohrer m drill

Boje f [boh-yuh] buoy

Bolzen m [**bol**tsen] bolt

Boot n [boht] boat

Bootsverleih m [bohts-fairl**i**] boat hire/rental

Bordkarte f [**bort**kart-uh] boarding card

böse [**burz**-uh] angry

Botschaft f [**boht**shaft] embassy

brachte [bra**к**н**t**-uh], brachtest, brachten brought

Branchenverzeichnis n [br**ang**shen-fairts**y**shniss] yellow pages

Brand m [brant] fire

Brandstiftung f [brant-sht**i**ftoong] arson

Bratpfanne f [bra**ht**-pfann-uh]

frying pan
Bräu n [broy] brew
Brauch m [browKH] custom
brauchen [browKHen] to need
Brauerei f brewery
Brauereiabfüllung bottled in
the brewery
braun [brown] brown
braungebrannt [brown-gebrannt]
tanned
**BRD (Bundesrepublik
Deutschland)** [bay-air-day]
FRG (Federal Republic of
Germany)
breit [brite] wide
Breite f [bryt-uh] width
Bremse f [bremz-uh] brake
bremsen [bremzen] to brake
Bremsflüssigkeit f [brems-
flOOssishkite] brake fluid
brennbar combustible
brennen to burn
Brief m [breef] letter
Brieffreund m [breef-froynt],
Brieffreundin f pen pal
Briefkasten m [breefkasten]
letterbox, mailbox
Briefmarke f [breefmark-uh]
stamp
Brieftasche f [breeftash-uh]
wallet
Briefträger m [breeftrayger]
postman
Briefträgerin f [breeftraygerin]
postwoman
Brille f [brill-uh] glasses,
eyeglasses
bringen to bring
Brosche f [brosh-uh] brooch

Broschüre f [broshOOr-uh]
brochure
Bruch m [brooKH] fracture
Brücke f [brOOck-uh] bridge
Bruder m [brOOder] brother
Brunnen m [broonnen] fountain
Brust f [broost] breast; chest
Buch n [bookKH] book
buchen [bookKHen] to book
Bücherei f [bOOsher-ī] library
Bücher und Zeitschriften
books and magazines
Buchhandlung f [bOOKH-
hantloong] bookshop,
bookstore
Bucht f [bookKHt] bay
Bügeleisen n [bOOgel-īzen] iron
Bügelfalte f [bOOgel-falt-uh]
crease
bügeln [bOOgeln] to iron
Bühne f [bOOn-uh] stage
Bundesautobahn federal
motorway/highway
Bundesgesundheitsminister m
German Minister of Health
**Der
Bundesgesundheitsminister:
Rauchen gefährdet Ihre
Gesundheit** government
warning: smoking can
damage your health
Bundeskanzler m [boondess-
kantsler] chancellor
Bundesrepublik Deutschland f
[boondess-repOObleek doytchlant]
Federal Republic of Germany
Bundesstraße f [boondess-
shtrahss-uh] major road,
A-road

Bundestag m [**boo**ndess-tahk]
 German parliament
Burg f [boork] castle
Bürgersteig m [**boo**rger-shtike]
 pavement, sidewalk
Büro n [b**oo**ro] office
Büroartikel office supplies
Bürste f [b**oo**rst-uh] brush
Busbahnhof m [b**oo**ss-bahnhof]
 bus station
Bushaltestelle f [b**oo**ss-halt-uh-
 sht**e**ll-uh] bus stop
bzw. (beziehungsweise) or

C

Café n [kaff**ay**] café, serving
 mainly cakes, coffee and tea
 etc
Campingbedarf camping
 equipment
Campingliege f [k**e**mping-leeg-
 uh] campbed
Campingplatz m [k**e**mpingplats]
 campsite; caravan site, trailer
 park
CD-Spieler m [tsay-**day**-shpeeler]
 CD player
Charterflug m [charter-fl**oo**k]
 charter flight
Chauvi m [sh**oh**vee] male
 chauvinist pig
Chef m [shef], **Chefin f** boss
chemische Reinigung f
 [sh**ay**mish-uh r**y**nigoong] dry
 cleaner's
Chinarestaurant n [sheena-
 restor**o**ng] Chinese restaurant
chinesisch [sheen**ay**zish]
 Chinese
Chirurg m [sheer**oo**rk], **Chirurgin
 f** surgeon
Coiffeur m [kwaff**ur**] hairdresser

D

da there; as; since
Dach n [daкн] roof
Dachboden m [d**a**кнbohden]
 attic
Dachgepäckträger m [d**a**кн-
 gepeck-trayger] roof rack
dafür [daf**oo**r] for that; on that;
 in that; in favour; then again;
 considering
daher [dah**air**] from there;
 that's why
Dame f [d**a**hm-uh] lady
Damen ladies' (toilet), ladies'
 room
Damenbinde f [d**a**hmenbind-uh]
 sanitary towel/napkin
Damenkleidung f [d**a**hmen-
 kl**y**doong] ladies' clothing
Damenmoden ladies' fashions
Damensalon m [d**a**hmen-zalong]
 ladies' hairdresser's
Damentoilette f [d**a**hmen-twalett-
 uh] ladies' (toilet), ladies'
 room
Damenunterwäsche f [d**a**hmen-
 oontervesh-uh] lingerie
damit so that; with it
Dampfer m steamer
danach [dan**a**кн] after that;
 accordingly
Dänemark n [d**ay**n-uh-mark]
 Denmark

dänisch [daynish] Danish

dankbar grateful

danke [dank-uh] thank you, thanks

danke gleichfalls [glyshfals] the same to you

danken to thank

dann then

darf am allowed to; is allowed to; may

darfst are allowed to; may

Darlehen n [dahrlay-en] loan

darum [daroom] about it; that's why

das the; who; that; which

dass that

Datum n [dahtoom] date

Dauerwelle f [dowervell-uh] perm

Daumen m [dowmen] thumb

davon from there; of it; of them; from it; from them

DB (Deutsche (Bundes)bahn) German Railways

Decke f [deck-uh] blanket; ceiling

Deckel m lid

defekt out of order; faulty

dein(e) [dine(-uh)] your

denken to think

Denkmal n [denkmahl] monument

denn for, because; than

deprimiert [deprimeert] depressed

der [dair] the; who; that

deshalb [dess-halp] therefore

Desinfektionsmittel n [desinfekts-yohns-mittel]

disinfectant

deutsch [doytch] German

Deutsche m/f [doytch-uh] German

deutsches Erzeugnis made in Germany

Deutschland n [doytchlant] Germany

Deutschlandlied n [doytchlant-leet] German national anthem

d.h. (das heißt) i.e.

Dia n [dee-ah] slide

Diabetiker m [dee-ah-baytiker], Diabetikerin f diabetic

Diamant m [dee-ah-mant] diamond

Diät f [dee-ayt] diet

dich [dish] you

Dichter m [dishter] poet

dick fat; thick

die [dee] the; who; that; which

Dieb m [deep] thief

Diebstahl m [deep-shtahl] theft

Dienstag m [deenstahk] Tuesday

dienstbereit [deenst-berite] on duty

dies [deess] this (one); that (one)

diese [deez-uh] this (one); that (one); these (ones); those (ones)

dieser [deezer] this (one); that (one)

dieses [deezess] this (one); that (one)

diesseits [deess-zites] on this side (of)

Ding n thing

dir [deer] (to) you

Direktflug m [deerekt-flook] non-stop flight

diskutieren [diskooteeren] to discuss

DJH (Deutsche Jugendherberge) German Youth Hostel Association

DLRG (Deutsche Lebensrettungsgesellschaft) [day-el-air-gay] German lifeguards association

DM (Deutsche Mark) DM, German mark

doch! [dokh] oh yes it is!; oh yes I am! etc

Dolmetscher m [dolmetcher], Dolmetscherin f interpreter

Dom m [dohm] cathedral

Donau f [dohnow] Danube

Donner m thunder

Donnerstag m [donnerstahk] Thursday

doof [dohf] stupid

Doppelbett n double bed

doppelt double

Doppelzimmer n [doppel-tsimmer] double room

Dorf n village

dort there

dort drüben [drooben] over there; up there

dort oben [ohben] over there; up there

Dose f [dohz-uh] can

Dosenöffner m [dohzen-urfner] tin opener

Dragees npl [draJayss] sugar-coated tablets

Draht m wire

Drahtseilbahn f [drahtzilebahn] cable car

Dreck m dirt

drehen [dray-en] to turn

drei [dry] three

dreimal täglich einzunehmen to be taken three times a day

dreißig [dryssish] thirty

dreizehn [dry-tsayn] thirteen

dringend [dring-ent] urgent

dritte(r,s) [dritt-uh,-er,-ess] third

Droge f [drohg-uh] drug

Drogerie f [drohgeree] chemist's, toiletries shop

Druck m [droock] pressure

drücken [droocken] to push

Drucker m [droocker] printer

Drucksache f printed matter

DSD (Duales System Deutschland) recycling scheme

du [doo] you

du lieber Gott! [leeber gott] good God!

du liebe Zeit! [leeb-uh tsite] struth!

Duft m [dooft] smell; fragrance

dumm [doomm] stupid

Dummheit f [doommhite] stupidity

Dummkopf m [doommkopf] idiot

Dünen fpl [doonen] sand dunes

dunkel [doonkel] dark

Dunkelheit f [doonkelhite] darkness

dünn [doonn] thin; skinny

durch [doorsh] through; by; well-done

Durcheinander n [doorsh-ine-ander] mess

Durchfall m [doorshfal] diarrhoea

Durchgang m [doorshgang] passage

Durchgangsverkehr through traffic

durchgehend geöffnet open 24 hours

Durchschnitt m [doorsh-shnitt] average

durchstreichen [doorsh-shtryshen] to cross out, to delete

Durchsuchung f [doorsh-zooKHoong] search

Durchwahl direct dialling

dürfen [doorfen] to be allowed to

Durst m [doorst] thirst
  Durst haben [hahben] to be thirsty

Dusche f [doosh-uh] shower

duschen [dooshen] to have a shower

Düsenflugzeug n [doozen-flooktsoyk] jet plane

Dutzend n [dootsent] dozen

duzen: sich duzen [zish dootsen] to use the familiar 'du' form

D-Zug [day-tsook] express train

E

Ebbe f [ebb-uh] low tide

echt [esht] genuine

Ecke f [eck-uh] corner

Edelstein m [aydel-shtine] precious stone

EG (Europäische Gemeinschaft) [ay-gay] EC, European Community

ehe [ay-uh] before

Ehe f [ay-uh] marriage

Ehefrau f [ay-uh-frow] wife

Ehemann m [ay-uh-man] husband

ehrlich [airlish] honest; sincere

Ehrlichkeit f [airlishkite] honesty

Eiche f [ish-uh] oak

Eieruhr f [ier-oor] egg timer

eifersüchtig [iferzooshtish] jealous

eigen [igen] own

eigenartig [igen-artish] strange

eigentlich [igentlish] actual; actually

Eigentümer m [igentoomer], **Eigentümerin** f owner

Eilzug m [ile-tsook] fast local train

Eimer m [ime-er] bucket

ein(e) [ine-(uh)] a; one

Einbahnstraße f [ine-bahn-shtrahss-uh] one-way street

Einbrecher m [ine-bresher] burglar

Einbruch m [ine-brooKH] burglary

einchecken [ine-checken] to check in

Eindruck m [ine-droock] impression

eine [ine-uh] a

einfach [ine-faKH] simple; single

einfache Fahrt one-way journey; single; one way

Einfahrt f [ine-fahrt] entrance, way in

Einfahrt freihalten keep entrance clear

Eingang m [ine-gang] entrance, way in

Eingang um die Ecke entrance round corner

eingeschränktes Halteverbot restricted parking

eingetragenes Warenzeichen registered trademark

Einheit f [ine-hite] unit

Einheitspreis flat rate

einige [ine-ig-uh] a few; some

Einkauf m [ine-kowf] shopping

einkaufen: einkaufen gehen [ine-kowfen gay-en] to go shopping

Einkaufskorb m [ine-kowfss-korp] shopping basket

Einkaufstasche f [ine-kowfss-tash-uh] shopping bag

Einkaufswagen m [ine-kowfss-vahgen] shopping trolley

Einkaufszentrum n [ine-kowfss-tsentroom] shopping centre

einladen [ine-lahden] to invite

Einladung f [ine-lahdoong] invitation

Einlass m [ine-lass] admission

einmal [ine-mahl] once

nicht einmal not even

einmalig [ine-mahlish] unique

einpacken [ine-packen] to wrap

einreiben [ine-ryben] to rub in

Einrichtung f [ine-rishtoong] furnishing; organization

eins [ine-ss] one

einsam [ine-zahm] lonely

einschalten [ine-shalten] to switch on

einschenken [ine-shenken] to pour

einschlafen [ine-shlahfen] to fall asleep

einschl. (einschließlich) incl., inclusive

einschließlich 15% Bedienung 15% service charge included

Einschreiben n [ine-shryben] registered letter

Einschreibsendungen registered mail

einsteigen [ine-shtygen] to get in

Einstieg hinten enter at the rear

Einstieg nur mit Fahrausweis obtain a ticket before boarding

Einstieg vorn enter at the front

eintreten in [ine-trayten] to enter

Eintritt m [ine-tritt] entry

Eintritt frei admission free

Eintrittskarte f [ine-tritts-kart-uh] ticket

Eintrittspreise admission

einverstanden! [ine-fair-shtanden] OK!; agreed

einwerfen [ine-vairfen] to insert

Einzahlungen deposits

Einzelbett n [ine-tselbett] single bed

Einzelfahrkarte f [ine-tsel-fahrkart-uh] single/one-way ticket

Einzelhändler m [ine-tsel-hentler] retailer

Einzelheit f [ine-tselhite] detail

Einzelpreis m [ine-tsel-price] (unit) price

Einzelzimmer n [ine-tsel-tsimmer] single room

Eiscafé n [ice-kaffay] ice cream parlour (also serves coffee and liqueurs)

Eisenbahn f [izenbahn] railway

Eisenwarenhandlung f [izenvahren-hantloong] hardware store

Eisstadion n [ice-shtahdee-on] ice rink

Eiter m [ite-er] pus

Elektriker m [aylektriker] electrician

Elektrizität f [aylektritsitayt] electricity

Elektroartikel mpl [aylektro-arteekel] electrical goods

Elektrogeräte npl [aylektro-gerayt-uh] electrical equipment

elf eleven

Elfmeter m [elfmayter] penalty

Ei: Ellbogen m [ell-bohgen] elbow

Eltern parents

Eltern haften für ihre Kinder parents are responsible for their children

Empfang m reception

Empfänger m [emp-fenger] addressee

empfehlen [emp-faylen] to recommend

Ende der Autobahn end of motorway/highway

Ende der Vorfahrtsstraße end of priority

endlich [entlish] at last; finally

Endstation f [ent-shtats-yohn] terminus

eng narrow; tight

Engländer m [eng-lender] Englishman

Engländerin f [eng-lenderin] English girl/woman

englisch [eng-lish] English; rare (meat)

Enkel m grandson

Enkelin f granddaughter

entdecken to discover

entfernt [entfairnt] away; distant

Entfernung f [entfairnoong] distance

entführen [entfooren] to kidnap, to abduct

Entgleisung f [ent-glyzoong] derailment

enthält ... contains ...

entlang along(side)

entscheiden [ent-shyden] to decide

entschlossen [ent-shlossen] determined

entschuldigen: sich entschuldigen [zish entshooldigen] to apologize

entschuldigen Sie bitte [zee bitt-uh] excuse me

Entschuldigung [entshooldigoong] sorry, excuse me

entsetzlich [entzetslish] appalling

enttäuscht [ent-**toy**sht]
disappointed

Enttäuschung f [ent-**toy**shoong]
disappointment

entweder ... oder ... [**ent**vayder
ohder] either ... or ...

Entwerter m [ent**vair**ter] ticket-
stamping machine

entwickeln [ent**vick**eln] to
develop

Entzündung f [ent-ts**oo**ndoong]
infection

er [air] he

Erde f [aird-uh] earth

Erdgeschoss n [**airt**-geshoss]
ground floor, (US) first floor

Erfahrung f [airfahroong]
experience

Erfolg m [air**foll**k] success

Erfrischung f [airfrishoong]
refreshment

ergibt die doppelte/dreifache
Menge makes twice/three
times as much

erhalten [air**hal**ten] to receive

erholen: sich erholen [zish
air**hoh**len] to recover

Erholungsgebiet n [airhoh**loo**ngs-
gebeet] recreational area

erinnern: sich erinnern an [zish
air-**inn**ern] to remember

Erinnerung f [air-**inn**eroong]
memory

erkälten: sich erkälten [zish
air**kel**ten] to catch cold

erkältet: erkältet sein [air**kel**tet]
to have a cold

Erkältung f [air**kel**toong] cold

erkennen [air**kenn**en] to
recognize

erklären [airk**lair**en] to explain

erlauben [air**low**ben] to allow

Erlaubnis f [air**low**pniss]
permission

Erlebnis n [air**layp**niss]
experience

Ermäßigte Preise reduced
prices

Ermäßigungen reductions;
concessions

ermorden [air**mor**den] to
murder

ernst [airnst] serious

Ersatzreifen m [air**zatz**-ryfen]
spare tyre

Ersatzteile npl [air**zatz**-tile-uh]
spare parts

erschießen [air**shee**ssen] to
shoot (and kill)

Ersparnisse fpl [airsh**pahr**niss-
uh] savings

erst [airst] only just; only

erstatten [airsh**tatt**en] to refund

erstaunlich [airsh**town**lish]
astonishing

erste(r,s) [**air**st-uh, -er, -es] first

Erste Hilfe f [**air**st-uh hilf-uh]
first aid

erste Klasse [**air**st-uh klass-uh]
first class

erstens [**air**stens] first; firstly

erster Stock m [**air**ster shtock]
first floor, (US) second floor

ersticken [airsh**tick**en] to
suffocate

ertrinken [air**trink**en] to drown

Erwachsene m/f [air**vak**sen-uh]
adult

erwähnen [airvaynen] to mention

es [ess] it

essbar [essbar] edible

essen to eat

Essen n food

Esslöffel m [ess-lurffel] tablespoon

Etage f [aytahJ-uh] floor, storey

Etagenbett n [aytahJen-bett] bunk beds

Etat m [aytah] budget

Etikett n label

etwa [etvah] about; perhaps

etwas [etvass] something; some; somewhat

etwas anderes [anderess] something else

euch [oysh] you

euer [oyer] your

eure [oyr-uh] your

europäisch [oyro-pay-ish] European

Euroscheck m [oyrosheck] Eurocheque

ev. (evangelisch) Protestant

evangelisch [evangaylish] Protestant

Er

Explosionsgefahr f [eksplohz-yohns-gefahr] danger of explosion

F

Fabrik f [fabreek] factory

Fach n [faKH] subject; pigeonhole

Facharzt m: Facharzt für ... [faKHartst foor] specialist for ...

Fachmann m [faKHmann] specialist

Faden m [fahden] string; thread

Fahne f [fahn-uh] flag

Fahrausweis m [fahr-owssvice] ticket

Fahrausweise sind auf Verlangen vorzuzeigen tickets must be displayed on request

Fahrbahn f roadway

Fähre f [fair-uh] ferry

fahren to drive; to go

Fahrer m driver

Fahrgäste passengers

Fahrkarte f [fahrkart-uh] ticket

Fahrkartenautomat m [fahrkarten-owtomaht] ticket machine

Fahrkartenschalter m [fahrkarten-shalter] ticket office

Fahrplan m [fahrplahn] timetable, (US) schedule

Fahrpreise mpl [fahrprize-uh] fares

Fahrrad n [fahr-raht] bicycle

Fahrräder bicycles

Fahrradkarte f [fahr-rahtkart-uh] bicycle ticket

Fahrradverleih m [fahr-raht-fairlी] bicycles for hire/to rent

Fahrradweg m [fahr-raht-vayk] cycle path

Fahrschein m [fahr-shine] ticket

Fahrscheinkauf nur beim Fahrer buy your ticket from the driver

Fahrstuhl m [fahr-shtool] lift, elevator

Fahrt f journey

Fahrtziele destinations

Fahrzeug n [fahr-tsoyk] vehicle

Fall m [fal] fall; case

fallen [fal-en] to fall

fallenlassen [fal-en-lassen] to drop

falls [falss] if

falsch [falsh] wrong; false

falten to fold

Familie f [fameelee-yuh] family

Familienpackung f family pack

fand [fant], fanden found

fangen to catch

Farbe f [farb-uh] colour; paint

Farben und Lacke paints

Farbfilm m [farpfilm] colour film

Fasching m [fashing] annual carnival held in the pre-Lent period with fancy-dress processions and general celebrating

Fasse dich kurz! keep it brief!

fast [fasst] almost, nearly

faul [fowl] lazy; rotten

Feder f [fayder] feather; spring

Federbett n [fayderbett] quilt

Fehler m [fayler] mistake; defect

fehlerhaft [fayler-haft] faulty

Feierabend m [fy-erahbent] closing time; time to stop

Feiertag m [fy-ertahk] public holiday

Feinkostgeschäft n [fine-kost-gesheft] delicatessen

Feinschmecker m [fine-shmecker], Feinschmeckerin f gourmet

Feld n [felt] field

Felsen m [felzen] rock

Fenster n window

Fensterläden mpl [fenster-layden] shutters

Ferien fpl [fairee-en] holidays, vacation

Ferienwohnung f [fairee-en-vohnoong] holiday home

Ferngespräch n [fairn-geshpraysh] long-distance call

Fernlicht n [fairn-lisht] full beam

Fernschreiben n [fairn-shryben] telex

Fernsehen n [fairnzay-en] television

Fernsprecher m telephone

Ferse f [fairz-uh] heel

fertig [fairtish] ready; finished

fest fixed; firm; definite

festnehmen [festnaymen] to arrest

Fete f [fayt-uh] party

fett greasy

Fett n fat

Fettgehalt fat content

feucht [foysht] damp

Feuchtigkeitscreme f [foyshtish-kites-kraym] moisturizer; cold cream

Feuer n [foyer] fire

Feuergefahr f [foyer-gefahr] fire hazard

Feuerlöscher m [foyerlursher] fire extinguisher

Feuertreppe f [foyertrepp-uh] fire escape

Feuerwehr f [foyervair] fire

brigade

Feuerwehrausfahrt fire brigade exit

Feuerwerk n [foyervairk] fireworks

Feuerzeug n [foyer-tsoyk] lighter

Fieber n [feeber] fever

Filmmusik f [film-moozeek] soundtrack

Filzstift m [filts-shtift] felt-tip pen

finden [fin-den] to find

Fingernagel m [fing-er-nahgel] fingernail

Firma f [feermah] company

Fischgeschäft n [fish-gesheft] fishmonger's

FKK [ef-kah-kah] nudism

flach [flakH] flat

Flasche f [flash-uh] bottle

Flaschenöffner m [flashen-urfner] bottle-opener

Fleck m stain; spot

Fleischerei f [flysher-ī] butcher's

Fliege f [fleeg-uh] fly; bow tie

fliegen [fleegen] to fly

fließend [fleessent] fluent

Flitterwochen fpl [flittervoKHen] honeymoon

Flucht f [flooKHt] escape

flüchten [flOOshten] to escape

Flug m [flook] flight

Flugdauer f [flook-dower] flight time

Flügel m [floogel] wing

Fluggast m [flook-gast] air passenger

Fluggeschwindigkeit f [flook-geshwindish-kite] flight speed

Fluggesellschaft f [flook-gezellshafft] airline

Flughafen m [flook-hahfen] airport

Flughafenbus m [flook-hahfen-booss] airport bus

Flughöhe f [flook-hur-uh] altitude

Flugkarte f [flook-kart-uh] flight ticket

Fluglinie f [flook-leen-yuh] airline

Fluglotse m [flook-lohts-uh] air traffic controller

Flugplan m [flookplahn] timetable, (US) schedule

Flugsteig m [flook-shtike] gate

Flugzeug n [flook-tsoyk] (aero)plane

Flugzeugabsturz m [flooktsoyk-apshtoorts] plane crash

Flur m [floor] corridor

Fluss m [flooss] river

Flut f [floot] high tide

fl.W. (fließendes Wasser) running water

folgen [fol-gen] to follow

folgende [folgend-uh] next

Fön® m [furn] hair dryer

fönen: sich fönen lassen [zish furnen] to have a blow-dry

fordern to demand

Formular n [formoolahr] form

Foto n [foto] photo(graph)

Fotoartikel mpl [foto-arteekel] photographic equipment

Fotograf m [fotorahf] photographer

fotografieren [foto-grafeeren] to

photograph
Fotografin f [fotograhfin]
photographer
Fr. (Frau) Mrs; Ms
Frage f [frahg-uh] question
fragen [frahgen] to ask
Frankreich n [frank-rysh] France
Franzose m [frantsohz-uh]
Frenchman
Französin f [frantsurzin] French
girl; French woman
französisch [frantsurzish]
French
Frau f [frow] woman; wife;
Mrs; Ms
Frauenarzt m [frowen-artst]
gynaecologist
Fräulein n [froyline] Miss
frech [fresh] cheeky
frei [fry] free, vacant
frei von Konservierungsstoffen
contains no preservatives
**frei von künstlichen
Aromastoffen** contains no
artificial flavouring
Freibad n [frybaht] outdoor
swimming pool
freigegeben ab ... Jahren
suitable for those over ...
years of age
Freikörperkultur f [fry-kurper-
kooltoor] nudism
Freitag m [frytahk] Friday
freiwillig [fry-villish] voluntary;
voluntarily
Freizeichen n [fry-tsyshen]
ringing tone
Freizeit f [fry-tsite] spare time;
leisure

Freizeitzentrum n [fry-tsite-
tsentroom] leisure centre
fremd [fremt] strange; foreign
Fremde m/f [fremd-uh] stranger;
foreigner
Fremdenzimmer npl [fremden-
tsimmer] room(s) to let/rent
freuen: sich freuen [zish froyen]
to be happy
Freund m [froynt] friend;
boyfriend
Freundin f [froyndin] friend;
girlfriend
freundlich [froyntlish] kind;
friendly
freut mich! [froyt mish] pleased
to meet you!
Frieden m [freeden] peace
Friedhof m [freet-hohf]
cemetery
frisch [frish] fresh
frisch gestrichen wet paint
Frischhaltepackung f airtight
pack
Friseur m [frizzur] barber;
hairdresser
Frisur f [frizzoor] hairstyle
Frittenbude f [fritten-bood-uh]
chip shop
Frl. (Fräulein) Miss
froh glad
frohes neues Jahr [froh-ess noyess yahr] happy New Year!
frohe Weihnachten! [froh-uh
vynaкHten] happy Christmas!
Frostschaden m [frost-shahden]
frost damage
Frostschutzmittel n [frost-
shoots-mittel] antifreeze

früh [froo] early

Frühling m [frooling] spring

Frühstück n [frooshtoock] breakfast

frühstücken [frooshtoocken] to have breakfast

fühlen: (sich) fühlen [(zish) foolen] to feel

fuhr [foor], fuhren drove; went; travelled

führen [fooren] to lead
wir führen ... we stock ...

Führer m [foorer] guide; guidebook

Führerin f [foorerin] guide

Führerschein m [foorer-shine] driving licence

fuhrst [foorst] drove; went

Führung f [fooroong] guided tour

füllen [foollen] to fill

Fundbüro n [foont-booro] lost property office

fünf [foonf] five

fünfzehn [foonf-tsayn] fifteen

fünfzig [foonf-tsish] fifty

Fünfzigmarkschein m [foonftsish-mark-shine] fifty-mark note/bill

Funktaxi n [foonk-taksee] radio taxi

funktionieren [foonkts-yohneeren] to work

für [foor] for

Furcht f [foorsht] fear

furchtbar [foorshtbar] terrible

fürchten: sich fürchten [zish foorshten] to be afraid

fürs [foorss] for the

Fuß m [fooss] foot
zu Fuß on foot

Fußball m [foossbal] football

Fußballplatz m [foossbal-plats] football ground

Fußballstadion n [foossbal-shtahdee-on] football stadium

Fußgänger m [fooss-geng-er], Fußgängerin f pedestrian

Fußgänger bitte andere Straßenseite benutzen pedestrians please use other side of road

Fußgängerüberweg m [foossgeng-er-oobervayk] pedestrian crossing

Fußgängerzone f [foossgeng-er-tsohn-uh] pedestrian precinct

G

gab [gahp] gave

Gabel f [gahbel] fork; hook

gaben [gahben], gabst [gahpst] gave

gähnen [gaynen] to yawn

Gang m corridor; gear; walk; course

ganz [gants] whole; quite; very
den ganzen Tag all day
ganz gut [goot] pretty good

Garderobe f [garderohb-uh] cloakroom
für Garderobe wird nicht gehaftet the management accepts no liability for items left here

Garten m garden

Gaspedal n [gahss-pedahl] accelerator

Gast m guest

Gastarbeiter m [gast-arbyter], Gastarbeiterin f foreign worker

Gästebuch n [gest-uh-bookh] visitors' register

Gastfreundschaft f [gastfroynt-shafft] hospitality

Gastgeber m [gast-gayber] host

Gastgeberin f [gast-gayberin] hostess

Gasthaus n [gast-howss] inn

Gasthof m [gast-hohf] restaurant, inn

Gaststätte f [gast-shtett-uh] restaurant; pub; inn

Gastwirtschaft f [gast-veert-shafft] pub

geb. (geboren) born, née

Gebäude n [geboyd-uh] building

geben [gayben] to give

Gebiss n [gebiss] dentures

geblieben [gebleeben] stayed

geboren: geboren sein [gebohren zine] to be born

gebracht [gebrakht] brought

Gebrauch m [gebrowkh] use; custom

vor Gebrauch schütteln shake before using

gebrauchen [gebrowkhen] to use

Gebrauchsanleitung instructions for use

Gebrauchsanweisung beachten follow instructions

for use

gebraucht [gebrowkht] second-hand

gebrochen [gebrokhen] broken

gebt [gaypt] give

Gebühren fpl [gebooren] charges

gebührenpflichtig liable to charge

Geburt f [geboort] birth

Geburtsort m [geboorts-ort] place of birth

Geburtstag m [geboorts-tahk] birthday

Gedächtnis n [gedeshtnis] memory

Gedanke m [gedank-uh] thought

Gefahr f [gefahr] danger

gefahren travelled; gone; driven

gefährlich [gefairlish] dangerous

Gefährliche Einmündung dangerous junction; danger: concealed exit

Gefährliche Kurve dangerous bend

gefallen: das gefällt mir [dass gefellt meer] I like it

Gefangene m/f [gefangen-uh] prisoner

Gefängnis n [gefengniss] prison

Gefriertruhe f [gefreer-troo-uh] freezer

gefroren [gefrohren] frozen

Gefühl n [gefool] feeling

gefunden [gefoonden] found

gegangen [gegang-en] gone

gegeben [gegayben] given

gegen [gaygen] against

Gegenanzeige contra-
indications
Gegend f [gaygent] area
Gegenstand m [gaygenshtant]
object
Gegenteil n [gaygen-tile]
opposite
gegenüber [gaygen-oober]
opposite
Gegenverkehr hat Vorfahrt
oncoming traffic has right
of way
gegessen eaten
Gegner m [gaykner], Gegnerin f
opponent
gehabt [gehapt] had
geheim [gehime] secret
Geheimnis n [gehymnis] secret
Geheimzahl eingeben enter
personal number
gehen [gay-en] to go; to walk
geht das? is that OK?
das geht nicht that's not on
Gehirn n [geheern] brain
Gehirnerschütterung f [geheern-
airshootteroong] concussion
Gehör n [gehur] hearing
gehören [ge-hur-ren] to belong
(to)
Geisel f [gyzel] hostage
Geistlicher m [gystlisher] priest
gekommen come
gekonnt been able to; masterly
gekühlt haltbar bis ... if chilled
will keep until ...
gelassen relaxed; left
gelb [gelp] yellow
Gelbe Seiten [gelb-uh zyten]
yellow pages

Geld n [gelt] money
Geldautomat m [gelt-owtomaht]
cash dispenser, automatic
teller
Geld einwerfen insert money
Geldeinwurf insert money
Geldrückgabe returned coins
Geldschein m [geltshine]
banknote, (US) bill
Geldstrafe f [geltshtrahf-uh] fine
Geldwechsel m [geltveksel]
bureau de change
Gelegenheitskauf m [gelaygen-
hites-kowf] bargain
Gelenk n joint
Gemälde n [gemayld-uh]
painting
gemocht [gemoKHt] liked
Gemüsehändler m [gemooz-uh-
hentler] greengrocer
gemusst [gemoosst] had to
genau [genow] exact; exactly
Genf [genf] Geneva
genommen taken
genug [genook] enough
genug haben (von) to be fed
up (with)
geöffnet [guh-urfnet] open;
opened
geöffnet von ... bis ... open
from ... to ...
Gepäck n [gepeck] luggage,
baggage
Gepäckaufbewahrung f
[gepeck-owf-bevahroong] left
luggage, (US) baggage check
Gepäckausgabe f [gepeck-
owssgahb-uh] baggage claim
Gepäckkontrolle f [gepeck-

kontrol-uh] baggage check

Gepäckschließfach n [gepeck-shleessfakH] luggage locker

Gepäckträger m [gepeck-trayger] porter

gepflegt [gepflaykt] well looked after; refined

gerade [gerahd-uh] just; straight

geradeaus [gerahd-uh-owss] straight on

Gerät n [gerayt] device

gerecht [geresht] fair

Gericht n [gerisht] court; dish

gern(e) [gairn(uh)] gladly
etwas gern(e) tun to like doing something

Geruch m [gerOOKH] smell

Gesamtpreis m [gezamt-price] total

Geschäft n [gesheft] shop; business

Geschäftsfrau f [gesheftsfrow] businesswoman

Geschäftsführer m [gesheftsfOOrer] manager

Geschäftsführerin f [gesheftsfOOrerin] manageress

Geschäftsmann m [gesheftsmann] businessman

Geschäftsreise f [geshefts-rize-uh] business trip

Geschäftszeiten hours of business

geschehen [geshay-en] to happen

Geschenk n [geshenk] present, gift

Geschenkartikel gifts

Geschichte f [geshisht-uh] story; history

geschieden [gesheeden] divorced

Geschirr n [gesheerr] crockery

Geschirrtuch n [gesheerr-tOOKH] tea towel

Geschlecht n [geshlesht] sex

Geschlechtskrankheit f [geshleshts-krank-hite] VD

geschlossen closed

geschlossen von ... bis ... closed from ... to ...

Geschmack m [geshmack] taste; flavour

geschrieben [geshreeben] written

Geschwindigkeit f [geshvindish-kite] speed

Geschwindigkeitsbeschränkung f [geshvindish-kites-beshrenkoong] speed limit

Geschwindigkeitsbeschränkung beachten observe speed limit

geschwollen [geshvollen] swollen

gesehen [gezay-en] seen

Gesellschaft f [gezellshafft] society; company

Gesetz n [gezets] law

Gesicht n [gezisht] face

Gesichtscreme f [gezishts-kraym] face cream

gesperrt closed; no entry

Gesperrt für Fahrzeuge aller Art closed to all vehicles

Gespräch n [geshpraysh] call; conversation

Gestalt f [geshtalt] figure
gestattet [geshtattet] allowed
gestern [gestern] yesterday
gestorben [geshtorben] died
gesund [gezoont] healthy
Gesundheit f [gezoont-hite] health
Gesundheit! bless you!
getan [getahn] done
Getränkekarte f [getrenk-uh-kart-uh] drinks list
getrennt [getrennt] separate; separately
Getriebe n [getreeb-uh] gearbox
getrunken [getroonken] drunk
Gewehr n [gevair] gun
gewesen [gevayzen] been
Gewicht n [gevisht] weight
Gewichtsverlust durch Erhitzen weight loss through heating
Gewinn m [gevinn] prize; profit
gewinnen [gevinnen] to win
Gewitter n [gevitter] thunderstorm
Gewohnheit f [gevohnhite] habit
gewöhnlich [gevurnlish] usual; usually
geworden [gevorden] become
gewünschten Betrag wählen select required amount
gewünschte Rufnummer wählen dial number required
gewusst [gevoosst] known
Gezeiten [getsyten] tides
gibst [geepst] give
gibt [geept] gives
gibt es ...? is/are there ...?
es gibt ... there is/are ...

Gift n poison
giftig [giftish] poisonous
ging, gingen [ging-en], gingst went
Gips m plaster (of Paris)
Gipsverband m [gips-fairbant] plastercast
Girokonto n [Jeero-konto] current account
Giroverkehr m [Jeero-fairkair] giro transactions
Gitarre f [gitarr-uh] guitar
Glas n [glahss] glass
glatt slippery; smooth
Glatteis n [glatt-ice] black ice
Glatteisgefahr black ice
Glatze f [glats-uh] bald head
glauben [glowben] to believe
gleich [glysh] equal; same; in a moment
Gleis n [glice] platform, (US) track
zu den Gleisen to the platforms/tracks
Glocke f [glock-uh] bell
Glück n [glOOck] luck; happiness
zum Glück [tsoom] fortunately
glücklich [glOOcklish] lucky; happy
Glücksbringer m [glOOcks-bring-er] lucky charm
Glühbirne f [glOObeern-uh] light bulb
GmbH (Gesellschaft mit beschränkter Haftung) [gay-em-bay-hah] Ltd, limited company
Gott n God
Gottesdienst m [gottes-deenst]

church service; mass

Grab n [grahp] grave

Grammatik f grammar

Gras n [grahss] grass

gratis [grahtiss] free

grau [grow] grey

grausam [growzahm] cruel

Grenze f [grents-uh] border

Grenzkontrolle f [grents-kontroll-uh] border checkpoint

Griechenland n [greeshenlant] Greece

griechisch [greeshish] Greek

Griff m handle

grinsen [grinzen] to grin

Grippe f [gripp-uh] flu

Groschen m [groshen] 10 pfennig piece

groß [grohss] big, large; tall

Großbritannien n [grohss-britannee-en] Great Britain

Größe f [grurss-uh] size

Großmutter f [grohss-mootter] grandmother

Großpackung f [grohss-packoong] large size

Großvater m [grohss-fahter] grandfather

grün [grOOn] green

der grüne Punkt suitable for recycling

Grund m [groont] cause

Grundierungscreme f [groondeeroongs-kraym] foundation cream

Grundschule f [groont-shOOl-uh] primary school

Gruppe f [groopp-uh] group; party

Gruppenreise f [grooppen-rize-uh] group excursion

Gruss m [grOOss] greeting

schöne Grüße an ... [shurn-uh grOOss-uh] give my regards to ...

grüßen [grOOssen] to greet; to say hello to

grüß Gott [grOOss] hello (South German)

gültig [gOOltish] valid

Gummi n [goommee] rubber

Gummiband n [goommeebant] rubber band

günstig [gOOnstish] favourable; convenient; inexpensive

Gürtel m [gOOrtel] belt

gut [gOOt] good; well

gutaussehend [gOOt-owss-zay-ent] handsome; good-looking

gute Besserung! [gOOt-uh besseroong] get well soon!

guten Abend [gOOten ahbent] good evening

gute Nacht [gOOt-uh naKHt] good night

guten Appetit! [gOOten appeteet] enjoy your meal!

guten Morgen [gOOten] good morning

guten Tag [gOOten tahk] hello

guten Tag, freut mich [gOOten tahk froyt mish] how do you do, nice to meet you

gute Reise [gOOt-uh rize-uh] have a good trip

Güterzug m [gOOter-tsOOk] goods train

gutmütig [gOOtmOOtish] good-natured

Gutschein m [goot-shine] voucher

Gymnasium n [goom-nah-zee-oom] secondary school

H

H (Haltestelle) bus/tram stop

Haar n [hahr] hair

Haarfestiger m [hahrfestiger] conditioner

Haarschnitt m [hahrshnitt] haircut

Haarstudio n [hahr-shtoodee-oh] hairdressing studio

haben [hahben] to have

Hafen m [hahfen] harbour, port

Hafenpolizei f [hahfen-polits-ī] harbour police

Hafenrundfahrt f [hahfen-roontfahrt] boat trip round the harbour

Haft f custody

Häftling m [heftling] prisoner

Hagel m [hahgel] hail

Haken m [hahken] hook

halb [halp] half

halbe Stunde f [halb-uh shtoond-uh] half an hour

Halbpension f [halp-pangz-yohn] half board

Hälfte f [helft-uh] half

Hallenbad n [hallenbaht] indoor swimming pool

Hals n [halss] neck

Halskette f [halsskett-uh] necklace

Hals-Nasen-Ohren-Arzt m [halss-nahzen-ohren-artst] ear, nose and throat specialist

Halsschmerzen [halss-shmairtsen] sore throat

Halstabletten fpl [halss-tabletten] throat pastilles

halt! [hallt] stop!

Haltbar bis ... best before ...

Haltbarkeitsdatum best before date

Halte deine Stadt sauber keep your city clean

halten to hold; to stop

Haltestelle f [hallt-uh-shtell-uh] stop

Halteverbot no stopping; no waiting

hält nicht in ... does not stop in ...

Handarbeit f [hant-arbite] needlework

Handbremse f [hantbremz-uh] handbrake

Handel m deal; commerce

Handelsgesellschaft f (trading) company

Handelsbank f merchant bank

Handgelenk n [hant-gelenk] wrist

Handgepäck n [hant-gepeck] hand luggage/baggage

Handlung f [hantloong] shop; action

Handschuhe mpl [hant-shoo-uh] gloves

Handtasche f [hant-tash-uh] handbag, (US) purse

Handtuch n [hant-tooKH] towel

Handwerk n [hantvairk] crafts

Handzettel m [hant-tsettel] leaflet

Hansaplast® n [hanzaplast] Elastoplast®, (US) Band-Aid

hart hard

Hase m [hahz-uh] hare; rabbit

Hass m hatred

hassen to hate

hässlich [hesslish] ugly

hast have

hat has

hatte [hatt-uh] had

hätte [hett-uh] would have; had

hatten, hattest had

Haupt- [howpt] main

Hauptbahnhof m [howpt bahnhohf] central station

Hauptpost f [howpt-posst] main post office

Hauptprogramm n [howpt-programm] main feature

Hauptsaison f [howpt-zaysong] high season

Hauptstraße f [howpt-shtrahss-uh] main road; high street

Haus n [howss] house
zu Hause [tsoo howz-uh] at home
nach Hause gehen [naKH – gay-en] to go home

Haushaltsgeräte npl [howss-hallts-gerayt-uh] household equipment

Haushaltwaren [howss-hallt-vahren] household goods

Hausmeister m [howss-myster] caretaker, janitor

Hausnummer f [howss-noommer] street number

Hausordnung f [howss-ortnoong] house rules

Hausschuhe [howss-shoo-uh] slippers

Haustier n [howsteer] pet

Hauswirt m [howssveert] landlord

Hauswirtin f [howss-veertin] landlady

Haut f [howt] skin

Hautreiniger m [howt-ryniger] skin cleanser

Hbf (Hauptbahnhof) central station

Heft n exercise book

Heftzwecke f [heft-tsveck-uh] drawing pin

Heißlufttrockner m [hice-looft-trockner] hot-air hand-drier

heilen [hylen] to cure

Heiligabend m [hylish-ahbent] Christmas Eve

Heimwerkerbedarf DIY supplies

Heirat f [hyraht] marriage

heiraten [hyrahten] to get married

heiß [hice] hot

heißen [hyssen] to be called
wie heißen Sie? [vee] what's your name?

Heißwachs m [hice-vaks] hot wax

Heizdecke f [hites-deck-uh] electric blanket

Heizgerät n [hites-gerayt] heater

Heizung f [hytsoong] heating

helfen to help

hell light; bright

Hemd n [hemt] shirt

herabgesetzt reduced

zu stark herabgesetzten Preisen prices slashed

Herbergsmutter f [hairbairks-mootter] warden

Herbergsvater m [hairbairks-fahter] warden

Herbst m [hairpst] autumn, (US) fall

herein! [hair-ine] come in!

hergestellt in ... made in ...

Herr m [hair] Mr; gentleman

Herren gents' (toilet), men's room

Herrenkleidung f [hairen-klydoong] menswear

Herrenmoden men's fashions

Herrensalon m [hairen-zalong] men's hairdresser

Herrentoilette f [hairen-twalett-uh] gents' (toilet), men's room

herrlich [hairlish] lovely

Hersteller m manufacturer

Herz n [hairts] heart

Herzinfarkt m [hairts-infarkt] heart attack

herzlich willkommen [hairtslish villkommen] welcome

herzlichen Glückwunsch! [hairtslishen glOOckvoonsh] congratulations!; happy birthday!; happy anniversary!

Heufieber n [hoyfeeber] hay fever

heute [hoyt-uh] today

heute abend [ahbent] tonight

heute geschlossen closed today

hier [heer] here

hier abreißen tear off here

hier abschneiden cut off here

hier einreißen tear off here

hier einsteigen enter here

hierher [heerhair] here

hierhin here

hier öffnen open here

hier Parkschein lösen buy parking permit here

Hilfe f [hilf-uh] help

Himmel m sky; heaven

hinlegen: sich hinlegen [zish hinlaygen] to lie down

hinsichtlich [hinzishtlish] with regard to

hinten at the back

hinter behind

Hintergrund m [hintergroont] background

Hinterhof m [hinterhohf] back yard

Hintern m bottom

Hinterrad n [hinter-raht] back wheel

Hirsch m [heersh] stag

Hitzewelle f [hits-uh-vell-uh] heat wave

hoch [hohKH] high

Hochschule f [hohKH-shOOl-uh] college; university

höchste [hurkst-uh] highest

Höchstgeschwindigkeit maximum speed

Hochzeit f [hoKH-tsite] wedding

Hochzeitstag m [hoKH-tsites-tahk] wedding anniversary

hoffen to hope

hoffentlich [hoffentlish]

hopefully

Hoffnung f [hoffnoong] hope

höflich [hurflish] polite

Höhe f [hur-uh] height

höher [hur-er] higher

höhere Schule f [hurer-uh shool-uh] secondary school

Höhle f [hurl-uh] cave

holen [hohlen] to fetch, to get

holländisch [hollendish] Dutch

Holz n [holts] wood

hören [hur-ren] to hear

Hörer m [hur-rer] receiver; listener

Hörer abnehmen lift receiver

Hörer einhängen replace receiver

Hörerin f [hur-rerin] listener

Hörgerat n [hur-gerayt] hearing aid

Höschen n [hurss-shen] panties

Hose f [hohz-uh] trousers, (US) pants

Hr. (Herr) Mr

hübsch [hoopsh] pretty

Hubschrauber m [hoop-shrowber] helicopter

Hüfte f [hooft-uh] hip

Hügel m [hoogel] hill

Hund m [hoont] dog

Hunde bitte anleinen dogs must be kept on a lead

hundert [hoondert] hundred

Hundertmarkschein m [hoondert-mark-shine] hundred-mark note/bill

Hunde sind an der Leine zu führen dogs must be kept on a lead

Hunger: Hunger haben [hoong-er hahben] to be hungry

Hupe f [hoop-uh] horn

Hupen verboten sounding horn forbidden

Husten m [hoosten] cough

Hut f [hoot] hat

Hypothek f [hoopotayk] mortgage

I

i.A. (im Auftrag) pp

ich [ish] I; me

Idee f [eeday] idea

i.d.T. (in der Trockenmasse) dry measure

ihm [eem] him; to him

ihn [een] him

ihnen them; to them

Ihnen [eenen] you; to you

ihr [eer] you; her; to her; their

Ihr [eer] your

ihre [eer-uh] her; their

Ihre [eer-uh] your

Illustrierte f [illoostreert-uh] magazine

im in (the)

immer always

Immobilienmakler m [immobeel-yen-mahkler] estate agent

Impfung f [impfoong] vaccination

indem [indaym] as; by

Industriegebiet n [indoostree-gebeet] industrial zone

infolge [in-folg-uh] as a result of

Infopostsendung f [info-posst-zendoong] printed matter

Informationsschalter m
[informats-**yoh**ns-shalter]
information desk

Inh. (Inhaber) proprietor

Inhalt contents

Initialen fpl [inits-**yah**len] initials

Inland domestic

Inlandsflüge domestic flights

Inlandsgespräch n [inlants-
gespraysh] inland call

Inlandsporto n [inlants-porto]
inland postage

innen (im/in) inside

innerhalb [**inn**er-halp] within

ins into the; to the

Insektenschutzmittel n
[inzekten-shoots-mittel] insect
repellent

Insel f [**inzel**] island

insgesamt altogether

Installateur m [inshtala**tur**]
plumber

Intensivstation f [intenzeef-
shtats-**yoh**n] intensive care unit

interessant interesting

Interesse n [interess-uh] interest

irgend etwas [**eer**gent etvass]
something; anything

irgend jemand [**eer**gent **yay**mant]
somebody; anybody

irgendwo [**eer**gent-vo]
somewhere

irisch [**eer**ish] Irish

isst eat; eats

ist is

Italien n [i**tah**lee-en] Italy

italienisch [ital-**yay**nish] Italian

J

ja [yah] yes

Jacht f [yaκHt] yacht

Jachthafen m [yaκHt-hahfen]
marina

Jacke f [yack-uh] jacket;
cardigan

Jahr n [yahr] year

Jahreszeit f [**yah**ress-tsite]
season

Jahrhundert n [yahr-**hoo**ndert]
century

Jahrmarkt m [**yahr**markt] fair

Jalousie f [Jal**oo**zee] Venetian
blind

Jausenstation f [**yow**zen-shtats-
yohn] snack bar

je [yay] ever

jede [**yay**d-uh] each; every

jeden Tag [**yay**den tahk] every
day

jeder [**yay**der] everyone; each

jedes [**yay**dess] each

jedesmal [**yay**dessmahl] every
time

je ... desto ... [yay **des**to] the ...
the ...

jemals [**yay**mahlss] ever

jemand [**yay**mant] somebody

jenseits [**yay**n-zites] on the
other side (of); beyond

jetzt [yetst] now

JH (Jugendherberge) youth
hostel

joggen: joggen gehen [dJoggen
gay-en] to go jogging

Jucken n [**yoo**cken] itch

jüdisch [y00dish] Jewish

Jugendherberge f [y00gent-hairbairg-uh] youth hostel

Jugendklub m [y00gent-kloop] youth club

Jugendliche: für Jugendliche ab ... Jahren for young people over the age of ...

Juli m [y00lee] July

jung [yoong] young

Junge m [yoong-uh] boy

junge Leute [yoong-uh loyt-uh] young people

Junge Mode fashions for the young

Junggeselle m [yoong-gezell-uh] bachelor

Juni m [y00nee] June

Juwel m [yoovayl] jewel

Juwelier m [yoov-uh-leer] jeweller's

K

Kabel n [kahbel] cable

Kabine f [kabeen-uh] cabin

Kaffeefilter m [kaffay-filter] coffee filter

Kaffeehaus n [kaffay-howss] café

kahl bald

Kai m [ki] quay

Kalender m calendar; diary

kalt cold

kam [kahm], kamen came

Kamin m [kameen] chimney; fireplace

Kamm m comb

Kampf m fight

kämpfen [kempfen] to fight

kamst [kahmst] came

Kanadier m [kanahdee-er], Kanadierin f Canadian

kanadisch [kanahdish] Canadian

Kanal m [kanahl] canal; Channel

Kaninchen n [kaneenshen] rabbit

kann can

Kännchen n [kennshen] pot

Kanne f [kann-uh] (tea/coffee) pot

kannst can

Kanu n [kahn00] canoe

Kapitän m [kapitayn] captain

Kappe f [kapp-uh] cap

kaputt [kap00tt] broken

Karfreitag m [karfrytahk] Good Friday

Karneval m [karn-uh-val] annual carnival held in the pre-Lent period with fancy-dress processions and general celebrating

Karte f [kart-uh] card; ticket

Karten tickets

Kartenleser m [karten-layzer] card reader

Kartenspiel n [kartenshpeel] card game

Kartentelefon n [karten-telefohn] cardphone

Kasse f [kass-uh] cashdesk, till, cashier; box office

Katalysator m [katal00zahtohr] catalytic converter

Kater m [kahter] hangover;

tomcat

kath. (katholisch) Catholic

Katze f [kats-uh] cat

kaufen [kowfen] to buy

Kaufhaus n [kowfhowss] department store

kaum [kowm] hardly

Kaution f [kowts-yohn] deposit

Kehle f [kayl-uh] throat

Keilriemen m [kile-reemen] fan belt

kein(e) ... [kine(-uh)] no ...; not ...

keine Ahnung [kine-uh ahnoong] no idea

ich habe keine [ish hahb-uh kine-uh] I don't have any

keine ... mehr [kine-uh mair] no more ...

kein ... mehr [kine mair] no more ...

kein Ausstieg no exit

keine heiße Asche einfüllen do not put hot ashes in this container

kein Einstieg no entry

keine Selbstbedienung no self-service

keine Zufahrt no entry

kein Trinkwasser not drinking water

kein Verkauf an Jugendliche unter ... Jahren sales forbidden to minors under the age of ...

kein Zugang no entry

kein Zutritt no admittance; no entrance

kein Zutritt fur Jugendliche

unter ... Jahren no admission to minors under the age of ...

Keller m cellar

Kellner m waiter

Kellnerin f waitress

kennen to know

Keramik f [kairahmik] china

Kerze f [kairts-uh] candle

Kette f [kett-uh] chain

Keuchhusten m [koysh-hoosten] whooping cough

Kiefer m [keefer] jaw; pine

Kind n [kint] child

Kinder npl children

für Kinder ab ... Jahren for children from the age of ...

Kinderarzt m [kinder-artst], **Kinderärztin f** pediatrician

Kinderbett n cot

Kinderkleidung f [kinder-klydoong] children's clothing

Kindermoden children's fashions

Kindersitz m [kinder-zits] child seat

Kinderspielplatz m [kinder-shpeelplats] children's playground

Kindervorstellung f [kinder-forshtelloong] children's performance

Kinderwagen m [kindervahgen] pram

Kinn n chin

Kino n [keeno] cinema, movie theater

Kinocenter n [keeno-senter] multiplex cinema/movie

theater
Kirche f [**keersh**-uh] church
Klang m sound
klar clear; OK, sure
Klasse f [**klass**-uh] class
klebrig [**klaybrish**] sticky
Kleid n [klite] dress
Kleider [**klyder**] clothes
Kleiderbügel m [**klyder**-b00gel] (coat)hanger
klein [kline] small
Kleinbus m [kl**ine**-booss] van
Kleingeld n [kl**ine**-gelt] change
Klempner m plumber
Klima n [**klee**mah] climate
Klimaanlage f [**klee**mah-anlahg-uh] air-conditioning
klimatisiert [klimatee**zeert**] air-conditioned
Klingel f bell
klingeln to ring
Klippe f [**klipp**-uh] cliff
Klo n [kloh] loo
Kloster n [**kloh**ster] convent; monastery
klug [kl00k] clever
Kneipe f [k-**nipe**-uh] pub, bar
Knie n [k-nee] knee
Knöchel m [k-**nursh**el] ankle
Knochen m [k-**no**KHen] bone
Knopf m [k-nopf] button
Knoten m [k-**noh**ten] knot
Koch m [koKH] cook
Kochgeschirr n [ko**KH**-gesh**eerr**] cooking utensils
Köchin f [**kursh**in] cook
Kochnische f [ko**KH**neesh-uh] kitchenette
Kochtopf m [**ko**KHtopf] saucepan

Koffer m bag; suitcase
Kofferkuli m [**koffer**00lee] luggage/baggage trolley
Kofferraum m [**koffer**-rowm] boot, (US) trunk
Kohle f [**kohl**-uh] coal
Kollege m [koll**ayg**-uh], **Kollegin** f colleague
Köln [kurln] Cologne
Kölnisch Wasser [**kur**lnish **vasser**] eau de Cologne
komisch [**koh**mish] funny
kommen to come
das kommt darauf an [**dah**rowf] it depends
Komödie f [kom**urdee**-uh] comedy
kompliziert [komplits**eert**] complicated
Konditorei f [kondeetor-**ī**] cake shop
Kondom n [kond**ohm**] condom
König m [**kur**nish] king
Königin f [**kur**nigin] queen
Konkurrenz f [konkoo**rents**] competition
können [**kur**nen] to be able to; can
können Sie ...? [zee] can you ...?
könnte [**kurnt**-uh], **könnten**, **könntest** could
konnte [**konnt**-uh], **konnten**, **konntest** could
Konservierungsstoffe preservatives
Konsulat n [konz00**laht**] consulate
Kontaktlinsen fpl [kont**akt**-linzen]

Ko

contact lenses
Konto n account
Kontrolle f [kontrol-uh] control
kontrollieren [kontrolleeren] to control
Konzert n [kontsairt] concert
Kopf m head
Kopfkissen n pillow
Kopfschmerzmittel n [kopfshmairts-mittel] aspirin
Kopfstütze f [kopf-shtoots-uh] headrest
Kopftuch n [kopftooKH] scarf
Kopfweh n [kopf-vay] headache
Kopie f [kopee] copy
kopieren [kopeeren] to copy
Korb m [korp] basket
Korkenzieher m [korken-tsee-er] corkscrew
Körper m [kurper] body
Körperpuder m [kurper-pooder] talcum powder
Kosmetika npl [kosmaytikah] cosmetics
kostbar [kost-bar] precious
kosten to cost
kostenlos [kosten-lohss] free of charge
köstlich [kurstlish] delicious
Kostüm n [kostoom] ladies' suit
Kragen m [krahgen] collar
Krampf m cramp
krank ill, sick
Kranke m/f [krank-uh] sick person
Krankenhaus n [kranken-howss] hospital
Krankenkasse f [krankenkass-uh] medical insurance

Krankenpfleger m [kranken-pflayger] male nurse
Krankenschein m [kranken-shine] health insurance certificate
Krankenschein nicht vergessen don't forget your health insurance certificate
Krankenschwester f [kranken-shvester] nurse
Krankenwagen m [krankenvahgen] ambulance
Krankheit f [krank-hite] disease
Krawatte f [kravatt-uh] tie, necktie
Krebs m [krayps] cancer
Kreditabteilung accounts department
Kredite [kraydeet-uh] loans
Kreditkarte f [kraydeetkart-uh] credit card
Kreis m [krice] circle
Kreisverkehr m [krice-fairkair] roundabout
Kreuz n [kroyts] cross
Kreuzfahrt f [kroytsfahrt] cruise
Kreuzung f [kroytsoong] junction; crossroads, intersection
Kreuzworträtsel n [kroytsvort-raytsel] crossword puzzle
Kriechspur crawler lane
Krieg m [kreek] war
kriegen [kreegen] to get
Krücken fpl [krooken] crutches
Krug m [krook] jug
Küche f [koosh-uh] cooking, cuisine; kitchen
Küchenbedarf for the kitchen

Kugel f [koogel] ball

Kugelschreiber m [koogel-shryber] biro®

Kuh f [koo] cow

kühl [kool] cool

Kühler m [kooler] radiator (on car)

kühl lagern keep in a cool place

Kühlschrank m [kool-shrank] fridge

kühl servieren serve chilled

Kultur f [kooltoor] culture

Kulturbeutel m [kooltoor-boytel] toilet bag

Kumpel m [koompel] pal

Kunde m [koond-uh], Kundin f customer

Der Kunde ist König the customer is always right

Kundenparkplatz customer car park/parking lot

Kunst f [koonst] art

Kunstgalerie f [koonst-galeree] art gallery

Kunsthalle f [koonst-hal-uh] art gallery

Künstler m [koonstler], Künstlerin f artist

künstlich [koonstlish] artificial

Kupplung f [kooploong] clutch

Kurbelwelle f [koorbel-vell-uh] crankshaft

Kurort m [koor-ort] spa

Kurs m [koorss] rate; exchange rate; course

Kurswagen m [koors-vahgen] through coach

Kurve f [koorv-uh] bend

Kurvenreiche Strecke bends

kurz [koorts] short

kurz nach [naкн] just after

kurz vor [for] just before

kurzsichtig [koorts-zishtish] shortsighted

Kurzstrecke f [koorts-shtreck-uh] short journey

Kurzwaren fpl [koortsvahren] haberdashery

Kusine f [koozeen-uh] cousin

Kuss m [kooss] kiss

küssen [koossen] to kiss

Küste f [koost-uh] coast

Küstenwacht f [koosten-vaкнt] coastguard

L

l (Liter) litre

Labor n [labohr] laboratory

lächeln [lesheln] to smile

Lächeln n smile

lachen [laкнen] to laugh

lächerlich [lesherlish] ridiculous

Laden m [lahden] shop

Ladenstraße f [lahdenshtrahss-uh] shopping street

Laken n [lahken] sheet

Lampe f [lamp-uh] lamp

Land n [lant] country

landen to land

Länder npl [lender] administrative districts of Germany, each with its own parliament

Landeskennzahl f [landess-kenntsahl] country dialling code

Landkarte f [**lant**kart-uh] map
Landschaft f [**lant**shafft]
countryside; landscape;
scenery
Landstraße f [lant-**shtrahss**-uh]
country road
Landtag m [lant-tahk] regional
parliament
Land- und forstwirtschaftlicher
Verkehr frei agricultural and
forestry vehicles only
lang long
lange [lang-uh] for a long time
Länge f [leng-uh] length
langsam [langzahm] slow;
slowly
Langsam fahren drive slowly
langweilig [langvile-ish] boring
Lärm m [lairm] noise
lassen to let; to leave
lässig [lessish] relaxed
Laster m lorry, truck
Lastwagen m [lasst-vahgen]
lorry, truck
Latzhose f [lats-hohz-uh]
dungarees
laufen [lowfen] to run
Läufer m [loyfer] runner; rug
laut [lowt] loud; noisy
lauwarm [low-varm] lukewarm
Lawine f [laveen-uh] avalanche
Lawinengefahr danger of
avalanches
Leben n [layben] life
leben to live
lebendig [lebendish] alive
Lebensgefahr f [laybens-gefahr]
danger
Lebenshaltungskosten pl

[laybens-haltoongs-kosten] cost
of living
Lebenslauf m [laybens-lowf]
CV, résumé
Lebensmittel npl [laybens-mittel]
groceries
Lebensmittelhandlung f
[laybensmittel-hantloong] grocer's
Lebensmittelvergiftung f
[laybensmittel-fairgiftoong] food
poisoning
Leber f [layber] liver
Leck n leak
lecker tasty
Leder n [layder] leather
Lederwaren leather goods
ledig [laydish] single
leer [lair] empty
Leerung f [lairoong] collection
Nächste Leerung next
collection
legen [laygen] to put
Lehrer m [lairer], **Lehrerin f**
teacher; instructor
leicht [lysht] easy; light
leicht verderblich will not
keep, perishable
leiden [lyden] to suffer
leider [lyder] unfortunately
leid: tut mir leid [toot meer lite]
I'm sorry
leihen [ly-en] to borrow; to
lend
Leihgebühr f [ly-geboor] rental
Leim m [lime] glue
Leiter f [lyter] ladder
Leiter m, Leiterin f leader;
manager
Lenkrad n [lenkraht] steering

wheel
Lenkung f [lenkoong] steering
lernen [lairnen] to learn
lesen [layzen] to read
Leser m [layzer], **Leserin f** reader
letzte(r,s) [letst-uh, -er, -ess] last
Leute pl [loyt-uh] people
Licht n [lisht] light
Licht einschalten turn on lights
Lichtspiele cinema, movie theater
Lidschatten m [leet-shatten] eye shadow
Liebe f [leeb-uh] love
lieben [leeben] to love
lieber [leeber] rather
Liebhaber m [leep-hahber], **Liebhaberin f** lover
Lieblings- [leeplings] favourite
Lied n [leet] song
Lieferant m [leeferant] supplier
liefern to deliver
liegen [leegen] to lie; to be situated
Liegestuhl f [leeg-uh-shtool] deckchair
Liegewagen f [leeg-uh-vahgen] couchette
lila [leelah] purple
Limousine f [limoozeen-uh] saloon car
Linie f [leen-yuh] line; airline
Linienflug m [leen-yen-flook] scheduled flight
links left
links (von) [fon] on the left (of)
Linksabbieger left filter

Links halten keep left
linkshändig [links-hendish] left-handed
Linse f [linz-uh] lens
Lippe f [lipp-uh] lip
Lippenstift m [lippen-shtift] lipstick
Liste f [list-uh] list
Lkw m [el-kah-vay] lorry, truck; heavy goods vehicle, HGV
Loch n [lokh] hole
Locke f [lock-uh] curl
Lockenwickler m [locken-vickler] curler
Löffel m [lurfel] spoon
los [lohss] loose
los! come on!
was ist los? what's up?
Löwe m [lurv-uh] lion
Lücke f [lÜck-uh] gap
Luft f [looft] air
luftdicht verpackt airtight pack
Luftdruck m [looft-droock] air pressure
Luftkissenboot n [looftkissen-boht] hovercraft
Luftpost: per Luftpost [pair looftposst] by airmail
Luftpostsendungen airmail
lügen [lÜgen] to lie
Lunge f [loong-uh] lung
Lungenentzündung f [loongen-ent-tsÜndoong] pneumonia
Lust haben auf [loost hahben owf] to feel like
Luxus m [looksoos] luxury

M

machen [maĸHen] to make; to do

mach schon! [maĸH shohn] get on with it!

mach's gut [goot] take care

Mädchen n [mayt-shen] girl

Mädchenname m [mayt-shen-nahm-uh] maiden name

mag [mahk] like; likes; may

Magen m [mahgen] stomach

Magenschmerzen mpl [mahgen-shmairtsen] stomach ache

Magenverstimmung f [mahgen-fairshtimmoong] indigestion

magst [mahkst] like

Mahlzeit f [mahl-tsite] meal

nach den Mahlzeiten einzunehmen to be taken after meals

vor den Mahlzeiten einzunehmen to be taken before meals

Mai m [my] May

Mal n [mahl] time

zum ersten Mal [tsoom airsten] for the first time

malen [mahlen] to paint

man one; you

man spricht Englisch English spoken

manchmal [manshmahl] sometimes

Mandelentzündung f [mandel-ent-tsoondoong] tonsillitis

Mandeln fpl tonsils

Mangel m shortage

Mann m man; husband

Mann! boy!

männlich [mennlish] male

Mannschaft f [mannshafft] team; crew

Mantel m coat

Markt m market

Markthalle f [markt-hal-uh] indoor market

März m [mairts] March

Masern [mahzern] measles

Massenmedien npl [massen-mayd-yen] mass media

Matratze f [matrats-uh] mattress

Mauer f [mower] wall

Maus f [mowss] mouse

maximale Belastbarkeit maximum load

Mechaniker m [meshahneeker] mechanic

Medikament n medicine

Meer n [mair] sea

mehr [mair] more

mehrere [mairer-uh] several

Mehrfachstecker m [mairfaĸH-shtecker] adaptor

Mehrfahrtenkarte f [mairfahrten-kart-uh] multi-journey ticket

Mehrheit f [mairhite] majority

Mehrwertsteuer f [mairvairt-shtoyer] Value Added Tax, VAT

mein [mine], meine [mine-uh] my

Meinung f [mynoong] opinion

meiste: das meiste (von) [myst-uh (fon)] most (of)

Melone f [melohn-uh] melon; bowler hat

Menge f [meng-uh] crowd

Mensch m [mensh] person

Mensch! wow!

Menschen people

menschlich [menshlish] human

Messe f [mess-uh] (trade) fair

Messegelände n [messuh-gelenduh] fair (site)

Messer n knife

Meter m [mayter] metre

Metzger m [metsger] butcher

Metzgerei f [metsger-ī] butcher's

mich [mish] me

Mietauto n [meet-owto] hire car, rental car

Miete f [meet-uh] rent

mieten [meeten] to rent

Mietkauf m [meetkowf] lease purchase

Militärisches Sperrgebiet keep off: military zone

Milliardär m [mill-yardair], Milliardärin f billionaire

Millionär m [mill-yonair], Millionärin f millionaire

min. (Minute) minute

Minderheit f [minderhite] minority

Mindestens haltbar bis ... will keep at least until ...

mindestens at least

Mineralölsteuer f [minerahl-url-shtoyer] oil tax

Minirock m miniskirt

mir [meer] me; to me

mir geht's gut [gayts goot] I'm OK

Mischung f [mishoong] mixture

Missbrauch strafbar penalty for misuse

Missgeschick n [miss-geshick] mishap

Missverständnis n [miss-fairshtentnis] misunderstanding

Mist! bugger!, shit!

Miststück n [mist-shtoock] bitch

mit with

Mitbringen von Hunden nicht gestattet no dogs allowed

Mitfahrzentrale f [mitfahr-tsentrahl-uh] agency for arranging lifts

Mitleid n [mit-lite] pity

mitnehmen [mit-naymen] to take; to give a lift to

zum Mitnehmen to take away, (US) to go

Mittag m [mittahk] midday

Mittagessen n [mittahk-essen] lunch

mittags [mittahks] at midday

mittags geschlossen closed at lunchtime

Mitte f [mitt-uh] middle

Mitteilung f [mit-tyloong] message

Mittel n means

Mittelalter n [mittel-alter] Middle Ages

mittelgroß [mittel-grohss] medium-sized

Mittelmeer n [mittel-mair] Mediterranean

Mitternacht f [mitternaкнт] midnight

Mittwoch m [mittvoкн]

Wednesday
Möbel pl [murbel] furniture
möbliert [mur-bleert] furnished
möchte [mursht-uh] would like to
ich möchte gern [gairn] I would like
Mode f [mohd-uh] fashion
Modeartikel fashions
modisch [mohdish] fashionable
Mofa n [mohfah] small moped
mögen [murgen] to like
möglich [murklish] possible
Möglichkeit f [murklishkite] possibility
Monat m [mohnaht] month
Monatskarte f [mohnats-kart-uh] monthly ticket
Monatsraten [mohnahts-rahten] monthly instalments
Mond m [mohnt] moon
Montag m [mohntahk] Monday
Mord m [mort] murder
Mörder m [murder], **Mörderin f** murderer
morgen tomorrow
Morgen m [morgen] morning
morgens in the morning
Motor abstellen switch off engine
Motorboot n [mohtorboht] motorboat
Motorhaube f [mohtohr-howb-uh] bonnet, (US) hood
Motorrad n [motohr-raht] motorbike
Möwe f [murv-uh] seagull
müde [mood-uh] tired
Mühe f [moo-uh] trouble

Müll abladen verboten no tipping (rubbish/garbage)
Mülltonne f [mooll-tonn-uh] dustbin, trashcan
München [moonshen] Munich
Mund m [moont] mouth
Münzeinwurf insert coin here
Münzen [moontsen] coins
Münztank m [moonts-tank] coin-operated pump
Muschel f [mooshel] shell; mussel
Muskel m [mooskel] muscle
muss [mooss] must
müssen [moossen] to have to
musst [moosst], **müßt** [moosst] must
musste [moosst-uh], **mussten, musstest** had to
Muster n [mooster] pattern; specimen
mutig [mootish] brave
Mutter f [mootter] mother; nut
Mutti f [moottee] mum
Mütze f [moots-uh] cap
MWSt (Mehrwertsteuer) VAT

N

nach [naкн] after; to; according to
Nachbar m [naкнbar], **Nachbarin f** neighbour
nachdem [naкнdaym] after; afterwards
nachher [naкн-hair] afterwards
Nachmittag m [naкнmittahk] afternoon
Nachmittags geschlossen

closed in the afternoons

Nachname m [na**KH**nahm-uh] surname

Nachricht f [na**KH**risht] message

Nachrichten fpl [na**KH**rishten] news

nachsenden [na**KH**zenden] to forward

nächste [na**y**kst-uh] next; nearest

nächstes Jahr next year

Nacht f [na**KH**t] night

Nachtdienst m [na**KH**t-deenst] late night chemist's/pharmacy

Nachteil m [na**KH**tile] disadvantage

Nachthemd n [na**KH**t-hemt] nightdress

Nachtportier m [na**KH**t-port-yay] night porter

Nachtruhe f [na**KH**troo-uh] sleep

nachts [na**KH**ts] at night

Nacken m nape of the neck

nackt naked

Nadel f [na**h**del] needle; pin

Nagel m [na**h**gel] nail

Nagelfeile f [na**h**gelfile-uh] nailfile

Nagellack m [na**h**gel-lack] nail polish

Nagellackentferner m [na**h**gel-lack-entfairner] nail polish remover

Nagelschere f [na**h**gel-shair-uh] nail clippers

nah(e) [na**h**(-uh)] near

Nähe: in der Nähe [in dair na**y**-uh] near here

nähen [na**y**-en] to sew

nahm, nahmen, nahmst took

Nahschnellverkehrszug m [nah-shnell-fairkairs-ts**oo**k] local train

Nahverkehrszug m local train

Narkose f [nark**oh**z-uh] anaesthetic

Nase f [na**h**z-uh] nose

Nasenbluten n [na**h**zenbl**oo**ten] nosebleed

nass wet

natürlich [nat**oo**rlish] natural; of course

Naturprodukt m natural produce

Nebel m [na**y**bel] fog

Nebelschlussleuchte f [na**y**bel-shl**oo**ss-loysht-uh] rear fog light

neben [na**y**ben] next to

Nebenstraße f [na**y**ben-shtrahss-uh] minor road

nee [nay] nope

Neffe m [neff-uh] nephew

nehmen [na**y**men] to take

Neid m [nite] envy

neidisch [n**y**dish] envious

nein [nine] no

Nerven mpl [n**ai**rfen] nerves

Nervenzusammenbruch m [n**ai**rfen-ts**oo**zammenbroo**KH**] nervous breakdown

nervös [nairv**u**rss] nervous

nett nice

Nettogewicht n net weight

Nettoinhalt m net contents

Netz n [nets] net; network

Netzkarte f [netskart-uh] travelcard, runabout ticket

neu [noy] new

Neubau m [noybow] new building

Neujahr n [noy-yar] New Year

neulich [noylish] recently; the other day

neun [noyn] nine

neunzehn [noyn-tsayn] nineteen

neunzig [noyn-tsish] ninety

nicht [nisht] not

nicht ... do not ...

nicht berühren do not touch

nicht betriebsbereit not ready

nicht bügeln do not iron

Nichte f [nisht-uh] niece

Nichtgefallen: bei Nichtgefallen Geld zurück money back if not satisfied

nicht hinauslehnen do not lean out

nicht hupen sounding horn forbidden

nicht in der Maschine waschen do not machine wash

nicht rauchen no smoking

Nichtraucher non-smokers

Nichtraucherabteil n [nishtrowкнer-aptile] non-smoking compartment

nichts [nishts] nothing

nicht schleudern do not spin-dry

nicht stürzen fragile

nicht zur innerlichen Anwendung not for internal use

Nichtzutreffendes bitte streichen please delete as appropriate

nie [nee] never

Niederlage f [neederlahg-uh] defeat

Niederlande pl [needer-land-uh] Netherlands

niederländisch [needer-lendish] Dutch

niemals [neemalss] never

niemand [neemant] nobody

Niere f [neer-uh] kidney

niesen [neezen] to sneeze

nimmst take

nimmt takes

nirgends [neergents] nowhere

noch [noкн] still; even; more

noch ein(e) ... [ine(-uh)] another ...

noch nicht [nisht] not yet

nochmal [noкнmahl] again

Norden m north

Nordfriesische Inseln fpl [nortfreezish-uh inzeln] North Frisian Islands

nordirisch [nort-eerish] Northern Irish

Nordirland n [nort-eerlant] Northern Ireland

nördliche Stadtteile city north

nördlich von [nurtlish fon] north of

Nordsee f [nortzay] North Sea

Normal n [normahl] two-star petrol, regular gas

Norwegen n [norvaygen] Norway

norwegisch [norvaygish] Norwegian

Notarzt m [noht-artst] emergency doctor

Notaufnahme f [noht-owfnahm-uh] casualty department, A&E

Notausgang m [noht-owssgang] emergency exit

Notausstieg m [noht-owss-shteek] emergency exit

Notbremse f [nohtbremz-uh] emergency brake

Notfall m [nohtfal] emergency **im Notfall Scheibe einschlagen** smash glass in case of emergency

Notfälle [noht-fell-uh] emergencies

nötig [nurtish] necessary

Notizbuch n [noteets-booKH] notebook

Notruf m [noht-roof] emergency call

Notrufsäule f [noht-roof-zoyl-uh] emergency telephone

notwendig [nohtvendish] necessary

Nr. (Nummer) No., number

nüchtern einzunehmen to be taken on an empty stomach

null [nooll] zero

Nummer f [noommer] number

Nummernschild n [noommern-shilt] number plate

nun [noon] now

nur [noor] only; just

nur begrenzt haltbar will keep for a limited period only

nur für Anlieger access for residents only

nur für Bedienstete staff only

nur für Busse buses only

nur für Erwachsene adults only

nur für Gäste (hotel) patrons only

nur gegen Voranmeldung by appointment only

nur im Notfall benutzen emergency use only

nur mit der Hand waschen hand wash only

nur solange der Vorrat reicht only as long as stocks last

nur werktags weekdays only

nur zur äußerlichen Anwendung for external use only

nützlich [nuutslish] useful

O

ob [op] whether; if

oben [ohben] top; at the top; upstairs

Obergeschoss n upper floor; top floor

Oberweite f bust measurement, chest measurement

Obst und Gemüse fruit and vegetables

obwohl [opvohl] although

oder [ohder] or

oder? isn't it?; don't you?; aren't I? etc; OK?

offen open

offensichtlich [offenzishtlish] obvious

öffentlich [urfentlish] public

Öffentlichkeit f [urfentlish-kite] public

öffnen **[ur**fnen] to open
Öffnung f **[ur**fnoong] opening
Nach Öffnung nur beschränkt
haltbar will keep for a limited
period only after opening
Öffnungszeiten **[ur**fnoongs-
tsyten] opening times
oft often
ohne **[ohn**-uh] without
ohne Konservierungsstoffe no
preservatives
ohne künstliche Aromastoffe
no artificial flavouring
Ohnmacht: in Ohnmacht fallen
[ohn-maкнt] to faint
Ohr n **[ohr]** ear
Oktoberfest n **[oktohb**erfest]
Munich beer festival (held in
September)
Ölstand m **[url**shtant] oil level
Ölwechsel sofort oil change
while you wait
Oma f **[ohm**ah] granny
Omnibus m **[omn**eebooss] bus
Onkel m uncle
Opa m **[ohp**ah] grandad
Oper f **[ohp**er] opera
Operationssaal m **[opairats-
yoh**ns-zahl] operating theatre
Opfer n victim
Optiker m optician
Ordner m **[ort**ner] folder;
steward
Ordnung f **[ort**noong] order
in Ordnung all right
Ort m town; place
örtliche Betäubung f **[urt**lish-uh
be**toy**boong] local anaesthetic
Ortsgespräch n **[orts-**

geshpr**aysh]** local call
Ortsnetz n **[orts**nets] local
network
Ortszeit f **[orts**-tsite] local time
Ossi m **[oss**ee] East German
Osten m east
Ostern n **[oh**stern] Easter
Österreich n **[ur**ster-rysh]
Austria
Österreicher m **[ur**ster-rysher]
Austrian
Österreicherin f **[ur**ster-rysherin]
Austrian (woman)
österreichisch **[ur**ster-ryshish]
Austrian
Ostfriesische Inseln fpl
[ostfreezish-uh **i**nzeln] East
Frisian Islands
östliche Stadtteile city east
östlich von **[urt**lish fon] east of
Ostsee f **[ost**zay] Baltic

P
▬

Paar n **[pahr]** pair
paar: ein paar ... a few ...
Päckchen n(pl) **[pe**ckshen] small
parcel(s)
packen to pack
Packung f **[pack**oong] pack
Paket n **[pak**ayt] parcel,
package
Paketannahme f **[pak**ayt-an-
nahm-uh] parcels counter
Palast m palace
Panne f **[pann**-uh] breakdown
Pannendreieck n **[pann**en-dry-
eck] emergency triangle
Pannenhilfe f **[pann**en-hilf-uh]

breakdown services

Papier n [papeer] paper; litter

Papier(hand)tücher npl [papeer-(hant)toosher] paper handkerchiefs, tissues

Pappe f [papp-uh] cardboard

Parfüm n [parfoom] perfume

Parkausweis m [park-owssvice] parking permit

Parkbucht f [parkbookHt] parking space

Parkdauer parking allowed for ...

parken to park

Parken nur mit Parkscheibe parking disc holders only

Parken nur mit Parkschein parking only with parking permit

Parken verboten no parking

Parkett n stalls

Parkhaus n [parkhowss] multistorey car park/parking garage

Parkplatz m [parkplats] car park, parking lot

Parkscheinautomat m [parkshine-owtomaht] car park/parking lot ticket vending machine

Parkschein entnehmen take a ticket

Parkuhr f [park-oor] parking meter

Parkverbot no parking

Pass m [pas] passport; pass

Passagier m [passah-jeer] passenger

Passkontrolle f [pas-kontrol-uh]

passport control

Pauschalreise f [powshahl-rize-uh] package tour

Pause f [powz-uh] interval, intermission; rest

Pech n [pesh] bad luck

peinlich [pine-lish] embarrassing

Pelz m [pelts] fur

Pelzmantel m [peltsmantel] fur coat

Pension f [pangz-yohn] guesthouse

Personalausweis m [pairzonahl-owssvice] identity card

Personaleingang m staff entrance

Personenzug m [pairzohnen-tsook] passenger train, stopping train

Perücke f [perOOck-uh] wig

Pf. (Pfennig) pfennig

Pfandleihe f [pfant-ly-uh] pawnbroker

Pfanne f [pfann-uh] frying pan

Pfd. (Pfund) pound (German pound = 500g)

Pfeife f [pfife-uh] pipe

Pferd n [pfairt] horse

Pferderennbahn f [pfaird-uh-rennbahn] race course

Pferdeschwanz m [pfaird-uh-shvants] ponytail

Pfingsten n Whitsun

Pflanze f [pflants-uh] plant

Pf. (Pfennig) pfennig (German unit of currency, 100 pf = DM 1)

Pfund n [pfoont] pound (German pound = 500g); pound (Sterling)

Phonoartikel hi-fi equipment

Pickel m spot

pikant savoury; spicy

Pille f [pill-uh] pill

Pinsel m [pinzel] paint brush

Pinzette f [pintsett-uh] tweezers

Pistole f [pistohl-uh] gun

Pkw m [pay-kah-vay] private car

Plakat n [plakaht] poster

Plakate ankleben verboten stick no bills

Plastik n plastic

Plastiktüte f [plastik-toot-uh] plastic bag

platt flat

Plattenspieler m [platten-shpeeler] record player

Platz m [plats] seat; square; place; space

Platzanweiserin f [plats-anvyzerin] usherette

Platzkarte f [plats-kart-uh] seat reservation

pleite [plite-uh] broke

Plombe f [plomb-uh] filling

plötzlich [plurtslish] suddenly

PLZ (Postleitzahl) postcode, zip code

Pokal m [pohkahl] cup

Polen n [pohlen] Poland

Politik f [politeek] politics

Politiker m [poleeticker], Politikerin f politician

politisch [poleetish] political

Polizei f [polits-ī] police

Polizeipräsidium n [polits-ī-prayzeedee-oom] police headquarters

Polizeiwache f [polits-ī-vaкн-uh] police station

Polizist m [politsist] policeman

Polizistin f [politsistin] policewoman

polnisch [pol-nish] Polish

Pony m [ponnee] fringe

Portemonnaie n [port-monnay] purse

Portier m [port-yay] porter

Porto n postage

portugiesisch [portoo-geezish] Portuguese

Porzellan n [portsellahn] porcelain; china

Post f [posst] mail; post office

Postamt n [posst-amt] post office

Postanweisung f [posst-anvyzoong] postal/money order

Postanweisungen money orders

Postkarte f [posstkart-uh] postcard

postlagernd [posst-lahgernt] poste restante

postlagernde Sendungen poste restante

Postleitzahl f [posst-lite-tsahl] postcode, zip code

Postscheckkonto n [posst-sheck-konto] (post office) giro account

Postsparkasse f [posst-shparkass-uh] post office savings bank

Postwertzeichen n(pl) [posst-vairt-tsyshen] postage stamp(s)

Postwertzeichen in kl. Mengen stamps in small quantities

praktisch [praktish] practical
praktische Ärztin f [praktish-uh airtstin] GP
praktischer Arzt m [praktisher artst] GP
Präservativ n [prezairvateef] condom
Praxis f [praksis] doctor's surgery; practice
Preis m [price] price
zum halben Preis half price
preisgünstig [price-gŏonstish] cheap; inexpensive
Preis reduziert price reduced
Preissenkung reduction
preiswert bargain price, inexpensive
prima! [preemah] good!
Prinz m [prints] prince
Prinzessin f [printsessin] princess
Privateigentum private property
Privatgrundstück private property
Privatparkplatz private car park/parking lot
pro: pro Woche [voKH-uh] per week
Probe f [prohb-uh] rehearsal; sample
probieren [probeeren] to taste; to try
Programmkino n [programm-keeno] arts cinema
Prospekt m [prohspekt] brochure
prost! [prohst] cheers!
Prozent n [prohtsent] per cent
Prozess m [proh-tsess] trial; process
prüfen [proofen] to check
Publikum n [pŏoblikoom] audience
Puder m [pŏoder] powder
Pumpe f [pŏomp-uh] pump
Punkt m [poonkt] point; dot; full stop
pünktlich [pŏonktlish] punctual
Puppe f [pŏopp-uh] doll
putzen [pootsen] to clean
Putzfrau f [pootsfrow] cleaning lady

Q

Qualität f [kvalitayt] quality
Qualitätsware quality goods
Qualle f [kvall-uh] jellyfish
Quatsch m [kvatsh] nonsense
Quelle f [kvell-uh] spring; source
Quittung f [kvittoong] receipt

R

Rabatt m reduction, discount
Rad n [raht] wheel
Radfahren n [raht-fahren] cycling
Radfahrer m [raht-fahrer] cyclist
Radfahrer frei cyclists only
Radfahrerin f [raht-fahrerin] cyclist
Radiergummi n [radeer-goommee] rubber, eraser
Radweg m [raht-vayk] cycle path
Radweg kreuzt cycle track

crossing

Rand m [rant] edge; rim

Rang m row; stalls; grade

Rasen m [rahzen] lawn

Rasierapparat m [razeer-apparaht] razor

Rasiercreme f [razeer-kraym] shaving cream

rasieren: sich rasieren [zish razeeren] to shave

Rasierklinge f [razeerkling-uh] razor blade

Rasierpinsel m [razeer-pinzel] shaving brush

Rasierseife f [razeerzife-uh] shaving foam

Rasierwasser n [razeervasser] aftershave

Raststätte f [rast-shtett-uh] services area

Rat m [raht] advice; council

Rate f [raht-uh] instalment; rate

raten [rahten] to guess; to advise

Ratenzahlung f [rahten-tsahloong] hire purchase, installment plan

Ratenzahlung möglich credit terms available

Rathaus n [raht-howss] town hall

Rätsel n [raytsel] puzzle

Ratskeller m [rahtskeller] restaurant and bar close to town hall

Ratte f [ratt-uh] rat

Rattengift n [rattengift] rat poison

Raub m [rowp] robbery

Raubüberfall m [rowp-oober-fal] armed robbery

Rauch m [rowKH] smoke

rauchen [rowKHen] to smoke

Rauchen einstellen no smoking

Rauchen und offenes Feuer verboten no smoking or naked lights

Rauchen verboten no smoking

Raucher smokers

Raucherabteil n [rowKHer-aptile] smoking compartment

rauh [row] rough

raus! [rowss] get out!

Rechner m [reshner] calculator; computer

Rechnung f [reshnoong] bill, (US) check

rechts [reshts] right

Rechtsabbieger right filter lane

Rechtsanwalt m [reshts-anvalt] lawyer

Rechtsanwältin f [reshts-anveltin] lawyer

rechts fahren keep to the right

rechts halten keep right

rechtshändig [reshts-hendish] right-handed

rechts (von) [reshts (fon)] on the right (of)

rechtzeitig [resht-tsytish] on time

reduziert reduced

Reformhaus n [reform-howss] health food shop

Reformkost f health food

Regen m [**ray**gen] rain

Regenmantel m [**ray**gen-mantel] raincoat

Regenschirm m [**ray**gen-sheerm] umbrella

Regierung f [reg**ee**roong] government

regnen [**ray**knen] to rain
es regnet [ess **ray**k-net] it's raining

regnerisch [**ray**knerish] rainy

Reh n [ray] roe deer

Reibe f [**ribe**-uh] grater

reich [rysh] rich

reichen: das reicht [rysht] that's enough

reif [rife] ripe

Reifen m [**ry**fen] tyre

Reifendruck m [**ry**fendroock] tyre pressure

Reifenpanne f [**ry**fenpann-uh] puncture

Reihe f [**ry**-uh] row; series

reine Baumwolle pure cotton

reine Schurwolle pure wool

reine Seide pure silk

reine Wolle pure wool

reinigen [**ry**nigen] to clean

Reinigung f [**ry**nigoong] laundry

Reinigungscreme f [**ry**nigoongs-kraym] cleansing cream

Reise f [**rize**-uh] journey

Reiseandenken souvenirs

Reiseapotheke f [**rize**-uh-apo**tayk**-uh] first aid kit

Reiseauskunft f [**rize**-uh-owsskoonft] travel information

Reisebedarf m [**rize**-uh-bedarf] travel requisites

Reisebüro n [**rize**-uh-b**oo**ro] travel agency

Reiseführer m [**rize**-uh-f**oo**rer] guide; guidebook

reisen [**rize**-en] to travel

Reisende [**ry**zend-uh] passengers

Reisepass m [**rize**-uh-pas] passport

Reiseproviant m [**rize**-uh-prohvee-**ant**] food for the journey

Reisescheck m [**rize**-uh-sheck] travellers' cheque

Reißverschluss m [**rice**-fairshlooss] zip

Reitsport m [**rite**-shport] horse riding

Reitweg m [**rite**-vayk] bridle path

Reklamationen complaints

Reklame f [rek**lah**m-uh] advertising; advertisement

Rennbahn f race track

Rentner m, Rentnerin f old-age pensioner

Reparaturen repairs

Reparaturwerkstatt f [reparat**oo**r-vairkshtatt] garage, repairs

reparieren [repar**ee**ren] to mend, to repair

Reportage f [reportah-J-uh] report

reservieren [rezair**vee**ren] to reserve

reserviert [rezer**vee**rt] reserved

Reservierung f [rezair**vee**roong] reservation

Restgeld wird zurückgegeben
change will be given
Rettungsring m [rettoongs-ring]
lifebelt
Rezept n [retsept] recipe;
prescription
rezeptpflichtig sold on
prescription only
Rhein m [rine] Rhine
Rheuma n [roymah]
rheumatism
Richter m [rishter] judge
Richterin f [rishterin] judge
richtig [rishtish] right; correct
Richtung f [rishtoong] direction
riechen [reeshen] to smell
Riegel m [reegel] bolt
Risiko n [reezeeko] risk
Rock m skirt; rock music
Rodelbahn f [rohdelbahn]
toboggan run
Rohr n [rohr] pipe
Rolle f [rol-uh] role; part
Rollsplitt loose chippings
Rollstuhl m [rol-shtool]
wheelchair
Rolltreppe f [rol-trepp-uh]
escalator
Roman m [romahn] novel
Röntgenaufnahme f [rurntgen-
owfnahm-uh] X-ray
rosa [rohza] pink
Rosenmontagszug m
[rohzen-mohntaks-tsook]
carnival procession held
on the Monday before Ash
Wednesday (public holiday)
rot [roht] red
Röteln [rurteln] German

measles
rothaarig [roht-hahrish] red-
headed
Rubin m [roobeen] ruby
Rücken m [roocken] back
Rückenschmerzen mpl
[roockenshmairtsen] backache
Rückfahrkarte f [roockfahrkart-
uh] return/round trip ticket
Rücklichter npl [roocklishter]
rear lights
Rückseite f [roockzite-uh] back;
reverse
rücksichtslos [roockzishts-lohss]
reckless
Rücksitz m [roockzits] back seat
Rückspiegel m [roock-shpeegel]
rearview mirror
rückwärts [roockvairts]
backwards
Rückwärtsgang m [roockvairts-
gang] reverse gear
Ruderboot n [rooderboht]
rowing boat
Ruf m [roof] call
ruf doch mal an somebody
somewhere wants a phonecall
from you
rufen [roofen] to call; to shout
Rufnummer f [roofnoommer]
telephone number
Rufsäule f [roofzoyl-uh]
emergency telephone
Ruhe f [roo-uh] quiet; rest
ruhestörender Lärm
disturbance of the peace
Ruhetag closed all day
ruhig [roo-ish] quiet
ruhige Lage peaceful, secluded

spot

rund [roont] round

Rundfahrt f [roontfahrt] guided tour

Rundgang m guided tour (on foot)

Rundreise f [roont-rize-uh] guided tour

russisch [roossish] Russian

Russland n [roosslant] Russia

S

Sache f [zaкн-uh] thing; matter; affair

Sachsen n [zakzen] Saxony

Sackgasse f [zack-gass-uh] cul-de-sac, dead end

sagen [zahgen] to say

man sagt, dass ... [zahkt] they say that ...

sagenhaft [zahgenhaft] terrific

sah [zah], sahen, sahst saw

Salbe f [zalb-uh] ointment

Salon m [zalong] lounge

salzig [zaltsish] salty

Sammelkarte f [zammel-kart-uh] multi-journey ticket

sammeln [zammeln] to collect

Sammlung f [zamloong] collection

Samstag m [zamstahk] Saturday

samstags [zamstahks] on Saturdays

Sandstrand m [zant-shtrant] sandy beach

Sanitäter m [zanee-tayter] ambulanceman

Sanitätsdienst m [zanitayts-deenst] ambulance service

Sanitätsstelle f [zanitayts-shtell-uh] first aid centre

Satz m [zats] sentence; rate

sauber [zowber] clean

säubern [zoybern] to clean

sauer [zower] sour; pissed off

Sauerstoff m [zowershtoff] oxygen

SB (Selbstbedienung) self service

S-Bahn f [ess-bahn] local urban railway

SB-Tankstelle f [ess-bay-tankshtell-uh] self-service petrol/gas station

Schachtel f [shaкнtel] box; packet

schade: das ist schade [shahd-uh] it's a pity

Schädel m [shaydel] skull

Schaden m [shahden] damage

Schaf n [shahf] sheep

Schaffner m [shaffner] conductor

schal [shahl] stale

Schal m [shahl] scarf

Schallplatte f [shallplatt-uh] record

Schalter m [shalter] counter; switch

Schalterstunden hours of business

Schaltknüppel m [shaltk-nooppel] gear lever

schämen: sich schämen [zish shaymen] to be ashamed

scharf [sharf] sharp; hot

Schatten m [shatten] shade

Schauer m [sh**ow**er] shower

Schaufenster n [sh**ow**-fenster] shop window

Scheck m [sheck] cheque, (US) check

Scheckheft n [sheck-heft] cheque book

Scheckkarte f [sheck-kart-uh] cheque card

Scheibe f [sh**ibe**-uh] slice

Scheibenwischer m [sh**yben**-visher] windscreen wiper

Schein m [sh**ine**] note, bill; appearance

Scheineingabe insert banknote

scheinen [sh**ynen**] to shine; to seem

Scheinwerfer mpl [sh**ine**-vairfer] headlights

Scheiße! [sh**ice**-uh] shit!

Scheißkerl m [sh**ice**-kairl] bastard

Schenkel m [shenkel] thigh

Schere f [shair-uh] scissors

scheu [shoy] shy

Schiedsrichter m [sh**eets**-rishter] referee

Schiff n [shiff] ship; boat

Schild n [shilt] sign

Schirm m [sheerm] umbrella; screen

Schlafanzug m [shl**ahf**-ants00k] pyjamas

schlafen [shl**ahf**en] to sleep

Schlaflosigkeit f [shl**ahf**lohzish-kite] insomnia

Schlafmittel n [shl**ahf**mittel] sleeping drug

Schlafraum m [shl**ahf**rowm] dormitory

Schlafsaal m [shl**ahf**zahl] dormitory

Schlafsack m [shl**ahf**zack] sleeping bag

Schlaftablette f [shl**ahf**-tablett-uh] sleeping pill

Schlafwagen m [shl**ahf**vahgen] sleeper, sleeping car

Schlafzimmer n [shl**ahf**-tsimmer] bedroom

Schlafzimmerbedarf for the bedroom

schlagen [shl**ahg**en] to hit

Schläger m [shl**ayg**er] racket; hooligan

Schlange f [shlang-uh] snake; queue

Schlange stehen [sht**ay**-en] to queue

schlank [shlank] slim

Schlauch m [shlowкн] inner tube

schlecht [shlesht] bad; badly; unwell

Schlechte Fahrbahn bad road surface

schlechter [shleshter] worse

schlechteste [shleshtest-uh] worst

Schleudergefahr danger of skidding

schleudern [shl**oy**dern] to skid

Schleuderpreise prices slashed

schließen [shl**eess**en] to close

Schließfach n [shl**eess**faкн] left luggage locker

Schließfächer luggage lockers

schloss [shloss] shut

Schloss n castle; lock

Schluckauf m [shloock-owf] hiccups

schlucken [shloocken] to swallow

Schluss m [shlooss] end

Schlüssel m [shlOOssel] key; spanner; wrench

schmackhaft [shmack-haft] tasty

schmecken [shmecken] to taste; to taste good

Schmerz m [shmairts] pain

schmerzen [shmairtsen] to hurt

schmerzhaft [shmairts-haft] painful

Schmerzmittel n [shmairts-mittel] painkiller

schminken: sich schminken [zish shminken] to do one's make-up

Schmuck m [shmoock] jewellery

schmutzig [shmootsish] dirty

schnarchen [shnarshen] to snore

Schnauze! [shnowts-uh] shut your mouth!

Schnee m [shnay] snow

schneebedeckt snow-covered

Schneeketten fpl snow chains

Schneeverhältnisse fpl [shnay-fair-heltniss-uh] snow conditions

Schneeverwehung f [shnay-fairvayoong] snow drift

schneiden [shnyden] to cut
  sich schneiden to cut oneself

Schneiderei f [shnyder-ī] tailor's

schneien [shny-en] to snow

schnell [shnell] fast

Schnellimbiss m [shnell-imbiss] snackbar

Schnellzug m [shnell-tsOOk] express train

Schnupfen m [shnoopfen] cold

Schnurrbart m [shnoorrbart] moustache

schön [shurn] beautiful; fine; nice

schon [shohn] already

Schönheitspflege f [shurnhites-pflayg-uh] beauty care

Schönheitssalon m [shurnhites-zalong] beauty salon

Schornstein m [shorn-shtine] chimney

Schotte m [shott-uh] Scotsman

Schottin f [shottin] Scotswoman

Schrank m [shrank] cupboard

Schranke f [shrank-uh] barrier

Schraube f [shrowb-uh] screw

Schraubenschlüssel m [shrowben-shlOOssel] spanner, wrench

Schraubenzieher m [shrowben-tsee-er] screwdriver

schreiben [shryben] to write

Schreibmaschine f [shripe-masheen-uh] typewriter

Schreibpapier n [shripe-papeer] writing paper

Schreibtisch m [shripe-tish] desk

Schreibwaren pl [shripe-vahren] stationery

Schreibwarenladen m [shripe-

vahren-lahden] stationer's
schreien [shry-en] to scream
schrieb [shreep], schriebst,
  schrieben wrote
Schriftsteller m [shrift-shteller],
  Schriftstellerin f writer
Schritt m [shritt] step
Schritt fahren drive at walking
  speed
schüchtern [shooshtern] shy
Schuhcreme f [shoo-kraym]
  shoe polish
Schuhe mpl [shoo-uh] shoes
Schuhmacher m [shoomakHer]
  shoe repairer
Schuhreparaturen shoe
  repairs, heelbar
Schulbedarf school items
Schulden fpl [shoolden] debts
schuld: er ist schuld [air ist
  shoolt] it's his fault
schuldig [shooldish] guilty
Schule f [shool-uh] school
Schüler und Studenten school
  children and students
Schulhof m [shool-hohf] school
  playground
Schulter f [shoolter] shoulder
Schüssel f [shoossel] bowl
Schutt abladen verboten no
  tipping
schützen [shootsen] to protect
Schützenfest n [shootsenfest]
  local carnival
Schwaben n [shvahben] Swabia
schwach [shvakH] weak
Schwachkopf m [shvakH-kopf]
  idiot, wally
Schwachsinn m [shvakH-zin]

rubbish
Schwager m [shvahger]
  brother-in-law
Schwägerin f [shvaygerin] sister-
  in-law
Schwamm m [shvamm] sponge
schwanger [shvang-er]
  pregnant
Schwanz m [shvants] tail
schwarz [shvartz] black
Schwarzes Brett n [shvartsess]
  noticeboard
Schwarzwald m [shvartsvalt]
  Black Forest
schwarz-weiß [shvarts-vice]
  black and white
Schwein n [shvine] pig
Schweiz f [shvites] Switzerland
Schweizer m [shvytser] Swiss
Schweizerin f [shvytserin] Swiss
  woman
schwer [shvair] heavy; difficult
Schwerlastverkehr heavy
  vehicles
Schwester f [shvester] sister
Schwiegermutter f [shveeger-
  mootter] mother-in-law
Schwiegersohn m
  [shveegerzohn] son-in-law
Schwiegertochter f [shveeger-
  tokHter] daughter-in-law
Schwiegervater m
  [shveegerfahter] father-in-law
schwierig [shveerish] difficult
Schwimmbad n [shvimmbaht]
  swimming pool
Schwimmen n [shvimmen]
  swimming
schwimmen to swim

schwimmen gehen [gay-en] to go swimming

Schwimmen verboten no swimming

Schwimmer m [shvimmer], Schwimmerin f swimmer

Schwimmweste f [shvimmvest-uh] life jacket

schwindlig [shvintlish] dizzy

schwitzen [shvitsen] to sweat

schwul [shvool] gay

sechs [zeks] six

sechzehn [zesh-tsayn] sixteen

sechzig [zesh-tsish] sixty

See m [zay] lake

See f sea

seekrank [zaykrank] seasick

Segelboot n [zaygelboht] sailing boat

Segeln n [zaygeln] sailing

Segler m [zaygler] yachtsman

Seglerin f [zayglerin] yachtswoman

sehen [zay-en] to see

Sehenswürdigkeit f [zay-ens-voordishkite] sight

sehr [zair] very

sei [zy] be

seid [zite] are

seien Sie [zy-en zee] be

Seide f [zide-uh] silk

Seife f [zife-uh] soap

Seil n [zile] rope

sein [zine] to be; his; its

seine [zine-uh] his; its

seit [zite] since

seitdem [zite-daym] since

Seite f [zite-uh] side; page

Seitenstreifen nicht befahrbar soft verges, keep off

Sekunde f [zekoond-uh] second

selbe [zelb-uh] same

selbst [zelpst] even

er/sie selbst himself/herself

Selbstbedienung f [zelpst-bedeenoong] self-service

selbstverständlich [zelpst-fairshtentlish] of course

Selbstwählferndienst direct long-distance dialling

seltsam [zeltzahm] strange

senden [zenden] to send

Sender m [zender] (radio/TV) station

Sendung f [zendoong] programme

sensibel [zenzeebel] sensitive

Serviervorschlag serving suggestion

Sessellift m [zessel-lift] chairlift

setzen [zetsen] to put

sich setzen to sit down

sexistisch [seksistish] sexist

sicher [zisher] sure; safe

Sicherheitsgurt m [zisherhites-goort] seat belt

Sicherheitsnadel f [zisherhites-nahdel] safety pin

Sicherung f [zisheroong] fuse

Sicht f [zisht] visibility

sie [zee] she; her; they; them

Sie you

sieben [zeeben] seven

siebzehn [zeep-tsayn] seventeen

siebzig [zeep-tsish] seventy

Sieg m [zeek] victory

siehe ... see ...

siehst [zeest] see

sieht [zeet] sees

siezen [zeetsen] to use the more formal 'Sie' form

Silber n [zilber] silver

silbern [zilbern] silver

Silvester n [zilvester] New Year's Eve

sind [zint] are

singen [zing-en] to sing

sinken [zinken] to sink

Sitz m [zits] seat

Sitz für Schwerbehinderte seat for handicapped

Sitzplätze seats

skifahren [sheefahren] to ski

Skifahren n skiing

Skigebiet n [shee-gebeet] skiing area

Skihose f [shee-hohzuh] ski pants

Skilehrer m [shee-lairer], Skilehrerin f ski instructor

Skipiste f [sheepist-uh] ski slope

Skistiefel mpl [shee-shteefel] ski boots

Skistock m [shee-shtock] ski pole

Smoking m dinner jacket

so [zo] so; this way

so ... wie [vee] as ... as

sobald [zohbalt] as soon as

Socke f [zock-uh] sock

Sodbrennen n [zohtbrennen] heartburn

sofort [zofort] immediately

Sohn m [zohn] son

solange [zohlang-uh] as long as

Sommer m [zommer] summer

Sommerfahrplan m [zommerfahrplahn] summer timetable/schedule

Sommerferien fpl [zommerfairee-en] summer holidays/vacation

Sommerschlussverkauf summer sale

Sonderangebot n [zonderangeboht] special offer

Sonderflug m [zonderflook] special flight

sondern [zondern] but

Sonderpreis m [zonder-price] special price

Sondervorstellung f [zonderforshtelloong] special performance

Sonnabend m [zonnahbent] Saturday

Sonne f [zonn-uh] sun

sonnenbaden [zonnenbahden] to sunbathe

Sonnenbrand m [zonnenbrant] sunburn

Sonnenbrille f [zonnenbrill-uh] sunglasses

Sonnenöl n [zonnen-url] suntan lotion; suntan oil

Sonnenschein m [zonnen-shine] sunshine

Sonnenstich m [zonnen-shtish] sunstroke

Sonnenuntergang m [zonnen-oontergang] sunset

sonnig [zonnish] sunny

Sonntag m [zonntahk] Sunday

Sonntagsfahrer m [zonntahksfahrer] roadhog, Sunday driver

sonn- und feiertags on

Sundays and public holidays

sonst [zonst] otherwise

Sorge f [zorg-uh] worry

sich Sorgen machen (um) [zish zorgen maKHen (oom)] to worry (about)

Sorte f [zort-uh] kind; sort

Souterrain n [zootereng] basement

soweit [zovite] as far as

sowieso [zoveezoh] anyway

sowohl ... als auch ... [zovohl alss owKH] both ... and ...

Spanien n [shpahnee-en] Spain

sparen [shpahren] to save

Sparguthaben n [shpahrgoot-hahben] savings account

Sparkasse f [shpahrkass-uh] savings bank

Spaß m [shpahss] fun; joke

spät [shpayt] late

wie spät ist es? [vee] what time is it?

Spaten m [shpahten] spade

Spätschalter m [shpayt-shalter] night counter

Spätvorstellung f [shpaytforshtelloong] late performance

spazieren gehen [shpatseeren gay-en] to go for a walk

Spaziergang m [shpatseergang] walk

Speiche f [shpysh-uh] spoke

Speisegaststätte f [shpize-uh-gast-shtett-uh] restaurant

Speiseraum m [shpize-uh-rowm] dining room

Speisesaal m [shpize-uh-zahl]

restaurant, dining room

Speisewagen m [shpize-uh-vahgen] restaurant car

Speisezimmer n [shpize-uh-tsimmer] dining room

Sperrgebiet prohibited area

Spiegel m [shpeegel] mirror

Spiel n [shpeel] game; match

spielen [shpeelen] to play

Spielende Kinder children at play

Spieler m [shpeeler], **Spielerin** f player; gambler

Spielkasino n [shpeel-kazeeno] casino

Spielplatz m [shpeelplats] playground

Spielwaren fpl [shpeel-vahren] toys

Spielzeug n [shpeeltsoyk] toy

Spinne f [shpinn-uh] spider

spinnen: du spinnst wohl! [doo shpinnst wohl] you've got to be joking!, you're out of your mind!

Spion m [shpee-ohn] spy

Spirale f [shpeerahl-uh] spiral; IUD

Spitze [shpits-uh] fantastic, magic

Spitzenqualität top quality

Spitzname m [shpitsnahm-uh] nickname

Sportartikel sports goods

Sportplatz m [shport-plats] sports ground

Sporttauchen n [shport-towKHen] skin-diving

Sportverein m [shport-fair-ine]

sports club
Sportwagen m [shport-vahgen] sports car; buggy
Sportzentrum n [shport-tsentroom] sports centre
Sprache f [shprahKH-uh] language
Sprachenschule f [shprahKHen-shool-uh] language school
Sprachführer m [shprahKH-foorer] phrasebook
sprechen [shpreshen] to speak; to talk
Sprechstunde f [shpresh-shtoond-uh] surgery
Sprechzimmer n [shpresh-tsimmer] surgery (room)
spricht [shprisht] speaks
wer spricht, bitte? [vair – bitt-uh] who's calling please?
springen [shpringen] to jump
Spritze f [shprits-uh] injection
Sprungschanze f [shproong-shants-uh] ski jump
Spüle f [shpool-uh] sink
spülen [shpoolen] to do the dishes; to rinse
Spülmittel n [shpool-mittel] washing-up liquid
Staat m [shtaht] state
Staatsangehörigkeit f [shtahts-an-gehur-rish-kite] nationality
Staatsanwalt m [shtahts-anvalt] public prosecutor
Stadion n [shtahdee-on] stadium
Stadt f [shtatt] town; city
Stadthalle f [shtatt-hal-uh] city hall
Stadtmitte f [shtatt-mitt-uh] city

centre
Stadtplan m [shtatt-plahn] map
Stadtzentrum n [shtatt-tsentroom] city centre
Stammgast m [shtammgast] regular customer
Stammtisch m [shtammtish] table for regulars
stand [shtant], **standen** [shtanden] stood
Standesamt n [shtandess-amt] registry office
Standlicht n [shtantlisht] sidelights
starb [shtarp], **starben** [shtarben] died
stark [shtark] strong; great
Starkes Gefälle steep gradient
Start m [shtart] start; take-off
Station f [shtats-yohn] (hospital) ward; stop
statt [shtatt] instead of
Stau m [shtow] tailback, traffic jam
Staub m [shtowp] dust
Staubsauger m [shtowp-zowger] vacuum cleaner
Std. (Stunde) hour
stechen [shteshen] to sting
Stechmücke f [shtesh-moock-uh] mosquito
Steckdose f [shteck-dohz-uh] socket
Stecker m [shtecker] plug
stehen [shtay-en] to stand
das steht mir [shtayt meer] it suits me
stehlen [shtaylen] to steal
Stehplätze mpl [shtayplets-uh]

standing room

steil [shtile] steep

Stein m [shtine] stone

Steinschlag falling rocks

Steinschlaggefahr danger of falling rocks

Stelle f [shtell-uh] place

stellen [shtellen] to put

Steppdecke f [shteppdeck-uh] continental quilt

sterben [shtairben] to die

Stereoanlage f [shtayray-oh-anlahg-uh] stereo system

Stern m [shtairn] star

Steuer f [shtoyer] tax

Steuer n steering wheel

Stiefel m [shteefel] boot

Stift m [shtift] pen

Stil m [shteel] style

Stille f [shtill-uh] silence

stillen [shtillen] to breastfeed

Stimme f [shtimm-uh] voice; vote

stimmt [shtimmt] that's right

Stimmung f [shtimmoong] mood

Stirn f [shteern] forehead

Stock m [shtock] floor, storey; stick

Stockwerk n [shtockvairk] floor, storey

Stoff m [shtoff] material; fabric

stolz [shtolts] proud

Stöpsel m [shturpsel] plug

stören [shtur-ren] to disturb

stört es Sie, wenn ich ...? [shturt ess zee venn ish] do you mind if I ...?

Störungsstelle f [shtur-roongs-shtell-uh] faults service

Stoßdämpfer m [shtohss-dempfer] shock-absorber

Stoßstange f [shtohss-shtang-uh] bumper, fender

Str. (Straße) street

Straßenbauarbeiten roadworks

Straßenkilometer kilometres by road

Strafe f [shtrahf-uh] penalty; punishment

Strand m [shtrant] beach

Strandgut n [shtrant-goot] flotsam and jetsam

Strandkorb m [shtrantkorp] wicker beach chair

Strandpromenade f [shtrant-promenahd-uh] promenade

Straße f [shtrahss-uh] street; road

Straßenbahn f [shtrahssenbahn] tram

Straßenbauarbeiten fpl [shtrahssenbow-arbyten] roadworks

Straßenschild n [shtrahssen-shilt] road sign

Straßenverkehrsordnung f [shtrahssen-fairkairs-ortnoong] highway code

Strecke f [shtreck-uh] route; stretch

streichen [shtryshen] to paint; to cancel

Streichholz n [shtrysh-holts] match

strengstens untersagt strictly prohibited

Streugut grit

stricken [shtricken] to knit

Strickwaren knitwear

Strom m [shtrohm] electricity; stream

Stromausfall m [shtrohm-owss-fal] power cut

Stromkosten [shtrohm-kosten] electricity costs

Strömung f [shtrurmoong] current

Strümpfe mpl [shtroompf-uh] stockings

Strumpfhose f [shtroompf-hohz-uh] tights, pantyhose

Stück n [shtoock] piece; play

Student m [shtoodent], Studentin f student

Stuhl m [shtool] chair

Stunde f [shtoond-uh] hour; lesson

Stundenplan m [shtoonden-plahn] timetable, (US) schedule

stündlich [shtoontlish] hourly

Sturm m [shtoorm] storm

stürmisch [shtoormish] stormy

Sturz m [shtoorts] fall

suchen [zooKHen] to look for

Sucher m [zooKHer] viewfinder

Süden m [zooden] south

südliche Stadtteile city south

südlich von [zootlish fon] south of

Summe f [zoomm-uh] sum

Super n [zooper] four-star petrol, premium (gas)

super [zooper] great

Suppenteller m [zooppenteller] soup plate

süß [zooss] sweet

T

Tabak m [tahbak] tobacco

Tabakwaren tobacconist's

Tabelle f [tabell-uh] (league) table

Tablett n tray

Tablette f [tablett-uh] pill, tablet

Tacho m [takHo] speedometer

Tafel f [tahfel] plate; blackboard

Tag m [tahk] day

Tag der Deutschen Einheit Day of German Unity, 3rd October, a public holiday

Tagebuch n [tahg-uh-booKH] diary

Tagesdecke f [tahgess-deck-uh] bedspread

Tageskarte f [tahgess-kart-uh] day ticket; menu of the day

Tageszeitung f [tahgess-tsytoong] daily newspaper

täglich [tayklish] daily

täglich frisch fresh every day

Taille f [tal-yuh] waist

Taillenweite f [tal-yen-vite-uh] waist measurement

Tal n [tahl] valley

Talsperre f [tahlshpair-uh] dam

Tankstelle f [tankshtell-uh] petrol/gas station

Tankwart m [tankvart] petrol/gas pump attendant

Tanne f [tann-uh] fir tree

Tante f [tant-uh] aunt

Tanz m [tants] dance

Tanzcafé n [tants-kaffay] café with dancing

tanzen [**tan**tsen] to dance

Tapete f [tap**ayt**-uh] wallpaper

tapezieren [tapayts**ee**ren] to wallpaper

tapfer brave

Tasche f [**tash**-uh] pocket; bag

Taschendieb m [**tash**en-deep] pickpocket

Taschenlampe f [**tash**en-lamp-uh] torch

Taschenmesser n [**tash**en-messer] penknife

Taschenrechner m [**tash**en-reshner] calculator

Taschentuch n [**tash**entooKH] handkerchief

Tasse f [**tass**-uh] cup

tat [taht], tatst, taten did

taub [towp] deaf

tauchen [**tow**KHen] to dive

Tauchen verboten no diving

tauschen [**tow**shen] to exchange

tausend [**tow**zent] thousand

Tauwetter n [**tow**-vetter] thaw

Taxistand m [**taksi**-shtant] taxi rank

TEE m [tay-ay-**ay**] Trans-Europe Express

Teekanne f [**tay**kann-uh] teapot

Teelöffel m [**tay**-lurfel] teaspoon

Teestube f [**tay**shtoob-uh] tea room

Teich m [tysh] pond

Teil m [tile] part

teilen [**ty**len] to share

teils ... teils ... [tiles] partly ... partly ...

Teilzahlung möglich credit

available

Telefax n fax

Telefonbuch n [tele**fohn**-booKH] phone book

Telefonieren ohne Münzen cardphone

Telefonkarte f [tele**fohn**kart-uh] phonecard

Telefonnummer f [tele**fohn**-noommer] phone number

Telefonzelle f [tele**fohn**-tsell-uh] phone box

Teller m [**tell**er] plate

Teppich m [**tepp**ish] carpet

Teppichboden fitted carpet

Termin m [**tair**meen] appointment

Terrasse f [tair**ass**-uh] patio

Tesafilm® m [**tay**zah-film] Sellotape®, Scotch tape®

teuer [**toy**er] dear; expensive

Theaterstück n [tay-**ah**tershtook] play

tief [teef] deep; low

Tiefe f [**teef**-uh] depth

Tiefgeschoss lower floor, basement

Tiefkühlkost frozen food

Tier n [teer] animal

Tierarzt m [**teer**-artst] vet

Tiergarten m [**teer**garten] zoo

Tierpark m [**teer**park] zoo

Tinte f [**tint**-uh] ink

Tisch m [tish] table

Tischdecke f [**tish**deck-uh] tablecloth

Tischtennis n [**tish**-tennis] table tennis

Tochter f [**to**KHter] daughter

Tod **m** [toht] death

Todesgefahr! danger of death!

Toilettenpapier **n** [twaletten-papeer] toilet paper

toll! tremendous!, brilliant!

Tollwutgefahr danger of rabies

Ton **m** [tohn] sound; clay

Topfpflanzen **fpl** [topf-pflantsen] pot plants

Tor **n** goal; gate

tot [toht] dead

Tote **m/f** [toht-uh] dead man/ woman

töten [turten] to kill

Trage **f** [trahg-uh] stretcher

tragen [trahgen] to carry

Tragödie **f** [tragurdee-uh] tragedy

Trainingsanzug **m** [traynings-antsook] tracksuit

trampen [trempen] to hitchhike

Trampen **n** [trempen] hitchhiking

trank, trankst, tranken drank

Trauer **f** [trower] sorrow

Traum **m** [trowm] dream

träumen [troymen] to dream

traurig [trowrish] sad

Trauring **m** [trowring] wedding ring

treffen to meet

Treffen **n** meeting

Treffpunkt **m** [treffpoonkt] meeting place

Treibstoff **m** [tripe-shtoff] fuel

Treppe **f** [trepp-uh] stairs

Treppenhaus **n** [treppen-howss] stairs; staircase; stairwell

treu [troy] faithful

Trikot **n** [treekoh] jersey

Trimm-dich-Pfad jogging track; keep-fit track

trinken to drink

Trinkgeld **n** [trink-gelt] tip

trocken dry

trocknen to dry

Tropfen **m** drop

trotz [trots] in spite of

trotzdem [trots-daym] in spite of that; all the same; nonetheless

tschüs [chooss] cheerio

Tuch **n** [tooKH] cloth

tun [toon] to do; to put

Tür **f** [toor] door

Türkei **f** [toor-ky] Turkey

Turm **m** [toorm] tower

Turnschuhe **mpl** [toornshoo-uh] trainers

TÜV **m** [tooff] (Technischer Überwachungs-Verein) MOT

Typ **m** [toop] guy, bloke

U

U-Bahn **f** [oo-bahn] underground, (US) subway

U-Bahnhof **m** [oo-bahnhohf] underground/subway station

über [oober] over; above

überall [oober-al] everywhere

überfahren [ooberfahren] to run over

Überfall **m** [oober-fal] attack

übergeben [oober-gayben] to hand over

sich übergeben to be sick

Übergewicht **n** [oobergevisht] overweight; excess baggage

überholen [ᴏᴏberhohlen] to overtake

Überholen verboten no overtaking

Überholverbot no overtaking

Überlebende m/f [ᴏᴏberlaybend-uh] survivor

übermorgen [ᴏᴏbermorgen] the day after tomorrow

Übernachtung f [ᴏᴏbernaкнtoong] night

Übernachtung mit Frühstück f [mit frᴏᴏshtᴏᴏck] bed and breakfast

überqueren [ᴏᴏber-kvairen] to cross

überraschend [ᴏᴏber-rashent] surprising

Überraschung f [ᴏᴏber-rashoong] surprise

überreden [ᴏᴏber-rayden] to persuade

Überschwemmung f [ᴏᴏbershvemmoong] flood

übersetzen [ᴏᴏberzetsen] to translate

Übersetzer m [ᴏᴏberzetser], Übersetzerin f translator

übertreiben [ᴏᴏbertryben] to exaggerate

Überweisung f [ᴏᴏber-vyzoong] transfer

überzeugen [ᴏᴏber-tsoygen] to convince

üblich [ᴏᴏplish] usual

Ufer n [ᴏᴏfer] shore

Uhr f [ᴏᴏr] clock; o'clock

Uhrmacher m [ᴏᴏrmaкнer] watchmaker

UKW (Ultrakurzwelle) [ᴏᴏ-kah-vay] FM

um [ᴏᴏm] around; at
um ... Uhr at ... o'clock
um zu in order to

umbringen [ᴏᴏmbring-en] to kill

Umgebung f [ᴏᴏmgayboong] surroundings; environment

Umgehungsstraße f detour; by-pass

Umkleidekabine f [ᴏᴏmklide-uh-kabeen-uh] changing room

Umleitung f [ᴏᴏm-lytoong] diversion

Umschlag m [ᴏᴏmshlahk] envelope

Umstandskleid n [ᴏᴏmshtants-klite] maternity dress

umsteigen [ᴏᴏm-shtygen] to change (trains etc)

umstoßen [ᴏᴏm-shtohssen] to knock over

umtauschen [ᴏᴏm-towshen] to exchange

Umtausch gegen bar ist nicht möglich goods cannot be exchanged for cash

Umtausch nur gegen Quittung goods may not be exchanged without a receipt

umziehen: sich umziehen [zish ᴏᴏmtsee-en] to change (clothes)

unabhängig [ᴏᴏnap-heng-ish] independent

unangenehm [ᴏᴏn-angenaym] unpleasant

unbedeutend [ᴏᴏn-bedoytent] unimportant

unbefugt unauthorized

unbekannt [oon-bekannt] unknown

und [oont] and

Unebenheiten uneven surface

Unentschieden n [oon-entsheeden] draw

Unfall m [oonfal] accident

Unfallgefahr accident black spot

Unfallrettung f [oonfal-rettoong] ambulance, emergency service

Unfallstation f [oonfal-shtats-yohn] casualty department

ungefähr [oon-gefair] approximately

ungeschickt [oon-geshickt] clumsy

unglaublich [oon-glowplish] incredible

Unglück n [oon-glϾck] disaster; accident; unhappiness

unglücklich [oon-glϾcklish] unhappy; unfortunate

ungültig [oon-gϾltish] invalid

unhöflich [oon-hurflish] impolite, rude

Unkosten pl [oon-kosten] overheads

unmöbliert [oon-mur-bleert] unfurnished

unmöglich [oon-murklish] impossible

uns [oonss] us

unschuldig [oon-shooldish] innocent

unser [oonzer], unsere [oonzer-uh] our

unsicher [oon-zisher] unsafe; unsure

Unsinn m [oonzinn] nonsense

unten [oonten] down; at the bottom; downstairs

unter [oonter] below, under; underneath; among

Unterbodenwäsche f [oonterbohden-vesh-uh] underbody cleaning

unterbrechen [oonterbreshen] to interrupt

Unterführung f [oonterfϾroong] underpass

Untergeschoss n [oonter-geshoss] basement

Unterhaltung f [oonterhaltoong] entertainment; conversation

Unterhemd n [oonter-hemt] vest, (US) undershirt

Unterkunft f [oonterkoonft] accommodation

Unternehmen n [oonternaymen] company; undertaking

Unterricht m [oonter-risht] lessons

untersagt prohibited

Unterschied m [oontersheet] difference

unterschreiben [oontershryben] to sign

Unterschrift f [oontershrift] signature

untersuchen [oonter-zooKHen] to examine

Untersuchung f [oonter-zooKHoong] examination; check-up

Untertasse f [oonter-tass-uh] saucer

Untertitel m [**oo**nterteetel] subtitle

Unterwäsche f [**oo**nter-vesh-uh] underwear

untreu [**oo**ntroy] unfaithful

unverbleit [**oo**nfairblite] unleaded

unverkäufliches Muster not for sale, sample only

unverschämt [**oo**nfairshaymt] outrageous

Unverschämtheit f [**oo**nfairshaymt-hite] cheek, nerve

unwichtig [**oo**nvishtish] unimportant

uralt [**oo**r-alt] ancient

Urlaub m [**oo**rlowp] holiday, vacation

Urlauber m [**oo**r-lowber], **Urlauberin f** holidaymaker

Urteil n [**oo**rtile] sentence; judgement

usw. (und so weiter) etc

V

vakuumverpackt vacuum-packed

Vater m [**fah**ter] father

Vati m [**vah**tee] dad

Ventil n [**ven**teel] valve

Ventilator m [ventil**ah**tor] fan

Verabredung f [fair-ap-raydoong] appointment

verantwortlich [fair-**a**ntvortlish] responsible

verärgert [fair-**air**gert] angry

Verband m [fairb**a**nt] bandage; association

verbergen [fairb**air**gen] to hide

verbessern [fairb**e**ssern] to improve

Verbindung f [fairb**i**ndoong] connection

verbleit [fairbl**i**te] leaded

verboten [fairb**oh**ten] forbidden, prohibited

Verbrauch m [fairbr**ow**KH] use; consumption

zum baldigen Verbrauch bestimmt will not keep

Verbraucher m [fairbr**ow**KHer], **Verbraucherin f** consumer

Verbrecher m [fairbr**e**sher], **Verbrecherin f** criminal

verbrennen: sich verbrennen [zish fairbr**e**nnen] to burn oneself

Verbrennung f [fairbr**e**nnoong] burn

verdammt (noch mal)! [fairda**mm**t (noKH mahl)] bloody hell!

verdienen [fairde**e**nen] to earn; to deserve

Verein m [fair-**ine**] club

Vereinigte Staaten f [fair-**ine**-isht-uh sht**ah**ten] United States

Vereinigtes Königreich n [fair-**ine**-ishtess k**u**rnish-rysh] United Kingdom

Verengte Fahrbahn road narrows

Verengte Fahrstreifen road narrows

Verfallsdatum n [fairfals-dahtoom] best before date

Vergaser m [fairg**a**hzer] carburettor

vergessen [fairg**e**ssen] to forget

Vergewaltigung f [fairgeval-tigoong] rape

vergleichen [fair-gl**y**shen] to compare

Vergnügen n [fairg-n**oo**gen] pleasure

vergriffen unavailable, out of stock

Vergrößerung f [fair-gr**u**rssseroong] enlargement

verhaften [fairh**a**ften] to arrest

verheiratet [fair-h**y**rahtet] married

verhindern [fairh**i**ndern] to prevent

Verhütungsmittel n [fair-h**oo**toongs-mittel] contraceptive

Verkauf m [fairk**ow**f] sale

verkaufen [fairk**ow**fen] to sell

zu verkaufen [ts**oo**] for sale

Verkauf nur gegen bar cash sales only

verkaufsoffener Samstag open on Saturday; Saturday opening

Verkehr m [fairk**ai**r] traffic

verkehren [fairk**ai**ren] to run

verkehrt alle ... Minuten runs every ... minutes

Verkehrspolizei f [fairk**ai**rs-poleets**i**] traffic police

Verkehrspolizist m [fairk**ai**rs-polits**i**st] traffic policeman

Verkehrsunfall m [fairk**ai**rs-oonfal] traffic accident

Verkehrszeichen n [fairk**ai**rs-tsyshen] roadsign

verlangen [fairl**a**ngen] to ask for

Verlängerungsschnur f [fairl**e**ngeroongs-shn**oo**r] extension lead

verlassen [fairl**a**ssen] to leave

verleihen: zu verleihen [ts**oo** fair-l**ī**-en] for hire, to rent

verletzt [fairl**e**tst] injured

verliebt [fairl**ee**pt] in love

verlieren [fairl**ee**ren] to lose

verlobt [fairl**oh**pt] engaged

Verlobte m/f [fairl**oh**pt-uh] fiancé; fiancée

Verlobung f [fairl**oh**boong] engagement

Verlust m [fairl**oo**st] loss

vermeiden [fairm**y**den] to avoid

vermieten: zu vermieten [ts**oo** fairm**ee**ten] for hire/to rent; to let

Vermieter m [fairm**ee**ter] landlord

Vermieterin f [fairm**ee**terin] landlady

vermissen [fairm**i**ssen] to miss

Vermittlung f [fairm**i**ttloong] operator

vernünftig [fairn**oo**nftish] sensible

verpassen [fairp**a**ssen] to miss

verriegeln [fair-r**ee**geln] to bolt

verrückt [fair-r**oo**ckt] mad

verschieden [fairsh**ee**den] different

verschlafen [fairshl**a**hfen] to oversleep

verschlucken [fairshl**oo**cken] to swallow

Verschluss m [fairshl**oo**ss]

shutter

verschmutzt [fairshm**oo**tst] polluted

verschwinden [fairshv**i**nden] to disappear

verschwinden Sie! go away!

Versicherung f [fairz**i**sheroong] insurance

Versicherungspolice f [fairz**i**sheroongs-pol**ee**ss-uh] insurance policy

verspätet [fairshp**ay**tet] late, delayed

Verspätung f [fairshp**ay**toong] delay

versprechen [fairshpr**e**shen] to promise

verstauchen [fairsht**ow**KHen] to sprain

verstehen [fairsht**ay**-en] to understand

ich verstehe nicht [fairsht**ay**-uh nisht] I don't understand

verstopft [fairsht**o**pft] blocked; constipated

Versuch m [fairz**oo**KH] attempt

versuchen [fairz**oo**KHen] to try

Verteiler m [fairt**y**ler] distributor

Vertrag m [fairtr**ah**k] contract; treaty

Vertreter m [fairtr**ay**ter], **Vertreterin f** representative; agent; sales rep

verwählen: sich verwählen [zish fairv**ay**len] to dial the wrong number

verwitwet [fairv**i**tvet] widowed

Verzeihung! [fair-ts**ī**-oong] I'm sorry; excuse me

Verzogen nach ... moved to ...

Verzögerung f [fairts**u**rgeroong] delay

verzollen [fairts**o**llen] to declare

Vetter m [f**e**tter] cousin

viel [feel] much, a lot (of)

viele [f**ee**l-uh] many

vielen Dank [f**ee**len] thanks a lot

viel Glück! [feel gl**oo**ck] good luck!

viel Glück zum Geburtstag! [tsoom geb**oo**rtstahk] happy birthday!

vielleicht [feel**y**sht] maybe

vier [feer] four

Viertel n [f**ee**rtel] quarter; district

Vierwaldstätter See m [v**ee**rvalt-shtetter zay] Lake Lucerne

vierzehn [f**ee**r-tsayn] fourteen

vierzig [f**ee**rtsish] forty

Visitenkarte f [veez**ee**ten-kart-uh] card; business card

Visum n [v**ee**zoom] visa

Vogel m [f**oh**gel] bird

Volk: das Volk [f**o**llk] the people

voll [fol] full; crowded

voll belegt full, no vacancies

vollklimatisiert fully air-conditioned

Vollnarkose f [f**o**l-narkohz-uh] general anaesthetic

Vollpension f [f**o**l-pangz-yohn] full board

volltanken [f**o**ltanken] to fill up

vom Umtausch ausgeschlossen cannot be exchanged

von [fon] of; by
von ... bis ... from ... to ...
von ... nach ... from ... to ...
vor [for] before; in front of
vor ... Tagen ... days ago
vor dem Frühstück before breakfast
vor Kindern schützen keep out of reach of children
vor dem Schlafengehen before going to bed
Vorausbuchung unbedingt erforderlich reserved seats only
voraus: **im voraus** [vorowss] in advance
vorbei [forby] over
vorbei an ... past ...
Vorderrad n [forder-raht] front wheel
Vorderseite f [forder-zite-uh] front
Vorfahr m [forfahr] ancestor
Vorfahrt f [forfahrt] right of way
Vorfahrt beachten give way
Vorfahrt gewähren give way
Vorfahrtsstraße f [forfahrts-shtrahss-uh] major road (vehicles having right of way)
vorgestern [forgestern] the day before yesterday
Vorhang m [forhang] curtain
vorher [forhair] before
Vorhersage f [forhairzahg-uh] forecast
Vorliebe f [forleeb-uh] liking
Vormittag m [formittahk] (late) morning
vorn [forn] at the front

Vorname m [fornahm-uh] Christian name, first name
Vorprogramm n [for-programm] supporting programme
Vorschlag m [forshlahk] proposal, suggestion
vorschlagen [forshlahgen] to propose
Vorsicht f [forzisht] caution; take care
Vorsicht bissiger Hund beware of the dog
vorsichtig [forzishtish] careful
vorsichtig fahren drive carefully
Vorsicht Stufe! mind the step!
Vorstadt f [forshtatt] suburbs
vorstellen [forshtellen] to introduce
Vorstellung f [forshtelloong] performance
nächste Vorstellung um ... next performance at ...
Vorteil m [fortile] advantage
Vorurteil n [for-oortile] prejudice
Vorwahl f [forvahl] dialling code
Vorwahlnummer f [forvahl-noommer] dialling code
vorziehen [fortsee-en] to prefer

W

wach [vaкн] awake
wachsen [vaksen] to grow
wagen [vahgen] to dare
Wagen m car; coach; carriage
Wagenheber m [vahgen-hayber] jack
Wagenstandanzeiger order of

carriages

Wahl f [vahl] choice; election

wählen [vaylen] to choose; to elect; to dial

Wahlkampf m [vahlkampf] election campaign

Wahnsinn m [vahnzinn] madness
Wahnsinn! fantastic!

wahr [vahr] true

während [vairent] during; while

Wahrheit f [vahr-hite] truth

wahrscheinlich [varshinelish] probable; probably

Währung f [vairoong] currency

Wald m [valt] forest

Waliser m [valeezer] Welshman

Waliserin f [valeezerin] Welshwoman

walisisch [valeezish] Welsh

Wand f [vant] wall

wandern [vandern] to hike, to walk

Wanderweg m [vandervayk] walk, route; trail

wann [van] when

war [var] was

waren [vahren] were

Waren fpl goods

Warenaufzug m [vahren-owfts00k] service lift

Warenhaus n [vahren-howss] department store

warm [varm] warm; hot

warst [varst], **wart** [vart] were

warten [varten] to wait

Wartesaal m [vart-uh-zahl] waiting room

Wartezimmer n [vart-uh-tsimmer] waiting room

warum? [varoom] why?

was? [vass] what?

Waschbecken n [vashbecken] washbasin

Wäsche f [vesh-uh] washing; laundry

waschen [vashen] to wash
sich waschen to wash (oneself)

Wäscherei f [vesher-ī] laundry

Waschlappen m [vashlappen] flannel; coward

Waschmaschine f [vashmasheen-uh] washing mashine

Waschpulver n [vashpoolver] washing powder

Waschraum m [vashrowm] wash room

Waschsalon m [vash-zalong] launderette, laundromat

Waschstraße f [vash-shtrahss-uh] car wash

Waschzeit washing time

Wasser n [vasser] water

wasserdicht [vasserdisht] waterproof

Wasserfall m [vasser-fal] waterfall

Wasserhahn m [vasser-hahn] tap, faucet

Wasserkessel m [vasser-kessel] kettle

wasserlöslich soluble in water

Wasserski n [vassershee] waterskiing

Wassersport m [vasser-shport]

water sports

Waterkant f [**vah**terkant] North German name for the North German coastal area

Watte f [**vatt**-uh] cotton wool, absorbent cotton

wechselhaft [**vek**selhaft] changeable

Wechselkurs m [**vek**sel-koors] exchange rate

wechseln [**vek**seln] to change

Wechselstube f [**vek**sel-shtoob-uh] bureau de change

wecken [**vec**ken] to wake up

Wecker m [**vec**ker] alarm clock

weder ... noch [**vay**der – noKH] neither ... nor ...

Weg m [vayk] path

wegen [**vay**gen] because of

Wegen Krankheit vorübergehend geschlossen temporarily closed due to illness

Wegen Umbauarbeiten geschlossen closed for alterations

weggehen [**vek**-gay-en] to go away

wegnehmen [**vek**-naymen] to take away

Wegweiser m [**vayk**-vyzer] signpost

wegwerfen [**vek**-vairfen] to throw away

weh tun: es tut weh [ess toot vay] it hurts

weiblich [**vipe**-lish] female

weich [vysh] soft

Weihnachten n [**vy**naKHten] Christmas

weil [vile] because

Weile f [**vile**-uh] while

weinen [**vy**nen] to cry

Weinhandlung f [**vine**-hantloong] wine shop

Weinprobe f [**vine**-prohb-uh] wine-tasting

Weinstraße f [**vine**-shtrahss-uh] route through wine-growing areas

Weinstube f [**vine**-shtoob-uh] wine bar (traditional style)

weiß [vice] know; knows; white

weißt [vysst] know

weit [vite] far; wide

weit entfernt far away

Weitzone f [**vite**-tsohn-uh] long-distance zone

welche? [**velsh**-uh] which?

Welle f [**vell**-uh] wave

Welt f [velt] world

wenden [**ven**den] to turn

sich wenden an to contact

wenig [**vay**nish] little; few

weniger [**vay**niger] less

wenn [venn] if

wenn vom Arzt nicht anders verordnet unless otherwise prescribed by your doctor

wer? [vair] who?

Werbung f [**vair**boong] advertising; publicity

werde [**vair**d-uh] will; become

werden [**vair**den] to become; will

werdet [**vair**det] will; become

werfen [**vair**fen] to throw

Werkstatt f [**vair**kshtatt] auto repairs

Werktag m [**vair**ktahk] weekday

Werkzeug n [**vair**k-tsoyk] tool

wert [vairt] worth

Wert m [vairt] value

Wertmünzen tokens

Wertsachen fpl [**vair**tzakHen] valuables

Wespe f [**ve**sp-uh] wasp

Wessi m [**ve**ssee] West German

Weste f [**ve**st-uh] waistcoat

Westen m [**ve**sten] west

westliche Stadtteile city west

westlich von [**ve**stlish fon] west of

Wette f [**ve**tt-uh] bet

wetten [**ve**tten] to bet

Wetter n [**ve**tter] weather

Wetterbericht m [**ve**tter-berisht] weather forecast

Wettervorhersage f [**ve**tter-for**hair**-zahg-uh] weather forecast

wichtig [**vi**shtish] important

wider [**vee**der] against

widerlich [**vee**derlish] disgusting

Widerrechtlich abgestellte Fahrzeuge werden kostenpflichtig abgeschleppt illegally parked vehicles will be removed at the owner's expense

widersprechen [veeder-shpreshen] to contradict

widerwärtig [**vee**der-vairtish] obnoxious

wie? [vee] how?

wie [vee] like

wie bitte? pardon (me)?, what did you say?

wie geht es Ihnen? [gayt ess **ee**nen] how are you?

wie geht's? how are things?

wieder [**vee**der] again

wiederholen [veeder-**ho**hlen] to repeat

Wiederhören: auf Wiederhören [owf **vee**der-hur-ren] goodbye (said on the phone)

wiegen [**vee**gen] to weigh

Wien [veen] Vienna

wieviel? [vee**feel**] how much?

wie viele? [vee **fee**l-uh] how many?

Wildleder n [**vi**ltlayder] suede

will [vill] want to; wants to

willkommen! [vill**ko**mmen] welcome!

willst [villst] want to

Wimperntusche f [**vi**mpern-toosh-uh] mascara

Windel f [**vi**ndel] nappy, diaper

windig [**vi**ndish] windy

Windschutzscheibe f [**vi**ntshoots-shibe-uh] windscreen

Winterfahrplan m [**vi**nterfahrplahn] winter timetable/schedule

Winterschlussverkauf m winter sales

wir [veer] we

wir müssen draußen bleiben sorry, no dogs

wir sind umgezogen we have moved

wird [veert] will; becomes

wirklich [veerklish] really

wirst [veerst] will; become

Wirt m [veert] landlord; host

Wirtin f [veertin] landlady; hostess

Wirtschaft f [veert-shafft] pub; economy

Wirtshaus n [veerts-howss] inn; pub

wissen [vissen] to know

wisst [vist] know

Witwe f [vitv-uh] widow

Witwer m [vitver] widower

Witz m [vits] joke

wo? [vo] where?

woanders [vo-anderss] elsewhere

Woche f [voKH-uh] week

Wochenende n [voKHen-end-uh] weekend

Wochenkarte f [voKHenkart-uh] weekly ticket

Woge f [vohg-uh] wave

woher? [vo-hair] where from?

wohin? [vo-hin] where to?

Wohnblock m [vohnblock] block of flats, apartment block

wohnen [vohnen] to live; to stay

Wohnmobil n [vohn-mobeel] caravan, (US) trailer

Wohnort m [vohn-ort] place of residence

Wohnung f [vohnoong] flat, apartment

Wohnwagen m [vohnvahgen] caravan, (US) trailer

Wohnzimmer n [vohn-tsimmer] living room

Wolke f [volk-uh] cloud

Wolle f [voll-uh] wool

wollen [vollen] to want

wollen Sie ...? do you want ...?

womit [vo-mit] with which; with what

worauf [vo-rowf] (up)on which

worden [vorden] been

worin [vo-rin] in which

Wort n [vort] word

Wörterbuch n [vurterbooKH] dictionary

wovon [vo-fon] from which; from what

wozu? [vo-tsoo] what for?

Wunde f [voond-uh] wound

wunderbar [voonderbar] wonderful

Wunsch m [voonsh] wish

wünschen [voonshen] to wish

wurde [voord-uh] was; became

würde [voord-uh] would

wurden [voorden], wurdest, wurdet were; became

würzen [voortsen] to season

würzig [voortsish] spicy

wusste [voosst-uh], wussten, wusstest knew

Wut f [voot] fury

wütend [vootent] furious

Z

zäh [tsay] tough

Zahl f [tsahl] number

zahlbar [tsahlbar] payable

zahlen [tsahlen] to pay

Zahlung f [tsahloong] payment

Zahn m [tsahn] tooth

Zahnarzt m [tsahn-artst], Zahnärztin f [tsahn-airtstin] dentist

Zahnbelag m [tsahn-belahk] plaque

Zahnersatz m [tsahn-airzats] dentures

Zahnklinik f [tsahn-kleenik] dental clinic

Zahnpasta f [tsahn-pastah] toothpaste

Zahnschmerzen mpl [tsahn-shmairtsen] toothache

Zange f [tsang-uh] pliers

Zapfsäule f [tsapf-zoyl-uh] petrol/gas pump

Zaun m [tsown] fence

z.B. (zum Beispiel) eg

ZDF (Zweites Deutsches Fernsehen) [tset-day-eff] Second German Television Channel

Zebrastreifen m [tsaybrah-shtryfen] zebra crossing

Zehe f [tsay-uh] toe

zehn [tsayn] ten

Zehnmarkschein m [tsayn-mark-shine] ten-mark note/bill

Zeichen n [tsyshen] sign

zeichnen [tsyshnen] to draw

zeigen [tsygen] to show; to point

Zeit f [tsite] time

Zeitansage f [tsite-anzahg-uh] speaking clock

Zeitschrift f [tsite-shrift] magazine

Zeitung f [tsytoong] newspaper

Zelt n [tselt] tent

Zelten verboten no camping

Zeltplatz m [tseltplats] campsite

Zentimeter m [tsentimayter] centimetre

Zentner m [tsentner] 50 kilos

Zentralheizung f [tsentrahl-hytsoong] central heating

Zentrum n [tsentroom] centre

zerbrechen [tsairbreshen] to break

zerstören [tsairshtur-ren] to destroy

Zettel m [tsettel] piece of paper

Zeuge m [tsoyg-uh], Zeugin f witness

Ziege f [tseeg-uh] goat

ziehen [tsee-en] to pull

Ziel n [tseel] aim; destination

ziemlich [tseemlish] rather

Zigarre f [tsigarr-uh] cigar

Zimmer n [tsimmer] room

Zimmer frei room(s) to let/ rent, vacancies

Zimmermädchen n [tsimmer-maytshen] chambermaid

Zimmernachweis m [tsimmer-naкнvice] accommodation service

Zimmerservice m [tsimmer-'service'] room service

Zimmer zu vermieten rooms to let/rent

Zinsen pl [tsinzen] interest

Zinssatz m [tsinss-zats] interest rate

Zoll m [tsol] Customs

Zollbeamte m [tsoll-buh-amt-uh], Zollbeamtin f customs officer zollfrei [tsolfry] duty-free

zollfreie Waren **fpl** [tsolfry-uh **vah**ren] duty-free goods

Zone 30 zone with 30 km/h speed limit

zu [tsoo] to; too; shut

zubereiten [tsoo-beryten] to prepare

Zuckergehalt sugar content

zufrieden [tsoofreeden] pleased

Zug **m** [tsook] train; draught

zu den Zügen to the trains

Zugabe **f** [tsoogahb-uh] encore

zugelassen für ... Personen carries ... persons

zuhören [tsoo-hur-ren] to listen

Zukunft **f** [tsookoonft] future

zum [tsoom] to the

zum Ochsen The Ox (pub etc name)

zunächst [tsoonaykst] first, firstly

Zunahme **f** [tsoonahm-uh] increase

Zuname **m** [tsoonahm-uh] surname

Zündkerze **f** [tsoont-kairts-uh] spark plug

Zündung **f** [tsoondoong] ignition

zunehmen [tsoonaymen] to increase; to put on weight

Zunge **f** [tsoong-uh] tongue

zur [tsoor] to the

zurück [tsooroock] back

zurückgeben [tsooroock-gayben] to give back

zurückkehren [tsooroock-kairen] to go back, to return

zurückkommen [tsooroock-kommen] to come back

zusammen [tsoozammen] together

Zusammenstoß **m** [tsoozammen-shtohss] crash

Zuschauer **m** [tsooshower], Zuschauerin **f** spectator

Zuschlag **m** [tsooshlahk] supplement

zuschlagpflichtig [tsooshlahk-pflishtish] supplement payable

zustimmen [tsooshtimmen] to agree

Zutaten **fpl** [tsootahten] ingredients

Zutreffendes ankreuzen cross where applicable

Zutritt für Unbefugte verboten no admission to unauthorized persons

zuviel [tsoofeel] too much

Zuwiderhandlung wird strafrechtlich verfolgt we will prosecute

zwanzig [tsvantsish] twenty

Zwanzigmarkschein **m** [tsvantsish-mark-shine] twenty-mark note/bill

Zweck **m** [tsveck] purpose

zwei [tsvy] two

Zweibettzimmer **n** [tsvybett-tsimmer] twin room

Zweig **m** [tsvike] branch

Zweigstelle **f** [tsvike-shtell-uh] branch

Zweimal täglich einzunehmen to be taken twice a day

zweite(r,s) [tsvite-uh, -er, -ess]

second
zweite Klasse f [tsv**ite**-uh klass-uh] second class
zweiter Stock m [tsv**y**ter shtock] second floor, (US) third floor
zweite Wahl seconds
Zwillinge mpl [tsvilling-uh] twins
zwischen [tsv**i**shen] between
Zwischenlandung f [tsv**i**shen-landoong] intermediate stop; stopover
Zwischenmahlzeit f [tsv**i**shen-mahltsite] snack between meals
zwölf [tsv**u**rlf] twelve
z.Zt. (zur Zeit) at the moment

Zz

Menu
Reader:
Food

Essential Terms

bread das Brot [broht]
butter die Butter [bootter]
cup die Tasse [tass-uh]
dessert der Nachtisch [naKHtish]
fish der Fisch [fish]
fork die Gabel [gahbel]
glass: a glass of ... ein Glas ... [ine glahss]
knife das Messer
main course das Hauptgericht [howpt-gerisht]
meat das Fleisch [flysh]
menu die Speisekarte [shpize-uh-kart-uh]
pepper der Pfeffer
plate der Teller
salad der Salat [zalaht]
salt das Salz [zalts]
set menu die Tageskarte [tahgess-kart-uh]
soup die Suppe [zoop-uh]
spoon der Löffel [lurfel]
starter die Vorspeise [for-shpize-uh]
table der Tisch [tish]

another ..., please noch ein ..., bitte [noKH ine bitt-uh]
excuse me! Entschuldigung! [ent-shooldigoong]
could I have the bill, please? kann ich bitte bezahlen? [kan ish bitt-uh betsahlen]

Aal [ahl] eel

Aalsuppe [ahlzoop-uh] eel soup

Ananas [ananass] pineapple

angemacht mit prepared with

Äpfel [epfel] apples

Äpfel im Schlafrock [shlahfrock] baked apples in puff pastry

Apfelkompott stewed apples

Apfelkuchen [-kOOKHen] apple pie

Apfelmeerrettich [-mayr-rettish] horseradish with apple

Apfelmus [-mOOss] apple purée

Apfelrotkohl red cabbage cooked with apples

Apfelsinen [apfelzeenen] oranges

Apfelstrudel apple strudel

Apfeltasche [-tash-uh] apple turnover

Aprikosen [aprikohzen] apricots

Arme Ritter [arm-uh] bread soaked in milk and egg then fried

aromatisiert aromatic

Artischocken artichokes

Artischockenherz [-hairts] artichoke heart

Aspik [aspeek] aspic

Auberginen [ohbairJeenen] aubergines, eggplants

Auflauf [owf-lowf] (baked) pudding or omelette

Aufschnitt [owf-shnitt] sliced cold meats, cold cuts

Austern [owstern] oysters

Bachforelle [baKH-forell-uh] river trout

backen to bake

Backobst [backohpst] dried fruit

Backofen oven

Backpflaumen [-pflowmen] prunes

Baiser [bezzay] meringue

Balkansalat [balkahn-zalaht] cabbage and pepper salad

Bananen [banahnen] bananas

Bandnudeln [bantnOOdeln] ribbon noodles

Basilikum basil

Bauernauflauf [bowern-owflowf] bacon and potato omelette

Bauernfruhstück [-frOOshtOOk] bacon and potato omelette

Bauernomelett [-omlet] bacon and potato omelette

Baumkuchen [bowmkOOKHen] cylindrical, layered cake

Béchamelkartoffeln sliced potatoes in creamy sauce

Béchamelsoße [-zohss-uh] creamy sauce with onions and ham

Beilagen [bylahgen] side dishes; side salads, vegetables

belegtes Brot [belayktess broht] sandwich

Berliner (Ballen) [bairleener (ballen)] jam doughnut with icing

bestreut mit sprinkled with

Bienenstich [beenen-shtish] honey and almond tart

Bierschinken [beer-shinken] ham sausage

Biersuppe [beerzoop-uh] beer soup

Birnen [**bee**rnen] pears

Biskuit [bisk**weet**] sponge

Biskuitrolle [bisk**weet**-rol-uh] Swiss roll

Bismarckheringe [-**hairing**-uh] filleted pickled herrings

Blätterteig [bl**e**ttertike] puff pastry

Blattsalat [-zal**aht**] green salad

Blattspinat [-sphinaht] leaf spinach

blau [blow] boiled, au bleu

Blaufelchen [bl**ow**-faylshen] blue Lake Constance trout

Blaukraut [bl**ow**krowt] red cabbage

Blumenkohl [bl**oo**menkohl] cauliflower

Blumenkohlsuppe [-zoop-uh] cauliflower soup

blutig [bl**oo**tish] rare

Blutwurst [bl**oo**t-voorst] black pudding, blood sausage

Bockwurst large frankfurter

Bohnen beans

Bohneneintopf [-**ine**-topf] bean stew

Bohnensalat [-zal**aht**] bean salad

Bohnensuppe [-zoop-uh] bean soup

Bonbon [bongb**ong**] sweet

Bouillon [booly**ong**] clear soup

Bouletten meat balls

Braten [br**ah**ten] roast meat

braten to fry

Bratensoße [-zohss-uh] gravy

Brathähnchen [br**ah**t-haynshen] roast chicken

Bratheringe [-**hairing**-uh] (pickled) fried herrings (served cold)

Bratkartoffeln fried potatoes

Bratwurst [-**voorst**] grilled pork sausage

Brezel [br**ay**tsel] pretzel

Brombeeren [br**o**mbairen] blackberries

Brot [broht] bread

Brötchen [br**ur**tshen] roll

Brotsuppe [br**oh**tzoop-uh] bread soup

Brühwurst [br**oo**voorst] large frankfurter

Brunnenkresse [br**oo**nnen-kress-uh] watercress

Bückling [b**oo**kling] smoked red herring

bunte Platte [b**oo**nt-uh pl**a**t-uh] mixed platter

Burgundersoße [boorg**oo**nder-zohss-uh] Burgundy wine sauce

Butterbrezel [b**oo**tter-braytsel] butter pretzel

Buttercremetorte [b**oo**tterkraym-tort-uh] cream cake

Champignoncremesuppe [-kraym-zoop-uh] cream of mushroom soup

Champignons [shampinyongs] mushrooms

Champignonsoße [-zohss-uh] mushroom sauce

Chicorée [sh**i**koray] chicory

Chinakohl [sh**ee**na-kohl] Chinese leaf

216

Chips crisps, potato chips
Cordon bleu veal cordon bleu
Curryreis [-rice] curried rice
Currywurst [-voorst] curried pork sausage

Dampfnudeln [-noodeln] sweet yeast dumpling
dazu reichen wir ... served with ...
deutsches Beefsteak [doytshess] mince patty
dicke Bohnen [dick-uh] broad beans
Dillsoße [-zohss-uh] dill sauce
durchgebraten [doorsh-gebrahten] well-done
durchwachsen [doorsh-vacksen] with fat
durchwachsener Speck [shpeck] streaky bacon

Edelpilzkäse [aydelpilts-kayz-uh] blue cheese
Ei [I] egg
Eier [I-er] eggs
Eierauflauf [-owf-lowf] omelette
Eierkuchen [-kookнen] pancake
Eierpfannkuchen pancake
Eierspeise [-shpize-uh] egg dish
eingelegt [ine-gelaykt] pickled
eingelegte Bratheringe pickled herrings
eingemacht [ine-gemaкнt] preserved
ein paar ... some ...
Eintopf [ine-topf] stew
Eintopfgericht [-gerisht] stew
Eis [ice] ice; ice cream

Eis am Stiel [shteel] ice lolly
Eisbecher [-besher] sundae
Eisbein [-bine] knuckles of pork
Eisbergsalat [-bairk-zalaht] iceberg lettuce
Eisschokolade [-shockolahd-uh] iced chocolate
Eissplittertorte [-shplitter-tort-uh] ice chip cake
Endiviensalat [endeev-yen-zalaht] endive salad
englisch [eng-lish] rare
Ente [ent-uh] duck
Entenbraten [entenbrahten] roast duck
entgrätet boned
Entrecote sirloin steak
Erbsen [airpsen] peas
Erbsensuppe [-zoop-uh] pea soup
Erdäpfel [airt-epfel] potatoes
Erdbeeren [airtbairen] strawberries
Erdbeertorte [-tort-uh] strawberry gâteau
Erdnüsse [airtnooss-uh] peanuts
Essig vinegar

falscher Hase [fal-sher hahz-uh] meat loaf
Fasan [fazahn] pheasant
Faschierte Laibchen [fasheert-uh lipe-shen] rissoles
Faschiertes [fasheertess] minced meat
Feldsalat [feltzalaht] lamb's lettuce
Fenchel fennel
Filet [fillay] fillet (steak)

Fisch [fish] fish

Fischfilet fish fillet

Fischfrikadellen fishcakes

Fischgerichte fish dishes

Fischstäbchen [-shtaypshen] fish fingers

Flädlesuppe [flaydl-uh-zoop-uh] soup with strips of pasta

flambiert flambé

Fleisch [flysh] meat

Fleischbrühe [-broo-uh] bouillon

Fleischkäse [-kayz-uh] meat loaf

Fleischklößchen [-klurss-shen] meat ball(s)

Fleischpastete [-pastayt-uh] meat vol-au-vent

Fleischsalat [-zalaht] diced meat salad with mayonnaise

Fleischtomate [-tomaht-uh] beef tomato

Fleisch- und Wurstwaren meats and sausages

Fleischwurst [-voorst] pork sausage

Flugente [floog-ent-uh] wild duck

Folienkartoffel [fohl-yen-] baked potato

Fond [font] meat juices

Forelle [forell-uh] trout

Forelle blau [blow] trout au bleu

Forelle Müllerin (Art) [moollerin] trout coated with breadcrumbs and served with butter and lemon

Frikadelle [frickadell-uh] rissole

frisch gepresst freshly squeezed

Frischwurst [-voorst] fresh sausage

fritiert [friteert] (deep-)fried

Froschschenkel [frosh-shenkel] frogs' legs

Frühlingsgemüse [froolings-gemooz-uh] spring vegetables

Frühlingsrolle [-rol-uh] spring roll

Gabelrollmops [gahbel-] rolled pickled herring, rollmops

Gans [ganss] goose

Gänsebraten [genz-uh-brahten] roast goose

Gänseleber [-layber] goose liver

Gänseleberpastete [-pastayt-uh] goose liver pâté

gar cooked

garniert [garneert] garnished

Gebäck [gebeck] pastries, cakes

gebacken fried

gebeizt [gebytst] marinaded

gebraten [gebrahten] roast

gebunden [geboonden] thickened

gedämpft [gedempft] steamed

Gedeck set meal

gedünstet [gedoonstet] steamed

Geflügel [gefloogel] poultry

Geflügelleber [-layber] chicken liver

Geflügelleberragout [-ragoo] chicken liver ragout

Geflügelsalat [-zalaht] chicken/poultry salad

gefüllt [gefoolt] stuffed

gefüllte Kalbsbrust [kalpsbroost] veal roll

gegart cooked

gegrillt grilled

gehackt minced; chopped

Gehacktes minced meat

gekocht [gekoкнt] boiled

gekochtes Ei [ī] boiled egg

Gelee [Jellay] jelly

gemischter Salat [gemishter zalaht] mixed salad

gemischtes Eis [īce] assorted ice creams

Gemüse [gemooz-uh] vegetable(s)

Gemüseplatte [plat-uh] assorted vegetables

Gemüsereis [-rice] rice with vegetables

Gemüsesalat [-zalaht] vegetable salad

Gemüsesuppe [-zoop-uh] vegetable soup

gepökelt [gepurkelt] salted, pickled

geräuchert [geroyshert] smoked

gerieben [gereeben] grated

Germknödel [gairm-k-nurdel] yeast dumplings

geschlagen [geshlahgen] whipped

geschmort [geshmohrt] braised, stewed

geschnetzelt [geshnetselt] chopped

Geschnetzeltes strips of meat in thick sauce

Geselchtes [gezelshtess] salted

and smoked meat

gespickt mit ... larded with ...

geschwenkt [geshvenkt] sautéed

Gewürze [gevoorts-uh] spices

Gewürzgurken [-goorken] gherkins

Goldbarsch [goltbarsh] type of perch

Götterspeise [gurttershpize-uh] jelly

gratiniert [gratineert] au gratin

Grießklößchen [greessklurs-shen] semolina dumplings

Grießsuppe [-zoop-uh] semolina soup

grüne Bohnen [groon-uh] French beans

grüne Nudeln [noodeln] green pasta

grüner Aal [ahl] fresh eel

Grünkohl (curly) kale

Gugelhupf [googel-hoopf] ring-shaped cake

Gulasch goulash

Gulaschsuppe [-zoop-uh] goulash soup

Gurke [goork-uh] cucumber; gherkin

Gurkensalat [-zalaht] cucumber salad

Hackepeter [hack-uh-payter] minced meat

Hackfleisch [-flysh] minced meat

Hähnchen [haynshen] chicken

Hähnchenkeule [-koyl-uh] chicken leg

Haifischflossensuppe

[hyfishflossen-zoop-uh] shark-fin soup

halbes Hähnchen [haynshen] half chicken

Hammelbraten [-brahten] roast mutton

Hammelfleisch [-flysh] mutton

Hammelkeule [-koyl-uh] leg of mutton

Hammelrücken [-rㅇㅇcken] saddle of mutton

Handkäse [hant-kayz-uh] very strong-smelling cheese

hartgekochtes Ei [hartgekoㅋㅋtess ī] hard-boiled egg

Hartkäse [-kayz-uh] hard cheese

Haschee [hashay] hash

Haselnüsse [hahzelnㅇㅇss-uh] hazelnuts

Hasenbraten [hahzenbrahten] roast hare

Hasenkeule [-koyl-uh] haunch of hare

Hasenpfeffer jugged hare

Hauptgerichte main dishes

Hauptspeisen main courses

Hausfrauenart [howssfrowenart] home-made style

hausgemacht [howss-gemaㅋㅋt] homemade

Hausmacher (Art) [howssmaㅋㅋHer] home-made style

Hausmarke [howss-mark-uh] own brand

Hecht [hesht] pike

Hechtsuppe [-zoop-uh] pike soup

Heidelbeeren [hydelbairen] bilberries

Heilbutt [hile-boott] halibut

Heringssalat [hairings-zalaht] herring salad

Heringsstipp [-shtip] herring salad

Heringstopf pickled herrings

Herz [hairts] heart

Himbeeren [himbairen] raspberries

Himmel und Erde [oont aird-uh] potato and apple purée with liver sausage

Hirn [heern] brains

Hirschbraten [heershbrahten] roast venison

Hirschmedaillons [-medah-yongs] small venison fillets

Holsteiner Schnitzel [holshtyner shnitsel] breaded veal cutlet with vegetables, topped with a fried egg

Honig [hohnish] honey

Honigkuchen [-kㅇㅇKHen] honeycake

Honigmelone [-melohn-uh] honeydew melon

Hoppelpoppel bacon and potato omelette

Hüfte [hㅇㅇft-uh] haunch

Huhn [hㅇㅇn] chicken

Hühnerbrühe [hㅇㅇner-brㅇㅇ-uh] chicken broth

Hühnersuppe [-zoop-uh] chicken soup

Hülsenfrüchte [hㅇㅇlzenfrㅇㅇsht-uh] peas and beans, pulses

Hummer [hㅇㅇmmer] lobster

Imbiss [imbiss] snack
inbegriffen included
Inklusivpreis all-inclusive price

Jagdwurst [yahkt-voorst] ham
sausage with garlic
Jägerschnitzel [yaygershnitsel]
pork with mushrooms
junge Erbsen [yoong-uh airpzen]
spring peas

Kabeljau [kahbelyow] cod
Kaiserschmarren
[kyzershmarren] sugared
pancakes with raisins
Kalbfleisch [kalpflysh] veal
Kalbsbraten [-brahten] roast
veal
Kalbsbries [-breess]
sweetbread
Kalbsfrikassee veal fricassee
Kalbshaxe leg of veal
Kalbsmedaillons [-medah-yongs]
small veal fillets
Kalbsnierenbraten [-neeren-
brahten] roast veal with
kidney
Kalbsschnitzel [-shnitsel] veal
cutlet
kalte Platte cold meal
kalter Braten [brahten] cold
meat
kaltes Bufett cold buffet
kalte Speisen cold dishes
Kaltschale [kaltshahl-uh] cold
sweet fruit soup
kalt servieren serve cold
Kaninchen [kaneenshen] rabbit
Kaninchenbraten [-brahten]

roast rabbit
Kapern [kahpern] capers
Karbonade [karbonahd-uh]
carbonade, beef and onion
stew cooked in beer
Karfiol [karf-yohl] cauliflower
Karotten carrots
Karpfen carp
Karpfen blau [blow] carp au
bleu
Kartoffel potato
Kartoffelbrei [-bry] potato
purée
Kartoffelklöße [-klurss-uh]
potato dumplings
Kartoffelknödel [-k-nurdel]
potato dumplings
Kartoffeln potatoes
Kartoffelpuffer [-pooffer] potato
fritters
Kartoffelpüree [-pooray] potato
purée
Kartoffelsalat [-zalaht] potato
salad
Kartoffelsuppe [-zoop-uh]
potato soup
Käse [kayz-uh] cheese
Käsebrötchen [-brurtshen]
cheese roll
Käsegebäck [-gebeck] cheese
savouries
Käsekuchen [-kooKHen]
cheesecake
Käseplatte [-plat-uh] selection
of cheeses, cheeseboard
Käse-Sahne-Torte [-zahn-uh-
tort-uh] cream cheesecake
Käsesalat [-zalaht] cheese salad
Käseschnitzel [-shnitsel]

escalopes with cheese

Käsesoße [-zohss-uh] cheese sauce

Käsespätzle [-shpetz-luh] home-made noodles with cheese

Kasseler Rippenspeer [rippen-shpair] salted ribs of pork

Kasserolle [kasserol-uh] casserole

Kassler smoked and braised pork chops

Kastanien [kastahn-yen] chestnuts

Katenleberwurst [kahtenlayber-voorst] smoked liver sausage

Katenrauchwurst [-rowKH-voorst] smoked sausage

Keule [koyl-uh] leg, haunch

Kieler Sprotten [keeler shprotten] smoked sprats

Kinderteller children's portion

Kirschen [keershen] cherries

klare Brühe [klahr-uh broo-uh] clear soup

Klößchensuppe [klurss-shen-zoop-uh] clear soup with dumplings

Klöße [klurss-uh] dumplings

Knäckebrot [k-neck-uh-broht] crispbread

Knacker frankfurter(s)

Knackwurst [-voorst] frankfurter

Knoblauch [k-nohb-lowKH] garlic

Knoblauchbrot [-broht] garlic bread

Knochen [k-noKHen] bone

Knochenschinken [-shinken] ham on the bone

Knödel [k-nurdel] dumplings

kochen [koKHen] to cook; to boil

Kohl cabbage

Kohlrabi [-rahbee] kohlrabi (type of cabbage)

Kohlrouladen [-roolahden] stuffed cabbage leaves

Kohl und Pinkel cabbage, potatoes, sausage and smoked meat

Kompott stewed fruit

Konfitüre [konfitoor-uh] jam

Königinpastete [kurnigin-pastayt-uh] chicken vol-au-vent

Königsberger Klopse [kurniksbairger klops-uh] meatballs in caper sauce

Königskuchen [kurniks-kooKHen] type of fruit cake

Kopfsalat [kopfzalaht] lettuce

Kotelett [kotlet] chop

Krabben shrimps, prawns

Krabbencocktail prawn cocktail

Kraftbrühe [kraftbroo-uh] beef consommé, beef tea

Krapfen jam doughnut with icing

Kräuter [kroyter] herbs

Kräuterbutter [-booter] herb butter

Kräuterkäse [-kayz-uh] cheese flavoured with herbs

Kräutersoße [-zohss-uh] herb sauce

Krautsalat [krowtzalaht] coleslaw

Krautwickel [-vickel] stuffed cabbage leaves

Krebs [krayps] crayfish

Kren [krayn] horseradish

Kresse [kress-uh] cress

Kroketten croquettes

Kruste crust

Küche [kOOsh-uh] cooking; cuisine; kitchen

Kuchen [kOOKHen] cake; pie

Kümmel [kOOmel] caraway

Kümmelbraten [-brahten] roast with caraway seeds

Kürbis [kOOrbiss] pumpkin

Labskaus [lapskowss] meat, fish and potato stew

Lachs [lacks] salmon

Lachsersatz [-airzats] sliced and salted pollack

Lachsforelle [-forell-uh] sea trout

Lachsschinken [-shinken] smoked rolled fillet of ham

Lakritz liquorice

Lamm Lamb

Lammrücken [-rOOken] saddle of lamb

Languste [langoost-uh] crayfish

Lauch [lowKH] leek

Lauchsuppe [-zoop-uh] leek soup

Leber [layber] liver

Leberkäse [-kayz-uh] baked pork and beef loaf

Leberklöße [-klurss-uh] liver dumplings

Leberknödel [-k-nurdel] liver dumplings

Leberknödelsuppe [-zoop-uh] liver dumpling soup

Leberpastete [-pastayt-uh] liver pâté

Leberwurst [-voorst] liver sausage

Lebkuchen [layp-kOOKHen] type of gingerbread biscuit

legiert thickened

Leipziger Allerlei [lipe-tsiger al-er-ly] mixed vegetables

Lendensteak loin steak

Linseneintopf [linzen-inetopf] lentil stew

Linsensuppe [-zoop-uh] lentil soup

Lutscher [lootsher] lollipop

mager [mahger] lean

Majoran [mahyo-rahn] marjoram

Makrele [makrayl-uh] mackerel

Makronen [makrohnen] macaroons

Mandarine [mandareen-uh] tangerine

Mandeln almonds

Margarine [margareen-uh] margarine

Marille [marill-uh] apricot

Marinade [mareenahd-uh] marinade

mariniert marinaded, pickled

Markklößchen [-klurss-shen] marrow dumplings

Marmelade [marmelahd-uh] jam

Marmorkuchen [marmor-kOOKHen] marble cake

Maronen [marohnen] sweet

chestnuts

Matjesfilet [matyess-fillay] fillet of herring

Matjes(hering) [-hairing] young herring

Maultaschen [mowl-tashen] pasta filled with meat, vegetables or cheese

Medaillons [maydah-yongs] small fillets

Meeresfische [mairess-fish-uh] seafish

Meeresfrüchte [-frOOsht-uh] seafood

Meerrettich [mair-rettish] horseradish

Meerrettichsoße [-zohss-uh] horseradish sauce

Mehl [mayl] flour

Mehlspeise [-shpize-uh] sweet dish, flummery

Melone [melohn-uh] melon

Menü set menu

Miesmuscheln [meess-moosheln] mussels

Milch [milsh] milk

Milchreis [-rice] rice pudding

Mirabelle [meerabell-uh] small yellow plum

Mischbrot [mishbroht] rye and wheat bread

Mohnkuchen [mohnkOOKHen] poppyseed cake

Mohnstrudel poppy-seed strudel

Möhren [mur-ren] carrots

Mohrrüben [mohr-rOOben] carrots

Mus [mOOss] purée

Muscheln [moosheln] mussels

Muskat(nuss) [mooskaht(nooss)] nutmeg

nach Art des Hauses [howzess] à la maison

nach Hausfrauenart [howss-frowenart] home-made

nach Jahreszeit depending on season

Nachspeisen [naKH-shpyzen] desserts

Nachtisch [naKHtish] dessert

Napfkuchen [napf-kOOKHen] ring-shaped pound cake

natur [natOOr] plain

nicht gar underdone

Nierenragout [neeren-ragOO] kidney ragout

Nudeln [nOOdeln] pasta

Nudelsalat [-zalaht] noodle salad

Nudelsuppe [-zoop-uh] noodle soup

Nuss [nooss] nut

Nüsse [nOOss-uh] nuts

Obst [ohpst] fruit

Obstsalat [-zalaht] fruit salad

Ochsenschwanzsuppe [oksen-shvants-zoop-uh] oxtail soup

ohne Knochen filleted

Öl [url] oil

Oliven [oleeven] olives

Olivenöl olive oil

Omelett [omlet] omelette

Orangen [oron-Jen] oranges

Originalrezept original recipe

Palatschinken [pallatshinken] stuffed pancakes

Pampelmuse [pampel-mooz-uh] grapefruit

paniert [paneert] with breadcrumbs

Paprikarahmschnitzel [papreekah-rahmshnitsel] cutlet in creamy sauce with paprika

Paprikasalat [-zalaht] pepper salad

Paprikaschote [-shoht-uh] pepper

Paradeiser [paradyzer] tomatoes

Parmesankäse [parmezahnkayz-uh] Parmesan cheese

Pastete [pastayt-uh] vol-au-vent; pâté

Pellkartoffeln potatoes boiled in their jackets

Petersilie [payterzeel-yuh] parsley

Petersilienkartoffeln potatoes with parsley

Pfannengerichte fried dishes

Pfannkuchen [-kooкнen] pancake

Pfeffer pepper

Pfefferminz peppermint

Pfeffernüsse [-nooss-uh] gingerbread biscuits

Pfefferrahmsoße [-rahmzohss-uh] peppered creamy sauce

Pfifferlinge [pfifferling-uh] chanterelles

Pfirsiche [pfeerzish-uh] peaches

Pflaumen [pflowmen] plums

Pflaumenkuchen [-kooкнen]
plum tart

Pflaumenmus [-mooss] plum jam

Pichelsteiner Topf [pishelshtyner] vegetable stew with diced beef

Pilze [pilts-uh] mushrooms

Pilzsoße [pilts-zohss-uh] mushroom sauce

Pilzsuppe [-zoop-uh] mushroom soup

Platte [plat-uh] selection

Plätzchen [plets-shen] biscuit

pochiert [posheert] poached

Pökelfleisch [purkelflysh] salted meat

Pommes frites [pom frit] chips, French fries

Porree [porray] leek

Potthast [pot-hast] braised beef with sauce

Poularde [poollard-uh] young chicken

Preiselbeeren [pryzel-bairen] cranberries

Presskopf [presskopf] brawn

Prinzessbohnen [printsess-] unsliced runner beans

Pumpernickel black rye bread

Püree [pooray] (potato) purée

püriert [pooreert] puréed

Putenschenkel [pootenshenkel] turkey leg

Putenschnitzel [-shnitsel] turkey escalope

Puter [pooter] turkey

Quark [kvark] type of low-fat cream cheese, quark

Quarkspeise [-shpize-uh] dish made with low-fat cream cheese

Radieschen [radeess-shen] radishes

Rahm (sour) cream

Rahmschnitzel [-shnitsel] cutlet in creamy sauce

Räucheraal [roysher-ahl] smoked eel

Räucherhering [-hairing] kipper, smoked herring

Räucherlachs [-lacks] smoked salmon

Räucherspeck smoked bacon

Rauchfleisch [rowKH-flysh] smoked meat

Rehbraten [ray-brahten] roast venison

Rehkeule [-koyl-uh] haunch of venison

Rehrücken [-rooken] saddle of venison

Reibekuchen [ribe-uh-kooKHen] potato waffles

Reis [rice] rice

Reisauflauf [-owf-lowf] rice pudding

Reisbrei [rice-bry] creamed rice

Reisfleisch [-flysh] meat with rice and tomatoes

Reisrand [-rant] with rice

Reissalat [-zalaht] rice salad

Reissuppe [-zoop-uh] rice soup

Remoulade [remoolahd-uh] remoulade (mayonnaise and herb dressing)

Renke [renk-uh] whitefish

Rettich [rettish] radish

Rhabarber [rabarber] rhubarb

rheinischer Sauerbraten [rynisher zowerbrahten] braised beef

Rinderbraten [rinder-brahten] pot roast

Rinderfilet [-fillay] fillet steak

Rinderleber [-layber] ox liver

Rinderlende [-lend-uh] beef tenderloin

Rinderrouladen [-roolahden] stuffed beef rolls

Rinderschmorbraten [-shmohr-brahten] pot roast

Rinderzunge [-tsoong-uh] ox tongue

Rindfleisch [rintflysh] beef

Rindfleischsalat [-zalaht] beef salad

Rindfleischsuppe [-zoop-uh] beef broth

Rippchen [ripshen] spareribs

Rippe [ripp-uh] rib

Risi-Pisi [reezee-peezee] rice and peas

roh raw

Rohkostplatte [-plat-uh] selection of salads

Rollmops rolled-up pickled herring, rollmops

rosa rare to medium

Rosenkohl Brussels sprouts

Rosinen [rohzeenen] raisins

Rostbraten [-brahten] roast

Rostbratwurst [-braht-voorst] barbecued sausage

Rösti [rurshtee] fried potatoes and onions

Röstkartoffeln [**ru**rst-] fried potatoes

Rotbarsch [**roh**tbarsh] type of perch

rote Bete [**roh**t-uh **bay**t-uh] beetroot, red beet

rote Grütze [**roh**t-uh gr**oo**ts-uh] red fruit jelly

Rotkohl [**roh**t-] red cabbage

Rotkraut [-krowt] red cabbage

Roulade [r**oo**l**ah**d-uh] beef olive

Rührei [r**oo**r-ī-er] scrambled eggs

Russische Eier [r**oo**ssish-uh ī-er] egg mayonnaise

Sachertorte [**za**кHertort-uh] rich chocolate cake

Sahne [**zah**n-uh] cream

Sahnesoße [-zohss-uh] cream sauce

Sahnetorte [-tort-uh] cream gateau

Salat [**za**l**ah**t] salad; lettuce

Salate salads

Salatplatte [-plat-uh] selection of salads

Salatsoße [-zohss-uh] salad dressing

Salatteller side salad; selection of salads

Salz [**za**lts] salt

Salzburger Nockerln [**za**ltsboorger] sweet soufflés

Salzheringe [-hairing-uh] salted herrings

Salzkartoffeln boiled potatoes

Sandkuchen [**za**ntk**oo**кHen] type of Madeira cake

Sauerbraten [**zow**erbrahten] marinaded potroast

Sauerkraut [**zow**erkrowt] white cabbage, finely chopped and pickled

Sauerrahm [-rahm] sour cream

Schafskäse [sh**ah**fs-kayz-uh] sheep's milk cheese

Schaschlik [sh**a**shlik] (shish-) kebab

Schattenmorellen morello cherries

Schellfisch haddock

Schildkrötensuppe [shiltkrurten-zoop-uh] real turtle soup

Schillerlocken [sh**i**ller-] smoked haddock rolls

Schinken [sh**i**nken] ham

Schinkenbrötchen [-br**ur**tshen] ham roll

Schinkenröllchen [-r**ur**lshen] rolled ham

Schinkenspeck [-shpeck] bacon

Schinkenwurst [-voorst] ham sausage

Schlachtplatte [shl**a**кHtplat-uh] selection of fresh sausages

Schlagobers [shl**ah**k-obers] whipped cream

Schlagsahne [-zahn-uh] whipped cream

Schlei [shly] tench

Schmorbraten [shm**oh**rbrahten] pot roast

Schnecken [shn**e**cken] snails

Schnittlauch [shn**i**tt-lowкH] chives

Schnitzel [shn**i**tsel] cutlet

Schokolade [shokol**ah**d-uh]

227

chocolate

Scholle [sholl-uh] plaice

Schollenfilet [-fillay] fillet of plaice

Schulterstück [shoolter-shtöock] slice of shoulder

Schwarzbrot [shvartsbroht] dark rye bread

Schwarzwälder Kirschtorte [shvartsvelder keershtort-uh] Black Forest gateau

Schwarzwurzeln [-voortseln] salsifies

Schweinebauch [shvine-uh-bowĸн] belly of pork

Schweinebraten [-brahten] roast pork

Schweinefilet [-fillay] fillet of pork

Schweinefleisch [-flysh] pork

Schweinekotelett [-kotlet] pork chop

Schweineleber [-layber] pig's liver

Schweinerippe [-ripp-uh] cured pork chop

Schweinerollbraten [-rolbrahten] rolled roast of pork

Schweineschmorbraten [-shmohr-brahten] roast pork

Schweineschnitzel [-shnitsel] pork fillet

Schweinshaxe [shvine-ss-hacks-uh] knuckle of pork

Seelachs [zaylacks] pollack

Seezunge [-tsoong-uh] sole

Sellerie [zelleree] celery

Semmel [zemmel] bread roll

Semmelknödel [-k-nurdel] bread dumplings

Senf [zenf] mustard

Senfsahnesoße [-zahn-uh-zohss-uh] mustard and cream sauce

Senfsoße mustard sauce

serbisches Reisfleisch [zairbishess rice-flysh] diced pork, onions, tomatoes and rice

Sohle [zohl-uh] sole

Soleier [zohl-ī-er] pickled eggs

Soße [zohss-uh] sauce; gravy

Spanferkel [shpahn-fairkel] suckling pig

Spargel [shpargel] asparagus

Spargelcremesuppe [-kraym-zoop-uh] cream of asparagus soup

Spätzle [shpets-luh] home-made noodles

Speckkartoffeln [shpeck-] potatoes with bacon

Speckknödel [-k-nurdel] bacon dumplings

Speckstreifen [-shrtyfen] strips of bacon

Speisekarte [shpize-uh-kart-uh] menu

Spezialität des Hauses our speciality

Spiegeleier [shpeegel-ī-er] fried eggs

Spieß: am Spieß [shpeess] on the spit

Spießbraten [shpeess-brahten] joint roasted on a spit

Spinat [shpinaht] spinach

Spitzkohl [shpits-] white cabbage

Sprotten [shprotten] sprats

Stachelbeeren [shtaкнel-bairen] gooseberries

Stangenspargel [shtangen-shpargel] asparagus spears

Stangen(weiß)brot [shtangen-(vice-)broht] French bread

Steinbutt [shtine-boott] turbot

Steinpilze [-pilts-uh] type of mushroom

Stollen [shtollen] fruit loaf

Strammer Max [shtrammer] ham and fried egg on bread

Streuselkuchen [shtroyzel-kOOKнen] sponge cake with crumble topping

Sülze [zOOlts-uh] brawn

Suppe [zoop-uh] soup

Suppen soups

Suppengrün [zoopengrOOn] mixed herbs and vegetables (in soup)

Süßigkeiten [zOOssish-kyten] sweets

Süßspeisen [zOOss-shpyzen] sweet dishes

Süßwasserfische [zOOss-vasser-fish-uh] freshwater fish

Szegediner Gulasch [shegaydeener] goulash with pickled cabbage

Tafelspitz [tahfel-shpits] soured boiled rump

Tagesgericht [tahgess-gerisht] dish of the day

Tageskarte [-kart-uh] menu of the day; set menu

Tagessuppe [-zoop-uh] soup of the day

Tatar [tatahr] raw mince with spices

Taube [towb-uh] pigeon

Teigmantel [tike-mantel] pastry covering

Teigwaren [-vahren] pasta

Thunfisch [tOOnfish] tuna

Tintenfisch [-fish] squid

Tomate [tomahtuh] tomato

Tomatensalat [-zalaht] tomato salad

Tomatensuppe [-zoop-uh] tomato soup

Topfen quark

Törtchen [turtshen] tart(s)

Torte [tort-uh] gateau

Trauben [trowben] grapes

Truthahn [trOOt-] turkey

überbacken [OOberbacken] au gratin

Ungarisches Gulasch [OOngahrishess] Hungarian goulash

Vanilleeis [vanill-uh-ice] vanilla ice cream

Vanillesoße [-zohss-uh] vanilla sauce

vegetarisch [vegaytahrish] vegetarian

verlorene Eier [fairlohren-uh ī-er] poached eggs

Vollkornbrot [follkornbroht] dark rye bread

vom Grill grilled

vom Kalb veal

vom Lamm lamb

vom Rind beef
vom Rost grilled
vom Schwein pork
vorbereiten to prepare
Vorspeisen [**fo**rshpyzen] hors d'œuvres, starters

Waffeln [**va**ffeln] waffles
Waldmeister [**va**ltmyster] woodruff
Waldorfsalat [**va**ldorf-zal**aht**] salad with celery, apples and walnuts
Wassermelone [**va**sser-mel**ohn**-uh] water melon
Weichkäse [**vy**sh-kayz-uh] soft cheese
Weinbergschnecken [**vine**-bairk-shnecken] snails
Weincreme [**vine**-kraym] pudding with wine
Weinkraut [-krowt] sauerkraut
Weinschaumcreme [-**showm**-kraym] creamed pudding with wine
Weinsoße [-**zohss**-uh] wine sauce
Weintrauben [-**trowben**] grapes
Weißbrot [**vice**-broht] white bread
Weißkohl white cabbage
Weißkraut [-krowt] white cabbage
Weißwurst [-**voorst**] veal sausage
Wiener Schnitzel [**vee**ner shnitsel] veal in breadcrumbs
Wiener Würstchen [**voo**rstshen] frankfurter(s)

Wild [vilt] game
Wildbret [-brayt] venison
Wildgerichte venison dishes
Wildschweinkeule [**vi**ltshvine-koyl-uh] haunch of wild boar
Wildschweinsteak wild boar steak
Windbeutel [**vi**ntboytel] cream puff
Wirsing [**vee**rzing] savoy cabbage
Wurst [**voorst**] sausage
Wurstbrötchen [-**brurtshen**] roll with sausage meat
Würstchen [**voo**rstshen] frankfurter(s)
Wurstplatte [**voo**rst-plat-uh] selection of sausages
Wurstsülze [-z**oolts**-uh] sausage brawn
Würzfleisch [-flysh] spicy meat

Zander [**tsa**nder] pike-perch, zander
Zartbitterschokolade [**tsa**rtbitter-shokol**ahd**-uh] plain chocolate
Ziegenkäse [**tsee**gen-kayz-uh] goat's cheese
Zigeunerschnitzel [tsig**oy**ner-shnitsel] veal or pork with peppers and relishes
Zitrone [tsitr**ohn**-uh] lemon
Zucchini [tsook**ee**nee] courgettes, zucchini
Zucker [**tsoo**cker] sugar
Zuckererbsen [-**airp**sen] mangetout peas
Zunge [ts**oo**ng-uh] tongue

Zwiebel [ts**vee**bel] onion

Zwiebelringe [-ring-uh] onion rings

Zwiebelrostbraten [-rostbrahten] steak with fried onions

Zwiebelsuppe [-zoop-uh] onion soup

Zwiebeltorte [-tort-uh] onion tart

Zwischengerichte entrées

Menu Reader: Drink

Essential Terms

beer das Bier
bottle die Flasche [**fla**sh-uh]
brandy der Weinbrand [**vine**-brant]
coffee der Kaffee [**ka**ffay]
cup: a cup of ... eine Tasse ... [**ine**-uh **ta**ss-uh]
fruit juice der Fruchtsaft [**froo**KHtzaft]
gin der Gin
  a gin and tonic einen Gin Tonic [**ine**-en]
glass: a glass of ... ein Glas ... [ine **gla**hss]
milk die Milch [**mi**lsh]
mineral water das Mineralwasser [miner**ah**lvasser]
orange juice der Orangensaft [oron**J**en-zaft]
red wine der Rotwein [**roht**vine]
rosé der Roséwein [rohz**ay**-vine]
soda (water) das Sodawasser [**zoh**da-vasser]
soft drink das alkoholfreie Getränk [alkoh**ohl**fry-uh ge**tre**nk], der Soft
  drink
sugar der Zucker [ts**oo**cker]
tea der Tee [tay]
tonic (water) das Tonic
vodka der Wodka [**vo**dka]
water das Wasser [**va**sser]
whisky der Whisky
white wine der Weißwein [**vice**-vine]
wine der Wein [vine]
wine list die Weinkarte [**vine**-kart-uh]

another ..., please noch ein ..., bitte [noKH ine ... **bi**tt-uh]

alkoholfreies Bier [alkohohlfry-ess beer] alcohol-free beer

Alsterwasser [-vasser] shandy

Alt(bier) [alt(beer)] light brown beer, not sweet

Apfelsaft [apfelzaft] apple juice

Apfelschorle [-shorl-uh] sparkling apple juice

Apfelwein [-vine] cider

Äppelwoi [eppelvoy] cider

Auslese [owsslayz-uh] wine selected from ripest bunches of grapes in top wine category

Ausschankwein [owss-shank-vine] wine by the glass

Bananenmilch [banahnen-milsh] banana milk shake

Beerenauslese [bairen-owsslayz-uh] wine from specially selected single grapes in top wine category

Berliner Weiße [bairleener vice-uh] fizzy beer

Bier [beer] beer

Bockbier [bockbeer] strong beer

Bowle [bohl-uh] punch

Buttermilch [boottermilsh] buttermilk

Cidre [seed-ruh] cider

Doppelkorn grain schnapps

Eierlikör [Ier-likur] advocaat

Eiswein [ice-vine] wine made from grapes picked after frost

entkoffeiniert [entkoffay-eeneert] decaffeinated

Erdbeermilch [airtbair-milsh] strawberry milk shake

Erzeugerabfüllung estate bottled

Federweißer [fayder-vysser] new wine

Feuerzangenbowle [foyer-tsangen-bohl-uh] red wine punch with rum which has been flamed off

Flasche [flash-uh] bottle

Flaschenwein [flashen-vine] bottled wine

fruchtig [frooKHtish] fruity

Fruchtsaft [frooKHtzaft] fruit juice

Gespritzter [geshpritster] wine and soda, spritzer

Getränke beverages

Glühwein [gl00-vine] mulled wine

Grog hot water with rum and sugar

halbsüß [halp-z00ss] semi-sweet

halbtrocken [halp-] medium dry

Hefeweizen [hayf-uh-vytsen] fizzy beer made with yeast and wheat

Heidelbeergeist [hydelbair-gyst] blueberry brandy

heiße Zitrone [hice-uh tsitrohn-uh] hot lemon

heiße Milch [h**i**ce-uh m**i**lsh] hot milk

Helles [h**e**lless] lager

herb [hairp] very dry

Himbeergeist [h**i**mbair-gyst] raspberry brandy

Jahrgang [y**ah**rgang] vintage

Kabinett light, usually dry, wine in top wine category

Kaffee [kaff**ay**] coffee

Kaffee mit Milch [m**i**lsh] white coffee

Kakao [kak**ow**] cocoa; hot chocolate

Kännchen (Kaffee) [k**e**nnshen (kaff**ay**)] pot (of coffee)

Kellerei [k**e**ller-**ī**] (wine) producer's

Kir [keer] white wine with a dash of blackcurrant liqueur

Kir Royal [roy**ahl**] champagne with a dash of blackcurrant liqueur

koffeinfrei [koffay-**ee**n-fry] decaffeinated

Kognak [k**o**nyak] brandy

Korn type of schnapps

Kräuterlikör [kr**oy**terlikur] herbal liqueur

Kräutertee [-tay] herbal tea

Krimsekt [kr**i**mzekt] Crimean champagne

Landwein [l**a**ntvine] country wine

Likör [lik**ur**] liqueur

Limo [l**ee**mo] lemonade

Limonade [limon**ah**d-uh] lemonade

Liter [l**ee**ter] litre

Malzbier [m**a**ltsbeer] sweet stout

Maß [mahss] litre of beer (Bavaria)

Milchmixgetränk [m**i**lshmix-getrenk] milkshake

Mineralwasser [miner**ah**l-vasser] sparkling mineral water

mischen [m**i**shen] to mix

Mokka mocha

Most [mosst] fruit wine

Nektar fruit squash

neuer Wein [n**oy**er vine] new wine

Obstler [**oh**pstler] fruit schnapps

offener Wein [vine] wine by the glass

Orangensaft [or**o**nJenzaft] orange juice

Pikkolo quarter bottle of champagne

Portwein [-vine] port

Pulverkaffee [p**oo**lver-kaffay] instant coffee

Qualitätswein b.A. quality wine from a special wine-growing area

Qualitätswein m.P. top quality German wine

Radler(maß) [**rah**tler-mahss] shandy

Rosé(wein) [roh**zay**(vine)] rosé wine

Rotwein [**roh**tvine] red wine

Saft [zaft] juice

Schokolade [shokol**ah**d-uh] chocolate

Schokomilch [sh**o**ko-milsh] chocolate milk shake

schwarzer Tee [shv**a**rtser tay] tea

Sekt [zekt] sparkling wine, champagne

Spezi [sh**pay**tsee] cola and lemonade

Spirituosen spirits

Sprudel(wasser) [shpr**oo**del (-vasser)] mineral water

Steinhäger® [sht**i**ne-hayger] type of schnapps

Sturm [shtoorm] new wine

Tafelwasser [t**ah**fel-vasser] still mineral water

Tafelwein [t**ah**felvine] table wine

Tee [tay] tea

Trinkwasser [-vasser] drinking water

trocken dry

vollmundig [f**o**l-moondish] full-bodied

vom Fass [fom] draught

Wasser [v**a**sser] water

Wein [vine] wine

Weinberg [v**i**nebairk] vineyard

Weinbrand [v**i**ne-brant] brandy

Weingut [-g**oo**t] wine-growing estate

Weinkarte [-kart-uh] wine list

Weinkeller [-keller] wine cellar

Weinkellerei [-keller-**ī**] wine producer's

weiß [vice] white

Weißbier [v**i**cebeer] fizzy, light-coloured beer made with wheat

Weißherbst [-hairpst] type of rosé wine

Weißwein [-vine] white wine

Weizenbier [v**y**tsenbeer] wheat beer

Zitronentee [tsitr**oh**nen-tay] lemon tea

Zwetschenwasser [tsv**e**tshen-vasser] plum brandy

How the Language Works

Pronunciation

In this phrase book, the German has been written in a system of imitated pronunciation so that it can be read as though it were English. Bear in mind the notes on pronunciation given below:

ay	as in m**ay**
e	as in g**e**t
g	always hard as in **g**oat
ī	as the 'i' sound in m**i**ght
J	like the 's' sound in plea**s**ure
KH	as in the Scottish way of saying lo**ch**
oo	as in b**oo**k
oo	as in mons**oo**n
∞	like the 'ew' in f**ew** but without any 'y' sound
ow	as in c**ow**
uh	like the 'e' in butt**e**r
ur	as in f**ur** but without any 'r' sound

The common German sound 'ei', as in Einstein, is written either with a 'y' or as 'ine'/'ite'/'ile' etc as in f**ine**/k**ite**/wh**ile**.

Abbreviations

acc	accusative		m	masculine
adj	adjective		n	neuter
dat	dative		nom	nominative
f	feminine		pl	plural
gen	genitive		sing	singular

Notes

In the English-German section, when two forms of the verb are given in phrases such as 'can you ...?' **kannst du/können Sie ...?** the first is the familiar form and the second the polite form (see the entry for **you**).

An asterisk (*) next to a word means that you should refer to the **How the Language Works** section for further information.

Nouns

All German nouns begin with a capital letter. They have one of three genders – masculine, feminine or neuter. Usually, the gender of a noun will have to be learnt together with the word itself. Certain noun endings, however, are reliable indicators of gender. For example:

Masculine nouns: ending in -or

der Motor	**der Professor**
dair m**oh**tohr	dair prof**e**ssohr
the engine	the professor

Feminine nouns: ending in -ei, -heit, -in, -keit, -ung

die Polizei	**die Abtei**
dee pohlits-**ī**	dee ap-**ty**
the police	the abbey
die Freiheit	**die Gesundheit**
dee fr**y**-hite	dee gez**oo**nt-hite
freedom	health
die Engländerin	**die Schauspielerin**
dee **e**ng-lenderin	dee sh**ow**-shpeelerin
the Englishwoman	the actress
die Telefonistin	**die Flüssigkeit**
dee telefoh**ni**stin	dee fl**oo**ssish-kite
the telephonist	the liquid
die Geschwindigkeit	**die Reservierung**
dee geshv**i**ndish-kite	dee rezairv**ee**roong
the speed	the reservation

die Verbindung
dee fairb**i**ndoong
the connection

Neuter nouns: ending in -chen, -ment

das Mädchen
dass **may**tshen
the girl

das Verkehrszeichen
dass fairk**ai**rss-tsyshen
the road sign

das Kompliment
dass kompli**ment**
the compliment

das Medikament
dass medika**ment**
the medicine

Plurals

There are a certain number of general rules about the formation of plurals, but the plural of most German nouns, like their gender, will have to be learnt individually.

Many German nouns form their plural by adding -e, -n or -en.

der Berg
dair bairk
the mountain

die Berge
dee **bai**rg-uh
the mountains

die Reise
dee r**ize**-uh
the journey

die Reisen
dee r**y**zen
the journeys

die Mahlzeit
dee m**ah**ltsite
the meal

die Mahlzeiten
dee m**ah**ltsyten
the meals

Many nouns of foreign origin, though not all, form their plural by adding -s.

das Auto
dass **ow**to
the car

die Autos
dee **ow**tohss
the cars

but:

der Computer
dair 'computer'
the computer

die Computer
dee 'computer'
the computers

Some nouns do not change at all in the plural. Others add
-er. This is often, but not always, combined with a change
of vowel: a number of nouns which contain an **a**, an **o** or a **u**
have an umlaut (**ä**, **ö** or **ü**) in their plural form.

der Wagen	die Wagen
dair **vah**gen	dee **vah**gen
the car	the cars

der Apfel	die Äpfel
dair **a**pfel	dee **e**pfel
the apple	the apples

der Koch	die Köche
dair koKH	dee **kur**sh-uh
the cook	the cooks

das Tuch	die Tücher
dass tOOKH	dee **too**sher
the cloth	the cloths

The following list of regular noun endings should prove
useful:

noun ending	gender	plural
-ar	m	-are
-är	m	-äre
-chen	n	-chen
-eur	m	-eure
-ich	m	-iche
-heit	f	-heiten
-in	f	-innen
-ium	n	-ien
-keit	f	-keiten
-ling	m	-linge
-ment	n	-mente
-nis	n	-nisse
-or	m	-oren
-schaft	f	-schaften
-ung	f	-ungen

Articles and Cases

German has three genders, masculine (**m**), feminine (**f**) and neuter (**n**). Each gender has its own article.

For masculine nouns, the definite article ('the' in English) is **der** and the indefinite article ('a' in English) **ein**:

der Mann	**ein Mann**
dair man	ine man
the man	a man

For feminine nouns, the definite article is **die** and the indefinite article **eine**:

die Frau	**eine Frau**
dee frow	**ine**-uh frow
the woman	a woman

For neuter nouns, the definite article is **das** and the indefinite article **ein**:

das Kind	**ein Kind**
dass kint	ine kint
the child	a child

The plural form of the definite article, regardless of the gender of a noun, is **die**:

die Männer	**die Frauen**
dee menner	dee frowen
the men	the women

die Kinder
dee kinder
the children

There are four cases: nominative, accusative, genitive and dative. The form of the definite and indefinite articles changes in line with the case being used, as shown in the following tables:

The Definite Article

	m	f	n	pl
nom	der	die	das	die
acc	den	die	das	die
gen	des	der	des	der
dat	dem	der	dem	den

The Indefinite Article

	m	f	n
nom	ein	eine	ein
acc	einen	eine	ein
gen	eines	einer	eines
dat	einem	einer	einem

The nominative is the case used for words when they are the subject of the sentence:

der Wagen fährt schnell
dair **vah**gen fairt shnell
the car goes fast

The accusative is the case used for words when they are the object of the sentence:

ich habe den Wagen gestern gekauft
ish h**ah**b-uh dayn **vah**gen g**e**stern gek**owf**t
I bought the car yesterday

The genitive is the case used to show possession:

der Preis des Wagens war sehr hoch
dair price dess **vah**genss var zair hohкн
the price of the car was very high

The dative is the case used to show motion towards a person or an object:

er ging dem Wagen entgegen
air ging daym **vah**gen entg**ay**gen
he walked towards the car

Prepositions

Most German prepositions take either the accusative or the dative or both.

The accusative is used after the following prepositions:

bis	biss	until
durch	doorsh	through
für	foor	for
gegen	gaygen	against
ohne	ohn-uh	without
um	oom	around

wir gehen durch die Stadt
veer gayen doorsh dee shtatt
we walk through the town

ohne die Kinder
ohn-uh dee kinder
without the children

The dative is used after the following prepositions:

aus	owss	out of
außer	owsser	except
bei	by	at, near
gegenüber	gaygen-oober	opposite
mit		with
nach	naKH	to
seit	zite	since
von	fon	from
zu	tsoo	to, at

mit den Kindern
mit dayn kindern
with the children

seit dem letzten Jahr
zite daym letsten yar
since last year

The following prepositions can either take the accusative or the dative:

an		on, to
auf	owf	on
hinter		behind
in		in
neben	nayben	beside
über	oober	over, across
unter	oonter	under
vor	fohr	before, in front of
zwischen	tsvishen	between

The accusative is used whenever motion is shown, whereas the dative indicates position:

ich stelle die Vase auf den Tisch
ish shtell-uh dee vahz-uh owf dayn tish
I put the vase on the table

die Vase steht auf dem Tisch
dee vahz-uh shtayt owf daym tish
the vase is on the table

wir fahren über den Fluss
veer fahren oober dayn flooss
we are crossing the river

die Brücke über dem Fluss
dee brook-uh oober daym flooss
the bridge across the river

Adjectives and Adverbs

In German, there is no special ending to distinguish an adverb from an adjective (as '-ly' in English). The adverb is the same as the basic form of the adjective.

das Wetter ist schön
dass vetter ist shurn
the weather is beautiful

sie singt schön
zee zingt shurn
she sings beautifully

When an adjective is used on its own, ie not in front of a noun, it appears in its basic form, without an ending:

die Straße ist nass
dee shtrahss-uh ist nass
the road is wet

es ist zu spät
ess ist tsoo shpayt
it is too late

If, however, an adjective appears in front of a noun, it needs an ending in order to agree with the noun:

die nasse Straße
dee nass-uh shtrahss-uh
the wet road

ein später Zug
ine shpayter tsook
a late train

The adjective's ending further depends on whether it is used after a definite article (**der, die, das**) or after an indefinite article (**ein, eine**). As can be seen from the following tables, the endings vary according to gender and case of the noun.

Endings After Definite Articles

	m	f	n	pl
nom	-e	-e	-e	-en
acc	-en	-e	-e	-en
gen	-en	-en	-en	-en
dat	-en	-en	-en	-en

Endings After Indefinite Articles

	m	f	n
nom	-er	-e	-es
acc	-en	-e	-es
gen	-en	-en	-en
dat	-en	-en	-en

das große Hotel
dass grohss-uh hotel
the big hotel

ein großes Hotel
ine grohssess hotel
a big hotel

die großen Hotels
dee **groh**ssen hotelss
the big hotels

wir wohnen in dem großen Hotel
veer **voh**nen in daym **groh**ssen hotel
we are staying in the big hotel

die Zimmer eines großen Hotels
dee tsimmer **ine**-ess **groh**ssen hotelss
the rooms of a big hotel

Comparatives and Superlatives

The comparative form of an adjective or adverb is used to express that something is bigger, better, more interesting etc than something else. In German, as for a number of English adjectives, this is shown by adding **-er**.

klein	kleiner
kline	kliner
small	smaller

schön	schöner
shurn	sh**ur**ner
beautiful	more beautiful

The superlative form of an adjective or adverb is used to express that something is the biggest, the best, the most interesting etc of all. In German, this is shown by adding **-ste**.

billig	der/die/das billigste
billish	dair/dee/dass **bil**lishst-uh
cheap	the cheapest

weich	der/die/das weichste
vysh	dair/dee/dass **vy**shst-uh
soft	the softest

Note that if adjectives contain an **a**, **o** or **u**, these will frequently change to **ä**, **ö** or **ü** in comparative and superlative forms:

lang	länger	der/die/das längste
lang	lenger	dair/dee/dass lengst-uh
long	longer	the longest

groß	größer	der/die/das größte
grohss	grurrsser	dair/dee/dass grurrsst-uh
big, tall	bigger, taller	the biggest, the tallest

dumm	dümmer	der/die/das dümmste
doomm	doommer	dair/dee/dass doommst-uh
stupid	more stupid	the most stupid

Some comparative and superlative forms are irregular completely:

gut	besser	der/die/das beste
goot	besser	dair/dee/dass best-uh
good	better	the best

hoch	höher	der/die/das höchste
hohKH	hurher	dair/dee/dass hurkst-uh
high	higher	the highest

viel	mehr	der/die/das meiste
feel	mair	dair/dee/dass myst-uh
much	more	the most

The word for 'than' is **als**:

er ist größer als ich
air ist grurrsser alss ish
he is taller than me

Possessive Adjectives

Possessive adjectives are words like 'my', 'your', 'our' etc. In German, they have to agree with the gender and number of the noun they refer to:

		m	f	n	pl
my		**mein**	**meine**	**mein**	**meine**
		mine	m**ine**-uh	mine	m**ine**-uh
your	(sing, familiar)	**dein**	**deine**	**dein**	**deine**
		dine	d**ine**-uh	dine	d**ine**-uh
	(sing, polite)	**Ihr**	**Ihre**	**Ihr**	**Ihre**
		eer	**eer**-uh	eer	**eer**-uh
his		**sein**	**seine**	**sein**	**seine**
		zine	z**ine**-uh	zine	z**ine**-uh
her		**ihr**	**ihre**	**ihr**	**ihre**
		eer	**eer**-uh	eer	**eer**-uh
our		**unser**	**unsere**	**unser**	**unsere**
		oonzer	**oo**nzer-uh	**oo**nzer	**oo**nzer-uh
your	(pl, familiar)	**euer**	**eure**	**euer**	**eure**
		oyer	**oy**r-uh	**oy**er	**oy**r-uh
	(pl, polite)	**Ihr**	**Ihre**	**Ihr**	**Ihre**
		eer	**eer**-uh	eer	**eer**-uh
their		**ihr**	**ihre**	**ihr**	**ihre**
		eer	**eer**-uh	eer	**eer**-uh

hast du deine Fahrkarte?
hast d**oo** d**ine**-uh **fah**rkart-uh
have you got your ticket?

das ist mein Hotel
dass ist mine ho**tel**
this is my hotel

sind unsere Koffer schon hier?
zint **oo**nzer-uh **k**offer shohn heer
have our suitcases arrived yet?

Personal Pronouns

Subject Pronouns

I		ich	ish
you	(sing, familiar)	du[(1)]	doo
	(sing, polite)	Sie[(2)]	zee
he		er	air
she		sie	zee
it		es	ess
we		wir	veer
you	(pl, familiar)	ihr[(3)]	eer
	(pl, polite)	Sie[(2)]	zee
they		sie	zee

[(1)] **du** is used when speaking to one person and is the familiar form generally used when speaking to family, friends and children

[(2)] **Sie** is the polite form of address in the singular as well as the plural; it takes the third person plural of verbs

[(3)] **ihr** is the familiar form used when speaking to more than one person

Note that, when talking to strangers, unless they are children, you should always use **Sie**, never **du** or **ihr**.

It is important to remember that the German for 'it' is not automatically **es** but always depends on the noun which 'it' refers to. If the noun is masculine, use **er**; if it is feminine, use **sie**; only if the noun is neuter is **es** the pronoun to use.

ist der Zug schon da? – da kommt er
ist dair tsook shohn da – da kommt air
has the train arrived yet? – here it comes

wo ist die Zeitung? – da liegt sie
vo ist dee tsytoong – da leekt zee
where's the paper? – there it is

was macht das Kind? – es spielt

vass maкнt dass kint – ess shpeelt

what's the child doing? – he / she is playing

Direct Object Pronouns

These occur if you are using the pronoun as an object.

me		**mich** mish	it		**es**	ess
you	(sing, familiar)	**dich** dish	us		**uns**	oonss
	(sing, polite)	**Sie** zee	you	(pl, familiar)	**euch**	oysh
him		**ihn** een		(pl, polite)	**Sie**	zee
her		**sie** zee	them		**sie**	zee

ich habe sie gesehen

ish hahb-uh zee gezayen

I have seen her/them

kann ich dich morgen anrufen?

kann ish dish morgen anroofen

can I phone you tomorrow?

ich möchte euch einladen

ish murisht-uh oysh ine-lahden

I would like to invite you

Indirect Object Pronouns

If you are using an object pronoun to mean 'to me', 'to you' etc (although 'to' might not always be necessary in English), you use the following:

(to) me		**mir**	meer
(to) you	(sing, familiar)	**dir**	deer
	(sing, polite)	**Ihnen**	eenen
(to) him		**ihm**	eem
(to) her		**ihr**	eer
(to) it		**ihm**	eem
(to) us		**uns**	oonss
(to) you	(pl, familiar)	**euch**	oysh
	(pl, polite)	**Ihnen**	eenen
(to) them		**ihnen**	eenen

sie hat es mir gegeben
zee hat ess meer geg**ay**ben
she has given it to me

ich habe es ihm gesagt
ish h**ah**b-uh ess eem gez**ah**kt
I told him

er hat ihnen einen Brief geschrieben
air hat **ee**nen **ine**-en breef geshr**ee**ben
he has written them a letter

Reflexive Pronouns

These are used with reflexive verbs like **sich waschen** 'to wash (oneself)', **sich umdrehen** 'to turn around':

myself		**mich**	mish
yourself	(familiar)	**dich**	dish
	(polite)	**sich**	zish
himself		**sich**	zish
herself		**sich**	zish
itself		**sich**	zish
ourselves		**uns**	oonss
yourselves	(familiar)	**euch**	oysh
	(polite)	**sich**	zish
themselves		**sich**	zish

wir haben uns gut unterhalten
veer h**ah**ben oonss g**oo**t oonterh**a**lten
we enjoyed ourselves

Sie irren sich
zee **ee**rren zish
you are mistaken

ich habe mich geärgert
ish h**ah**b-uh mish ge-**ai**rgert
I was annoyed

Possessive Pronouns

Possessive adjectives are words like 'mine', 'yours', 'ours' etc. In German, they have to agree with the gender and number of the noun they refer to:

	m	f	n	pl
mine	**meiner**	**meine**	**meins**	**meine**
	m**i**ner	mine-uh	mine-ss	mine-uh
yours (sing, familiar)	**deiner**	**deine**	**deins**	**deine**
	d**i**ner	dine-uh	dine-ss	dine-uh
(sing, polite)	**Ihrer**	**Ihre**	**Ihres**	**Ihre**
	eerer	**ee**r-uh	**ee**ress	**ee**r-uh
his	**seiner**	**seine**	**seins**	**seine**
	z**i**ner	zine-uh	zine-ss	zine-uh
hers	**ihrer**	**ihre**	**ihres**	**ihre**
	eerer	**ee**r-uh	**ee**ress	**ee**r-uh
ours	**unserer**	**unsere**	**unseres**	**unsere**
	oonzerer	**oo**nzer-uh	**oo**nzer-ess	**oo**nzer-uh
yours (pl, familiar)	**eurer**	**eure**	**eures**	**eure**
	oyrer	**oy**r-uh	**oy**ress	**oy**r-uh
(pl, polite)	**Ihrer**	**Ihre**	**Ihres**	**Ihre**
	eerer	**ee**r-uh	**ee**ress	**ee**r-uh
theirs	**ihrer**	**ihre**	**ihres**	**ihre**
	eerer	**ee**r-uh	**ee**ress	**ee**r-uh

das sind meine
dass zint m**ine**-uh
these are mine

ist das mein Glas oder Ihres?
ist dass mine glahss **o**der **ee**ress
is that glass mine or yours?

möchten Sie Wein? – wir haben unseren schon bestellt
m**u**rshten zee vine – veer h**ah**ben **oo**nzeren shohn besht**e**llt
would you like some wine? – we've already ordered ours

Verbs

The basic form of German verbs (the infinitive) usually ends in
-**en**, occasionally in -**ln** or -**rn**.

gehen	to go, to walk
schlafen	to sleep
angeln	to fish

Present Tense

The present tense corresponds to 'I leave' and 'I am leaving' in English. To form the present tense in German, remove the verb ending (**-en** or **-n**) and add the endings to the stem of the verb, as shown in the tables below (the 'stem' of a verb is the past without the final '-en', '-eln' or '-ern'):

		machen (to do)		**reden** (to talk)
		maкн-en	rayd-en	
I		ich	mach-e	ich	red-e
you	(sing, familiar)	du	mach-st	du	red-est
	(sing, polite)	Sie	mach-en	Sie	red-en
he/she/it		er/sie/es	mach-t	er/sie/es	red-et
we		wir	mach-en	wir	red-en
you	(pl, familiar)	ihr	mach-t	ihr	red-et
	(pl, polite)	Sie	mach-en	Sie	red-en
they		sie	mach-en	sie	red-en

See the section on Subject Pronouns page 253 for the use of the different words for 'you'.

Note that verbs ending in **-t** or **-d**, as **reden** above, insert an additional **-e-** to form some of their tenses.

Some common verbs are irregular:

haben [hahben] to have			**sein** [zine] to be		
ich	habe	hahb-uh	ich	bin	
du	hast		du	bist	
Sie	haben	hahben	Sie	sind	zint
er/sie/es	hat		er/sie/es	ist	
wir	haben		wir	sind	
ihr	habt	hapt	ihr	seid	zite
Sie	haben		Sie	sind	
sie	haben		sie	sind	

257

dürfen [dოrfen] to be allowed to

ich	darf	
du	darfst	
Sie	dürfen	dოrfen
er/sie/es	darf	
wir	dürfen	
ihr	dürft	dოrft
Sie	dürfen	
sie	dürfen	

können [kurnen] to be able to

ich	kann	
du	kannst	
Sie	können	kurnen
er/sie/es	kann	
wir	können	
ihr	könnt	kurnt
Sie	können	
sie	können	

müssen [mოssen] to have to

ich	muss	mooss
du	musst	moosst
Sie	müssen	mოssen
er/sie/es	muss	
wir	müssen	
ihr	müßt	moosst
Sie	müssen	
sie	müssen	

werden [vairden] to become

ich	werde	vaird-uh
du	wirst	veerst
Sie	werden	vairden
er/sie/es	wird	veert
wir	werden	
ihr	werdet	vairdet
Sie	werden	
sie	werden	

fahren [fahren] to go, drive

ich	fahre	fahr-uh
du	fährst	fairst
Sie	fahren	fahren
er/sie/es	fährt	fairt
wir	fahren	
ihr	fahrt	
Sie	fahren	
sie	fahren	

mögen [murgen] to like

ich	mag	mahk
du	magst	mahkst
Sie	mögen	murgen
er/sie/es	mag	
wir	mögen	
ihr	mögt	murkt
Sie	mögen	
sie	mögen	

sehen [zayen] to see

ich	sehe	zay-uh
du	siehst	zeest
Sie	sehen	zayen
er/sie/es	sieht	zeet
wir	sehen	
ihr	seht	zayt
Sie	sehen	
sie	sehen	

wollen [vollen] to want

ich	will	vill
du	willst	villst
Sie	wollen	vollen
er/sie/es	will	
wir	wollen	
ihr	wollt	vollt
Sie	wollen	
sie	wollen	

Past Tense

To describe an action that has taken place in the past, both the imperfect and perfect tense can be used.

Imperfect

The imperfect describes events which have occurred once in the past or which were repeated, habitual or took place over a period of time. To form the imperfect, the following verb endings are used:

machen (to do)		reden (to talk)	
ich	mach-te	ich	red-ete
du	mach-test	du	red-etest
Sie	mach-ten	Sie	red-eten
er/sie/es	mach-te	er/sie/es	red-ete
wir	mach-ten	wir	red-eten
ihr	mach-tet	ihr	red-etet
Sie	mach-ten	Sie	red-eten
sie	mach-ten	sie	red-eten

als ich Student war, lebte ich in Köln
alss ish shtoodent var laypt-uh ish in kurln
when I was a student, I used to live in Cologne

wie war das Wetter in den Alpen?
vee var dass vetter in dayn alpen
what was the weather like in the Alps?

Both **haben** and **sein** are irregular in the imperfect tense:

haben [hahben] to have			sein [zine] to be	
ich	hatte	hatt-uh	ich	war	var
du	hattest		du	warst	varst
Sie	hatten		Sie	waren	vahren
er/sie/es	hatte		er/sie/es	war	
wir	hatten		wir	waren	
ihr	hattet		ihr	wart	vart
Sie	hatten		Sie	waren	
sie	hatten		sie	waren	

Perfect

The most common way of referring to the past is the perfect tense. The perfect is formed with the present tense of either **haben** or **sein** (see page 257) followed by the past participle of the verb. The past participle is formed by taking the stem of the verb and adding a prefix and ending as follows:

mach-en to do	**ge-mach-t** done
red-en to talk	**ge-red-et** talked

Most verbs take **haben** to form the perfect tense:

er hat es gemacht
air hat ess gem**a**KHt
he has done it, he did it

wir haben davon geredet
veer h**ah**ben daf**o**n ger**ay**det
we (have) talked about it

Some verbs take **sein**, mostly verbs of motion. Some of these are:

fahren to go, to drive	**ich bin gefahren**
fallen to fall	**ich bin gefallen**
fliegen to fly	**ich bin geflogen**
gehen to go	**ich bin gegangen**
kommen to come	**ich bin gekommen**
sein to be	**ich bin gewesen**
sterben to die	**ich bin gestorben**
werden to become	**ich bin geworden**

er ist nach London gefahren
air ist naKH l**o**ndon gef**ah**ren
he went to London

letztes Jahr sind wir in München gewesen
l**e**tstess yar zint veer in m**oo**nshen gev**ay**zen
last year we were in Munich

Some common verbs have irregular past tenses. The following list shows the infinitive, the third person singular of the imperfect tense and the past participle.

Some Common Irregular Verbs

beginnen	to begin	begann	begonnen
bleiben	to stay	blieb	geblieben
bringen	to bring	brachte	gebracht
dürfen	to be allowed to	durfte	gedurft
essen	to eat	aß	gegessen
fahren	to go, to drive	fuhr	gefahren
finden	to find	fand	gefunden
fliegen	to fly	flog	geflogen
geben	to give	gab	gegeben
gehen	to go	ging	gegangen
haben	to have	hatte	gehabt
kennen	to know	kannte	gekannt
kommen	to come	kam	gekommen
können	to be able to	konnte	gekonnt
lassen	to let, to allow	ließ	gelassen
lesen	to read	las	gelesen
liegen	to lie	lag	gelegen
müssen	to have to	musste	gemusst
nehmen	to take	nahm	genommen
schreiben	to write	schrieb	geschrieben
sehen	to see	sah	gesehen
sein	to be	war	gewesen
sitzen	to sit	saß	gesessen
sterben	to die	starb	gestorben
trinken	to drink	trank	getrunken
verlieren	to lose	verlor	verloren
werden	to become	wurde	geworden
wissen	to know	wusste	gewusst

Future

The future tense in German is formed by the verb **werden** and the infinitive of the verb concerned:

ich	werde	kommen	I will come etc
du	wirst	kommen	
Sie	werden	kommen	
er/sie/es	wird	kommen	
wir	werden	kommen	
ihr	werdet	kommen	
Sie	werden	kommen	
sie	werden	kommen	

er wird es nicht schaffen
air veert ess nisht shaffen
he's not going to manage it

was werden Sie morgen machen?
vass vairden zee morgen maкнen
what are you going to do tomorrow?

er wird morgen kommen
air veert morgen kommen
he'll come tomorrow

Note that German, like English, frequently uses the present tense for the future:

was machen Sie morgen?
vass maкнen zee morgen
what are you doing tomorrow?

er kommt morgen
air kommt morgen
he's coming tomorrow

Negatives

To make a sentence negative, German uses the word **nicht**:

ich verstehe	**ich verstehe nicht**
ish fairsht**ay**-uh	ish fairsht**ay**-uh nisht
I understand	I don't understand

If you want to say 'no' or 'not any' with nouns, use the word **kein** or **keine**:

ich habe kein Geld	**er hat keine Geduld**
ish h**ah**b-uh kine gelt	air hat k**i**ne-uh ged**oo**lt
I have no money	he hasn't got any patience

Imperatives

The imperative is used to express a command (such as 'come here!', 'let's go' etc). Generally, the imperative forms are similar to those of the infinitive. In fact, just adding **Sie** to the infinitive gives the polite form of the imperative:

warten to wait	**warten Sie!**
	v**a**rten zee
	wait!

The familiar form (singular) is identical with the infinitive without the final -n, or, in some cases, without the final -en:

warte!	but:	**komm!**
v**a**rt-uh		komm
wait!		come (here)!

The corresponding plural form adds a -t to the singular:

wartet!	**kommt!**
v**a**rtet	kommt
wait!	come (here)!

Questions

To form a question, the word order of subject and verb in the sentence change:

Sie sprechen Deutsch
zee shpr**e**shen doytch
you speak German

sprechen Sie Deutsch?
shpr**e**shen zee doytch
do you speak German?

Word order is also inverted in other cases, especially when a question word is used:

wann schließt das Museum?
van shleesst dass m00z**ay**oom
when does the museum close?

ist mein Gepäck schon angekommen?
ist mine gep**e**ck shohn **a**n-gekommen?
has my luggage arrived yet?

Dates

Dates are expressed with ordinal numbers (see below):

der erste Juli
dair **air**st-uh y**00**lee
the first of July

am ersten Juli
am **air**sten y**00**lee
on the first of July

der zwanzigste März
dair tsv**a**ntsishst-uh mairts
the twentieth of March

am zwanzigsten März
am tsv**a**ntsishsten mairts
on the twentieth of March

At the beginning of letters, the following form should be used:

Frankfurt, den 20. März
Frankfurt, March 20

Days

Monday	Montag [**moh**ntakh]
Tuesday	Dienstag [**dee**nstahk]
Wednesday	Mittwoch [**mitt**voKH]
Thursday	Donnerstag [**do**nnerstahk]
Friday	Freitag [**fry**tahk]
Saturday	Samstag [**zam**stahk]
Sunday	Sonntag [**zo**nntahk]

Months

January	Januar [**yan**ooar]
February	Februar [**fay**brooar]
March	März [mairts]
April	April [a-**prill**]
May	Mai [my]
June	Juni [**yoo**nee]
July	Juli [**yoo**lee]
August	August [owg**oo**st]
September	September [**zept**ember]
October	Oktober [ok**to**ber]
November	November [no**vo**Nbr]
December	Dezember [dayts**e**mber]

Time

what time is it? wie spät ist es? [vee shpayt ist ess]
one o'clock ein Uhr [ine oor]
two o'clock zwei Uhr [tsvy oor]
it's one o'clock es ist ein Uhr [ess ist ine oor]
it's two o'clock es ist zwei Uhr [ess ist tsvy oor]
it's ten o'clock es ist zehn Uhr [ess ist tsayn oor]
five past one fünf nach eins [foonf naKH ine-ss]
ten past two zehn nach zwei [tsayn nahKH tsvy]

quarter past one Viertel nach eins [**fee**rtel nahKH ine-ss]

quarter past two Viertel nach zwei [**fee**rtel naKH tsvy]

*half past ten halb elf [halp elf]

twenty to ten zwanzig vor zehn [**tsva**ntsish for tsayn]

quarter to two Viertel vor zwei [**fee**rtel for tsvy]

at half past four um halb fünf [oom halp foonf]

at eight o'clock um acht Uhr [oom aKHt oor]

14.00 14 Uhr [**fee**rtsayn oor]

17.30 siebzehn Uhr dreißig [**zee**ptsayn oor **dry**ssish]

2 a.m. 2 Uhr morgens [tsvy oor **mor**gens]

2 p.m. 2 Uhr nachmittags [tsvy oor na**hKH**mittahks]

10 a.m. 10 Uhr vormittags [tsayn oor **for**mittahks]

10 p.m. 10 Uhr abends [tsayn oor **ah**bents]

noon Mittag [**mi**ttahk]

midnight Mitternacht [**mi**tternaKHt]

an hour eine Stunde [**ine**-uh shtoond-uh]

a/one minute eine Minute [**ine**-uh min**oo**t-uh]

two minutes zwei Minuten [tsvy min**oo**ten]

a second eine Sekunde [**ine**-uh zek**oo**nd-uh]

a quarter of an hour eine Viertelstunde [**ine**-uh **fee**rtelshtoond-uh]

half an hour eine halbe Stunde [**ine**-uh halb-uh shtoond-uh]

three quarters of an hour eine Dreiviertelstunde [**ine**-uh **dry**feer-tel-shtoond-uh]

* Note the difference here. German for 'half past ten/three/
five' etc is, literally, 'half eleven/four/six' etc.

Numbers

0	null [nooll]	7	sieben [**zee**ben]
1	eins [ine-ss]	8	acht [aKHt]
2	zwei [tsvy]	9	neun [noyn]
3	drei [dry]	10	zehn [tsayn]
4	vier [feer]	11	elf [elf]
5	fünf [foonf]	12	zwölf [**tsvurlf**]
6	sechs [zeks]	13	dreizehn [**dry**-tsayn]
		14	vierzehn [**veer**-tsayn]

15	fünfzehn [**foo**nf-tsayn]	31	einunddreißig
16	sechzehn [**ze**sh-tsayn]		[**ine**-oont-dryssish]
17	siebzehn [**zee**p-tsayn]	40	vierzig [**fee**rtsish]
18	achtzehn [**a**KH-tsayn]	50	fünfzig [**foo**nftsish]
19	neunzehn [**noy**n-tsayn]	60	sechzig [**ze**shtsish]
20	zwanzig [tsvantsish]	70	siebzig [**zee**ptsish]
21	einundzwanzig	80	achtzig [**a**KHtsish]
	[**ine**-oont-tsvantsish]	90	neunzig [**noy**ntsish]
22	zweiundzwanzig	100	hundert [**hoo**ndert]
	[**tsvy**-oont-tsvantsish]	110	hundertzehn
23	dreiundzwanzig		[hoondert-ts**ay**n]
	[**dry**-oont-tsvantsish]	200	zweihundert
30	dreißig [**dry**ssish]		[tsv**y**-hoondert]

300	dreihundert [**dry**-hoondert]
1,000	tausend [**tow**zent]
2,000	zweitausend [**tsvy**-towzent]
10,000	zehntausend [**tsay**n-towzent]
50,000	fünfzigtausend [**foo**nftsish-towzent]
100,000	hunderttausend [**hoo**ndert-towzent]
1,000,000	eine Million [**ine**-uh mill-y**oh**n]

Ordinal numbers are formed by adding **-te** or **-ste** if the number ends in **-ig**. For example, **fünfte** [**foo**nft-uh] (fifth), **zwanzigste** [tsvantsishst-uh] (twentieth).

1st	erste [**air**st-uh]	6th	sechste [**ze**kst-uh]
2nd	zweite [**tsvi**te-uh]	7th	siebte [**zee**pt-uh]
3rd	dritte [**dri**tt-uh]	8th	achte [**a**KHt-uh]
4th	vierte [**fee**rt-uh]	9th	neunte [**noy**nt-uh]
5th	fünfte [**foo**nft-uh]	10th	zehnte [**tsay**nt-uh]

In German, thousands are written with a full-stop. A comma is used for decimals.

German	English
10.000	10,000
2,83	2.83

Conversion Tables

1 centimetre = 0.39 inches		1 inch = 2.54 cm
1 metre = 39.37 inches = 1.09 yards		1 foot = 30.48 cm
1 kilometre = 0.62 miles = 5/8 mile		1 yard = 0.91 m
		1 mile = 1.61 km

km	1	2	3	4	5	10	20	30	40	50	100
miles	0.6	1.2	1.9	2.5	3.1	6.2	12.4	18.6	24.8	31.0	62.1

miles	1	2	3	4	5	10	20	30	40	50	100
km	1.6	3.2	4.8	6.4	8.0	16.1	32.2	48.3	64.4	80.5	161

1 gram = 0.035 ounces   1 kilo = 1000 g = 2.2 pounds

g	100	250	500
oz	3.5	8.75	17.5

1 oz = 28.35 g
1 lb = 0.45 kg

kg	0.5	1	2	3	4	5	6	7	8	9	10
lb	1.1	2.2	4.4	6.6	8.8	11.0	13.2	15.4	17.6	19.8	22.0

kg	20	30	40	50	60	70	80	90	100
lb	44	66	88	110	132	154	176	198	220

lb	0.5	1	2	3	4	5	6	7	8	9	10	20
kg	0.2	0.5	0.9	1.4	1.8	2.3	2.7	3.2	3.6	4.1	4.5	9.0

1 litre = 1.75 UK pints / 2.13 US pints

1 UK pint = 0.57 l	1 UK gallon = 4.55 l
1 US pint = 0.47 l	1 US gallon = 3.79 l

centigrade / Celsius $°C = (°F - 32) × 5/9$

°C	-5	0	5	10	15	18	20	25	30	36.8	38
°F	23	32	41	50	59	64	68	77	86	98.4	100.4

Fahrenheit $°F = (°C × 9/5) + 32$

°F	23	32	40	50	60	65	70	80	85	98.4	101
°C	-5	0	4	10	16	18	21	27	29	36.8	38.3